The Hero and His Shadow

Also by Erel Shalit

Enemy, Cripple, Beggar:
Shadows in the Hero's Path
ISBN 978-0-9776076-7-9

Requiem:
A Tale of Exile and Return
978-1-926715-03-2

The Complex:
Path of Transformation from Archetype to Ego
978-0-919123-99-1

The Cycle of Life:
Themes and Tales of the Journey
978-1-926715-50-6

Will Fishes Fly in Aquarius—
Or WIll they Drown in the Bucket?
978-1-926715-40-7

The Hero and His Shadow

Psychopolitical Aspects of Myth
and Reality in Israel

Revised Edition

Erel Shalit

The Hero and His Shadow
Psychopolitical Aspects of Myth
and Reality in Israel

Published simultaneously in Canada, the United Kingdom, and the United States of America by Fisher King Press. For information on obtaining permission for use of material from this work, submit a written request to:

permissions@fisherkingpress.com
Fisher King Press
PO Box 222321
Carmel, CA 93922
www.fisherkingpress.com
info@fisherkingpress.com
+1-831-238-7799

Dedication

I dedicate this book to those, all too many, whose voices were silenced by man's evil.

I dedicate it to those, all too few, who raise their voice against fascism, who speak up in the struggle for peace and reconciliation, especially between Palestinians and Israelis, incessantly on the verge of yet another cycle of violence and hostilities.

I dedicate it to those who try to hold the vulnerable balance in that ultimate conflict of Abraham between Father and Son, divine and human, idea and implementation, past and future, ego and self.

I dedicate this book to the daughters and the sons whose future is endangered.

Contents

Preface   The Beggar in the Hero's Shadow   ix

Acknowledgments   xv

Chapter 1   Return to the Source   1

Chapter 2   From My Notebook   11

Chapter 3   From Dream to Reality   33

Chapter 4   Origins and Myths   45

Chapter 5   From Redemption to Shadow   55

Chapter 6   Wholeness Apart   95

Chapter 7   Myth, Shadow and Projection   111

Chapter 8   A Crack in the Mask   131

Chapter 9   The Death of the Mythical and the Voice of the Soul   151

Glossary   169

Bibliography   173

Index   181

Preface

The Beggar in the Hero's Shadow

In the beginning, Zionism was a myth of redemption. It became reality when a mere handful of inspired young men and women transformed the idea, the spirit, into matter, sometimes sacrificing their lives as they let personal identity merge with the Grand Idea. This conflation of individual and collective transformed Zionism from Utopia and Ideal into harsh reality. Hero-ideals were actualized in the personae of pioneer and farmer, guardsman and warrior. The heroic vision was personified by strength, determination, vigor and self-reliance. The crystallization of this vision, and the willingness to merge with it, was essential for the fulfillment of Zionism and the birth of a new nation.

However, behind the hero-ideal, and within the soul of each and everyone, linger shadowy images such as the beggar – shadowy images that like faithful phantoms follow in the footsteps of the venerable. The pioneer who revivifies the earth is far more attractive than the homeless beggar who depends on the charity of others. Indeed, Theodor Herzl called for the repudiation of philanthropy which he considered to be guilty of "breeding beggars" and debasing "the character of our people" (Bein 1962, p. 127). Yet, even as the freedom fighter raised his rifle in the Land of Israel, elsewhere, philanthropic funds were being collected.

We owe the beggar a debt, whether he stands at the corner of a street or dwells within our soul. We readily reject his presence and prefer to look the other way, as he stands at the gate pleading we take notice of him. As a metaphor, his hand stretching out from the shadow, carries the desire to walk the path of redemption. His hand holds the knowledge we tend to disregard and forget – the humble realization that our fate is not completely in our own hands, not determined only by ourselves, and that we are not, what ideally we would want to be. However imperative the hero's task, he does not stand unaccompanied. The guilt in the beggar's hand begs us to see, to reflect and to look deeper into what lingers in the darkness of the shadow. Herzl appears to have had a profound understanding of the beggar as representing our aspiration for redemption. The Jewish beggar outside the coffeehouse, a boy "hunched up against the cold, hugging himself with his arms and stamping his feet in the snow" manages to break through arrogance and apathy (Herzl 1961, p. 10). In his *Altneuland*, it is this beggar who speaks the words of Zionist redemption, "pronouncing a whole life's program in a few sentences" (p. 22). Behind the hope for redemption in the Land of Israel by means of strength and vision, as carried in the collective ideals of pioneer, warrior and hero, the beggar appears. And behind the beggar's facade of misery, we reveal his "determination and faith" (Herzl, p. 22).

Shadowy aspects thrive in the backyard of public events that take place in society, aspects we prefer to overlook and which we become aware of only as things go wrong. While shadows often are hard to spot, they sometimes cast their silhouette in public manifestations. The shadow lingered behind the coffin with Prime Minister Rabin's name inscribed on it, and the hangman's rope as a cross of vengeance, in a public protest foreboding his assassination. Even prominent participators in that demonstration claimed they "did not see." And perhaps they did not *see*, because in order to see, to understand, to light up our own shadow, there is a need for humbleness rather than arrogance.

In the darkness behind the conscious determination reflected in the proud stance of the pioneer, stands the beggar with torn clothes and penetrating gaze. In *A Beggar in Jerusalem*, Elie Wiesel (1970, p. 3) writes:

> Do you see him? There. Sitting on a tree stump, huddled in the shadows, as though in wait for someone, he scrutinizes those who come his way, intending perhaps to provoke or unmask them.

In Israel, the relationship between individual and collective carries unique features and is characterized by an unusually *close proximity* (see glossary) between them. At the personal level, this may be experienced as a sense of belonging, "we come from the same village," of sharing a common fate. Or, it may be felt as an incestuous over-intimacy from which one needs to escape, whereby the anonymity of New York becomes the dream, the epitome of freedom.

The collective processes of Israel – state-building, war, mass-immigration, rapid social change, changing borders, tension between society's subgroups (Jews and Arabs, Sephardic and Ashkenazi Jews, secular and religious) – are all-encompassing. Hardly anyone, no family, can refrain from active involvement. Existential anxiety, separation, loss, death, and identity-crises, are particularly evident at times of war. Such feelings were experienced, for instance, during the Gulf Missile War (or, the "Sealed Room War") January/February 1991, which had been preceded by six wars in four decades, and the Intifada, the Palestinian uprising, which began in December 1987 and persisted for years. This close proximity has been profound, as well, during the war of terror, waged against civilian Israeli society following the failed Camp David Talks in 2000, in which more than one out of every thousand Israelis was killed or injured, and every fifth citizen has had a family member or acquaintance directly hit by terror.

Israel's establishment in the shadow of annihilation made the intense mutuality between individual and collective historical processes inescapable. Permanent crisis and existential anxiety have influenced the development and identity-formation of both individual and society.

The individual's identification with the *Collective Idea* forms the core of Israeli society. It is the very basis of Zionism, which was realized only through the readiness of a 'handful enough' of individuals to become one with the *Idea*, and thereby concretely effect the return to Zion.

In individual as well as collective development, a gradual separation and differentiation must take place. A child goes through several stages of separation from his parents, and his conscious identity is shaped by constant differentiation (for instance between clean and dirty, good and bad, feminine and masculine). As pertaining to Israeli society, because of the particular close proximity, the differentiation between individual and collective is often not gradual but a drastic separation, for example, through emigration. Alternatively, it is defended against by clinging to rigid and restrictive collective norms and "national values," rejecting deviance as a sign of weakness, betrayal or animosity. One outcome of this is a tendency to "unify and purify" the collective identity. Thus, that which challenges our self-image and resides in the *shadow* is projected outward, onto the enemy, in denial of the fact that the spirit of evil perpetually resides within each and all, within each and every society.

In the Jewish collective psyche, the Nazi and the terrorist embody the archetypal images of the enemy. The archetypal enemy in Hebrew mythology is Amalek, son of Eliphaz, grandson of Esau. The Amalekites attacked the Jews, who were on their way from Egypt, as it says, for "no apparent reason." They ambushed, deceived, and attacked the weak and the sick. There is a Biblical command to "blot out" their memory, but in accordance with the Talmudic statement that the Assyrian king Sennacherib mixed up the ancient peoples, it is no longer possible to identify the Amalekites. Consequently, the enemy is no longer personal and identifiable, but becomes an archetypal abstraction, whose reality resides within everyone's soul.

And evil does reside within *the other* as well, and the imperfections disclosed by self-scrutiny sometimes cause identification with the aggressor and idealization of the other.

This book seeks to delineate a psychological view of the collective processes that underlie the creation and development of the State of Israel, and the relationship between the individual and the collective processes up to the present time.

Two disparate ways of relating to the world are combined. One is political, based on external collective reality, action, talking and doing. The other is psychological, emanating from the individual's inner, subjective reality. The internal and the external – the subjective and the objective, being and doing – are both valuable orientations, and influence each other. Observing one from the perspective of the other renders an opportunity to look into the shadows that the one casts at the other.

When psychologists confine themselves to the ivory tower of their treatment rooms without looking out of the window, with no outsight and not realizing that the world itself breathes and has a soul; when they turn away from external society denying its importance for the human soul, they soon lose touch with reality. In spite of increasing biologization of psychiatry, the environment's influence on the individual's psyche, emotions and behavior is undeniable. But society must also be observed from the psyche's perspective, in order not to be blind to the meaning and the value of reality. While the analyst is in danger of being imprisoned by the chains of the soul if he turns away from the world, so society runs the risk of being encaged in a soul-less lack of awareness. Neumann (1990, p. 31) puts it thus:

> The connection between the problems of the individual and those of the collective is far closer than generally realized. We are still by no means aware of the 'totality constellation' by virtue of which each single individual is an organ of the collective, whose common inner structure he bears in his collective unconscious.

To approach one worldview from the perspective of an opposite one, for example to observe psychology from a political point of view and politics from a psychological one, has in itself a balancing effect. Failing to account for what seems to lie hidden, seeing only that which is empirically visible, that which is consonant with the prevailing outlook and perspective, the collective consciousness, may lead to catastrophe as a result of being blind to soul and shadow. This may be the case when detachment is brought about through splitting-off weakness and vulnerability (the lack of a realistic appraisal prior to the Yom Kippur War). It may lead astray by virtue of psychological inflation (striving to set up a new order in Lebanon) and constriction of vision (being taken by surprise that the enemy actively struggles against occupation during the Intifada that began in 1987). The mass deportation in December 1992 of an uncompromising, murderous Hamas group was intended to be a "liberal," time-limited act, but the government failed to take into account the psychological meaning of deportation. For Palestinians, deportation – being driven from their land – is a core fear similar to the Israeli core fear of annihilation.

The spirit of hatred and fanaticism that spread across the nation, headed by extremist opposition to Prime Minister Rabin's peace efforts, was not accounted for until his assassination. Likewise, the blindness that follows from not relating to the other's needs and demands, letting him carry the load of too burdensome projections, leads to compulsive repetition of harmful behavior.

By means of a liberal perspective, the subject approaches *the other* in such a way that the object becomes less a target of projection (even if projection is always be present to some extent). However, this may sometimes lead to the failure to realize that the subject is, as well, the target of the other's projections – and those projections may be different than one's own. By the year 2000, a majority of Israelis had come to accept withdrawal from occupied territories and the establishment of a Palestinian state alongside Israel. Perhaps arrogantly, Israelis did not discern what was going on in the Palestinian backyard (just like they had previously failed to see what went on in their own piazzas). They did not see that those who met in the open to discuss peace had done so tactically, and had a more far-reaching strategic goal, which – so it seems – justified incitement and instigation to terror behind the scene.

However, it is the shadow side of the Zionist enterprise and Israeli society that this book attempts to bring to the foreground, the shortcomings that become helpful when we reflect upon them, when we permit ourselves to be provoked or unmasked by them, but dangerous when unrelated to.

A note on gender

The hero revived the idea of redemption from its slumber in the unconscious and turned it into a collectively conscious guiding myth. Whether enacted by man or woman, collective consciousness accentuated the masculine. In some early posters portraying the pioneer, *he*, the hero-ideal, stands upright with a visionary look into the future, while *she* sits, laboring the ground, doing the work. Thus, *he* has been predominantly used in this book, for simplicity and fluency. If, however, the hero-principle proceeds solely along the track of the male hero and masculine principles, as reflected for instance in the rays of Samson ("strength of sun"), without also walking the path of the heroine, who follows the reflective light of moonlit introspection, then the motif of Masada, or *the suicidal soldier*, may be acted out.

Acknowledgments

I wish to thank those with whom I have had the opportunity to share thoughts and ideas privately, in lectures and in seminars, in Israel and abroad.

When serving as Director of the Shalvata Community Mental Health Clinic, I was fortunate to work with the late Professor Shamai Davidson, Director of Shalvata Psychiatric Center. Psychoanalyst, Elie Wiesel Chair of Holocaust Studies and pioneer of community mental health in Israel, he valued and respected the integrity and the personal narrative of every individual, and was simultaneously keenly aware of the close proximity between individual and collective processes.

My thanks to Marcella London, who initiated, and the late Zeev Utitz who edited the book in Hebrew, both of the Hakibbutz Hameuchad Publishing House.

I want to thank Mel Mathews of Fisher King Press, who with warmth and skill has brought this edition of *The Hero and His Shadow* into publication.

I wish to thank Seffi Matiuk, who designed the cover of the book.

My very special thanks to Sonia, my wife, who with her continuous support has enabled this as well as other endeavors to materialize.

I want to express my thanks to Gunlög and Håkan Raihle, friends and colleagues, at the Center for Jungian Psychology, Stockholm, Sweden, for permission to quote from my booklet *Shadows in Jerusalem: Beyond the Hill of Evil Counsel, Towards the Valley of Hell* (1998).

I would like to express my thanks to Blackwell Publishers for permission to quote from my papers in *Political Psychology*, vol. 8: 365-378, 'Within Borders and Without – The Interaction Between Geopolitical and Personal Boundaries in Israel,' and vol. 15: 415-434, 'The Relationship Between Aggression and Fear of Annihilation in Israel.'

I would like to express my thanks to the Editor for permission to quote from my article in *Midstream,* November 1987: 29-31, 'To Lebanon and Back.'

I want to thank the Editor, Jackie Jakubowski, for permission to include my essay 'Behind the Veils of Deception' (Swedish translation by Svante Hansson, as 'Moralisk plikt att riva bort illusionens slöjor'), published in *Judisk Krönika*, 2003:1

Chapter 1

Return to the Source

Psychiatric diagnoses change in the course of time not only because of increasing knowledge and accumulated wisdom, but also according to the *zeitgeist*; that is, the prevailing collective consciousness. For instance, a biological understanding of mental phenomena is prominent during periods of conservatism, while environmental influences are accentuated during periods of greater liberalism (Group for the Advancement of Psychiatry [GAP] 1983, p. 14; Shalit & Davidson 1986, p. 61). When one view dominates, a compensatory one thrives in the backyard. When psychiatry and medicine are ruled by drugs, biology and technology, there is a complementary interest in alternative medicine and eco-psychology; when genes shape the soul, the psyche influences the immune system.

Psychopathology changes over time, and so, for example, anorexia – reminding us that there is a fatness of soul behind the fragility of body – takes the place of hysteria, which used to tell us that there is libido behind the girdle. The anger and the boredom of the borderline personality replace the guilt and the internal conflict of the neurotic. Meaninglessness and alienation substitute repression and anxiety.

A society's prevailing collective consciousness influences the perception of psychopathology. While visiting Moscow in the mid-1970's, I was surprised to see so many people walking in the street talking to themselves, freely hallucinating. I realized that private madness did not disrupt the delusion of the collective, while publicly

telling the truth was a malaise in need of hospital 'treatment.'
Psychologist and society are interrelated. This relationship becomes
particularly critical when society is governed by a powerful ideology
or _Weltanschauung_, with a concomitant stress on adaptation and
conformity, or in case of a totalitarian regime. During the years of the
military junta in Argentina, many of those seeking out the
psychoanalytic _temenos_, the protected space of therapeutic rapport,
needed to know the analyst's political stance in order to confide in
him or her and to feel protected from the persecuting authorities.

Psychology (and medicine) can be put in the hands of a totalitarian
regime and used for purposes of interrogation and torture. The
ultimate transformation from healer to killer, the mechanism by which
one is engulfed and participates in a regime's distortions, is described
by Lifton (1986) in _The Nazi Doctors_. On February 25, 1994 – half a
year after the Oslo accords, which marked the beginning of a process
which seemed to lead to reconciliation between Israelis and
Palestinians – the physician Baruch Goldstein brutally killed twenty-
nine praying Muslims from behind, in the Cave of Abraham, holy
both to Muslims and Jews. His act was carried out with the sharpness
of a surgeon's scalpel, in Hebron, that most sensitive spot on the
Middle East map of conflict, and may have caused an escalation in
Palestinian terrorist attacks. Yet, for both Palestinian and Israeli, all
too often it seems that the destruction that follows when the shadow is
cast onto the _other_, carries less weight than the burdensome
recognition of the shadow within oneself.

Lately, the role of Jungian theory and praxis in Nazi Germany has
been scrutinized (see Maidenbaum & Martin 1991; Samuels 1993,
chapters 11-12). The Nazi regime sought to control the development
and direction of psychoanalysis. While Freud's theories were
prohibited, Jung's were expected to play a role in the establishment of
a "German Psychotherapy" (von der Tann 1989, p. 54), conforming to
the requirements of the regime, which necessarily raises questions
about the theory, its founder and its followers. For example, the policy
of a quota against Jews is explained in an official 1995 pamphlet of
the Jungian Psychology Club in Zurich thus (see Shalit 1996, p. 103):

> Because the Club wished to remain small, membership had to be
> restricted in the mid-nineteen-thirties when there was an influx of
> foreigners to Switzerland from Nazi Germany. Many of the people who
> wished to join the Psychological Club were Dr. Erich Neumann's Jewish
> analysands. Fearing that the Swiss character of the Club would be lost
> with so many foreigners applying for membership, the Committee

decided to restrict the intake of foreign members by introducing a quota.... Later on, when there were fewer applications for membership by foreigners those who were eligible to join (Jews included) were able to do so. Canceling the quota was therefore overlooked until 1950.

The pamphlet does not mention why later on there were fewer (Jewish) applications...

This book does not deal with the politics of psychology. However, it may be claimed that the book itself is an expression of the politics of psychology. Nor do I profess neutrality, neither any pretensions for this to be an 'objective' laboratory study. Rather, the book is an effort to contribute to our understanding of past and present collective processes. The less conscious man is, the more he finds himself in the grip of events and circumstances; a situation in which he may become a passive bystander, or project evil onto his rival or enemy.

Psyche and Society

The psychoanalytic study of society can be seen as the study of the "interface of individual and collective identities" (Lifton 1983b, p. 106). This is, in fact, the essence of this work, which deals with the unique relationship between the individual and the collective in Israel. However, because of my personal proximity in space, and partly in time, to the topic – in which I am not a participant observer but a somewhat observing participator – I cannot claim the appropriate distance needed for a psychohistoric perspective.

According to Freud, social organization began with an imposition of the taboos of totemism which said that the totem animal must not be killed, and that "the members of the same totem are not allowed to enter into sexual relations with each other" (Freud 1946, p 7). These laws, in fact, coincided with repressed Oedipal wishes, i.e., the son's desire to "kill" his father and "marry" his mother. Freud's notion was that the Totem laws originated when "the expelled brothers joined forces, slew and ate the father, and thus put an end to the father's horde. Together they dared and accomplished what would have remained impossible for them singly" (ibid., p. 183). The guilt, remorse, and shame of the criminal deed turned into the prohibition against killing the Totem, thus forming the basis of religion, worship and sanctification. As the brothers shared in the crime, the basis was laid for fraternity and social consolidation. According to Neumann (1970, pp. 289-290), the totem ancestor represents the 'ancestral experience within us' which is incorporated in the body and is at the same time the basis of our individuality. ... [T]he group's totality, which is identical with the common totem ancestor, is simultaneously included in the body and the self.

The creation of society "becomes the working out and reworking of that perennially inherited imagery of rebellion, murder, 'oral incorporation,' and guilt" (Lifton 1983b, p. 103).

When Freud outlined his thesis, he presupposed the existence of a "psyche of the mass in which psychic processes occur as in the psychic life of the individual" and, he says, "we let the sense of guilt for a deed survive for thousands of years, remaining effective in generations which could not have known anything of this deed" (1946, p. 203). Thus, "repression that ensued as a consequence of historical, guilt-inducing actions was passed down from one generation to the next, giving rise to the 'archaic inheritance'" (Satinover 1986, p. 431). While cautious, Freud did take into account a "phylogenetically transmitted inheritance" (Laplanche and Pontalis 1988, p. 331).

Jung (1966) was more explicit. He considered mankind's phylogenetic development to be replicated in individual, ontogenetic psychological growth, which Neumann (1970) further elaborated upon. Jung postulated the existence of *archetypes*, universal psychological patterns manifesting as images, comparable to the concept of universal instincts at the biological level. Though he warned against *inflation*, that is, identification with an archetypal motif, which leads to a loss of ego, of conscious awareness, Jung fell victim to his own ideas. His initial fascination with the rise of Nazism stands out as an ugly chapter in his life, and casts a dark shadow on a theory so intimately and intuitively connected to its originator (see for instance the collection of papers in *Lingering Shadows: Jungians, Freudians and Antisemitism* (Maidenbaum & Martin 1991).

Though not referring to himself, after the Second World War Jung (1969b, p. 224-225) pointed out that sometimes

the ego proves too weak to offer the necessary resistance to the influx of unconscious contents and is thereupon assimilated by the unconscious, which produces a blurring or darkening of ego-consciousness and its identification with a preconscious wholeness. ... The psychic phenomena recently observable in Germany fall into this category. It is abundantly clear that such an ... overpowering of the ego by unconscious contents and the consequent identification with a preconscious wholeness, possesses a prodigious psychic virulence, or power of contagion, and is capable of the most disastrous results.

Like Freud, Jung saw the longing for mother, for a return to the source – that is, nature and the unconscious, the Great Mother – and the incest-taboo preventing the actual, physical satisfaction of that desire, as the origin of consciousness and society. Instead of regressing to our origin, instinctual energy is directed to cultural, collective needs. Freud called it sublimation, the alchemists spoke of converting the base to the noble (cf. Odajnyk 1976).

For the purpose of acculturation, instinctual *energy* is diverted to collective needs. Jung (1966, p. 150) illustrates this process with the example of a primitive tribe, which in its spring-ritual digs a hole in the ground and covers it with bushes to resemble a woman's genitals. The tribesmen then dance around the hole, "holding their spears in front of them in imitation of an erect penis" and "thrust their spears into the hole." By means of this rite, individual, instinctual energy is collectively transferred into the earth. The single individual's consciousness would otherwise not be strong enough to work the earth and reap the harvest. (The way in which this image applies to the origin and implementation of Zionism will be discussed later.)

At puberty the individual leaves childhood. Puberty and initiation rites, for example the *bar mitzvah* (at age 13, following which the Jewish boy becomes responsible for his moral and spiritual conduct), serve as a bridge from childhood attachments, channeling the *libido*, instinctual and psychic energy, to the collective ventures of society. In Israel, youth movements have played an important socializing function, enabling the young to separate from their *personal* parents and be initiated into the society of *collective* parents. Thus, the young person joins society in the sense of a greater belonging, going beyond childhood and the family circle. The connection to collective parents implies linking with and recognizing one's collective background – the ancestors and forebears of society, i.e., one's social heritage. By a variety of activities (for example, the chanting of rhymes and singing), libido is gathered and directed to the collective, forming the basis of the adolescent's social responsibility. Specific activities carry particular psychological connotations, such as, reinforcing the attachment to (Mother) Earth. Much of the activity involves fire, which is played with, gathered around, experienced. It may be approached as Logos (light, consciousness), as Eros (flame, relatedness, feeling), or as Thanatos (aggression, destruction, death).

In this way, the constructive use of fire is learned. Fire, the natural transformative energy, is inherently bipolar, as destructive as it can be constructive. The fire-rites entail the acculturation of fire, a Promethean act of stealing from the gods and handing it over to man, so that he can make purposeful use of it. These rites and activities constitute a transitional space where freedom from parental and social super-ego authority enables the young to experience their own feelings and their own fire, which now come under their sole control and responsibility.

The struggle to become more fully oneself can be likened to a hero's trial (cf. Neumann 1970). In this process, the person "partakes of the collective as a member of society," yet he also separates himself from the collective. When there is need to, he is able to raise his voice against the ingrained norms and values, against a worldview that has become obsolete. Thus he attains his own "unique combination of the potentials inherent in the collective as a whole" (Samuels, Shorter, & Plaut 1986, p. 32).

When, however, there is a complete break-up of ties and *boundaries*, the result is chaos and alienation. The response may be a reversal to national extremism, brotherhoods and clans, a search for protection by the strong leader, or a move to fundamentalist religion.

The origin and development of society necessitate channeling libido, instinctual and psychic energy, into shared collective efforts, and inducing (or projecting) into the collective a charismatic energy, *mana*, or libido with a concomitant regulation about the degree of intimacy. The collective venture back to the Mother, to Mother Earth, carries an erotic and libidinal element, as indicated by its romanticism, songs, and poems as well as the sense of intimacy among those who took part in it. The feeling of collective intimacy is an experience commonly reported by Israelis. Elon (1981, p. 242), for instance, speaks of "a degree of neighborliness infinitely more intense than that found in other urban societies. It can sometimes be excruciatingly hard to bear."

Additionally, the formation of society necessitates a separation between *Us* and *Them*, which entails the need and formation of boundaries. Similar to Freud's (1946) description, a sense of fraternity and togetherness is created. This, in turn, becomes instrumental in the essential process of boundary-formation. Later, the way in which this pertains to the establishment and developments of the State of Israel will be elaborated.

Onenenss, Identity, Shadow

Of particular interest to the area of our concern are three eminent psychoanalysts who have investigated the relationship between the individual and the collective: the Freudians *Erik H. Erikson* and *Erich Fromm*, and the Jungian *Erich Neumann*. Fromm and Neumann deal with man's separation from original oneness with society, and Erikson concerns himself with the issue of identity. Neumann further deals with the projection of our negative, dark side, and Fromm describes the conditions for a more sane society.

Erich Fromm outlines the relationship between the individual and society. He argues against Freud's belief that "there exists a basic dichotomy between man and society, and ... that human nature is evil at its roots" (Brown 1964, p. 149). Fromm criticizes Freud's biological orientation and static view of society, claiming the relationship between the individual and society to be constantly changing.

Erich Fromm

Fromm (1995) describes the beginning of man's history as emerging from a state of oneness with the rest of nature [or 'participation mystique,' an anthropological term Jung (1971, pp. 456-457) borrowed from Levi-Bruhl; see also the seminal work by Neumann (1970)]. In this original state, man is hardly aware of a separate existence of his own. He "has a minimum of self-awareness combined with a maximum of attachment to the *object*; hence the object can exercise a direct magical compulsion upon him" (Jung 1969b, p. 270). A feeling of complete identity between the individual and the collective prevails and serves as protection against the feeling of being alone in the world. Therefore man's soul is not necessarily located inside his body but could equally well be found in nature, outside his body-boundary. Likewise, "the unconscious mutual identity of persons is expressed in the fact that the group is responsible for the individual and that each individual, for his part, is regarded as an incarnation of the whole group" (Neumann 1990, p. 60). In the course of history, man has wrested himself out of this intimate bond with nature and complete dependency on society.

By the Middle Ages, man was no longer one with nature, but rather strongly tied to his social network. Society was static, with rigid and unchangeable social roles. The individual did not really exist by himself; he remained "bound to his society by primary ties, and full awareness of himself and others as separate beings had not yet developed" (Brown 1964, p. 156). Eventually, wealth took predominance over birth so that social mobility became more possible. However, "nineteenth-century Capitalism was first of all ruthless exploitation of the worker" (Fromm 1965, p. 82), and today science and technology, as well as the laws of the market rule over man (p. 83). The individual becomes powerless with an increasing sense of alienation, "being out of touch with himself as he is out of touch with any other person" (p. 111), estranged from himself. Fromm sees this as a pathological condition of the social world that causes the individual to attempt an escape from loneliness and helplessness. Fromm (1976) advocates a society not based solely on *having* but also on *being*. We may look at the pattern of separation from original oneness, as we contemplate the processes of modern Israel, in which the dis-identification of the individual from the collective ideology creates conditions of loneliness and alienation. These are then defended against on the collective level for instance by means of an exaggerated emphasis on consensus and wholeness.

Erik Erikson

Erik Erikson, who trained as a child analyst and was in analysis with Anna Freud, elaborated the concept of identity (e.g. Erikson 1968). He gave birth to his own personal identity, Erik the son of Erik, and he explored identity in its social context. In *Childhood and Society*, Erikson relates the individual ego to society and outlines the shift of psychoanalysis "from the concentrated study of the conditions which blunt and distort the individual ego to the study of the ego's roots in social organization" (p. 13). He scrutinizes society's influence on the individual's identity. His major concern is not the individual neurosis of political leaders, such as Hitler, (p. 310), but how the leader reflects collective conditions and the way "historical and geographic reality amplify familial patterns and to what extent ... these patterns influence a people's interpretation of reality" (p. 311).

Erikson (1968, pp. 193-195) specifically mentions the newborn Israeli nation to exemplify the importance of ideology for identity-formation. Ideology is the social institution that protects a sense of continuity and identity (p. 133), "for it is through their ideology that social systems enter into the fiber of the next generation" (p.134). When society fails to provide adequate goals, we may find "the sudden impulses to join in destructive behavior" which "are a joint expression of historical identity fragments waiting to be tied together by some ideology" (p. 195). In Israel we bear witness to disarray and fragmentation, as the powerful tie to ideology has dissipated. This is reflected, for instance, in the numerous small political parties. In the 1999 elections, thirty-three parties ran for a total of 120 Knesset seats.

Erich Neumann

Erich Neumann was Jung's prominent follower and colleague. He elaborated Jung's theories, particularly concerning the developmental aspects of the individual and the "evolution of consciousness in the life of humanity" (Neumann 1970, p. xvi). He outlined the relationship between ego and self, delineating the ego-Self axis. In *Depth Psychology and a New Ethic*, written in the shadow of the Second World War and the Holocaust, Neumann sees evil as the basic problem of modern man. The "disastrous results for both the individual and the collective" (ibid., p. 35) occur, when the dark side within us is denied. This happens "when the individual adapts to collective ideals by repression and suppression" (ibid. p. 37). Thus, by identification with the collective *persona*, in conformation with collective ethical values, the individual ego loses touch with the severed, dark contents within. He is easily accepted and affirmed as a well-adapted individual but he, as well as society-at-large, becomes one-dimensional and uniform, relying on projection of the shadow. Thereby society loses its capacity for self-scrutiny.

By identification with the collective, "the limited individual loses contact with his own limitations and becomes inhuman" (ibid., p. 43). Thus, while Erikson outlines the importance of ideology for identity-formation, identification with and uncritical adaptation to a prevailing ideology (i.e., the collective consciousness) causes a loss of selfhood. Neumann asserts that

> every self-identification of the ego with a transpersonal content – and that is the precise meaning of hubris, in which man imagines himself to be equal to the gods – inevitably results in downfall; the transpersonal content (that is, the gods) annihilates the ego (ibid., p. 43).

In troubled and unstable times, there are many who see themselves as 'God's messengers and identify with transpersonal contents, for instance intending to rebuild the Temple in Jerusalem. Rather than coming to grips with the inner meaning of the Temple, some are occupied with preparing ritual garments and breeding the *Red Heifer*, necessary for the required process of purification prior to the rebuilding of the Temple. In a society insensitive to its own limitations, such fundamentalism may find support. In the words of Israeli author Sami Michael, "In Iraq I learned that God is Great and the rabbis are small, while in Israel God is small and the rabbis are Big."

The old ethic, claims Neumann (1990, p. 45), "is based on the principle of opposites in conflict. The fight between good and evil, light and darkness is its basic problem." However, "the battle of the opposites is eternal. ... The world, nature and the human soul are the scene of a perpetual and inexhaustible rebirth of evil" (p. 46). Our dark side, our shadow,

> which is in conflict with acknowledged values, cannot be accepted as a negative part of one's own psyche and is therefore projected – that is, it is transferred to the outside world and experienced as an outside object. It is combated, punished, and exterminated as 'the alien out there' instead of being dealt with as 'one's own inner problem' (ibid., p. 50).

This intensifies the split between *Us* and *Them* (cf. Volkan 1988), as well as the tendency of scapegoating within the life of society (Neumann 1990, p. 74).

Neumann proposes exchanging the old ethic of repression and projection for the recognition of one's own evil.

Whereas in conflict-free regions of the world it seems relatively easy to tolerate the other, because he does not impinge and his presence may not be felt, in times of crisis and areas of conflict the recognition of one's own evil is much harder, precisely because its presence is ever-felt, and projection of the shadow onto the enemy is so much more accessible.

Chapter 2

From My Notebook

Fall 1984. The Orwellian year, which had ensured its undeniable place in an uncertain future, and which uncannily coincided with the Jewish year with the number-acronym of Tashmad (תשמ"ד) – destruction, persecution – is coming to an end.

I feel apprehensive as I take the brown envelope from the mailbox. I know its contents – a call-up for reserve-duty in Lebanon. Though expected for weeks, it becomes real only through the all too familiar envelope, and inevitable a few days later when I can no longer postpone confirming that I have indeed received the letter. I am reminded of those patients with deep scars from the wars, whose anxiety sets in when the brown army envelope arrives. For days they treat it as a letter bomb. They fear it, put it away in a drawer, and avoid the drawer. They live in the shadow of its message, of the memories and the wounds. They bring it to me, hand it over unopened, and remain silent while their facial expressions barely hide the underlying fear, helplessness or despair.

During the weeks and days preceding mobilization, fear and anger gradually build up. So does the will to stay alive. Every experience is intensified. The meaning of simple, ordinary things becomes unmistakably clear. I grapple with the inescapable thoughts about death and meaning. I try to enjoy those close to me. On the last Sabbath before leaving, I take my two daughters, I'layah and No'ah, then five and two years old, to the beach. A long walk on stony paths, laughing, running, singing, playing, gathering shells. The joy of life coupled with a streak of fear. A double life of dread and delight. For a split second, a memory runs through my mind: a year ago, just before my last term in Lebanon, I'layah steps into the bathroom, declaring that she is off for the battle field "to look for Daddy." She goes searching, but "he's lost." A little later she has found him in a hospital. "He's dead, his eyes are closed." Quickly I join the wild dance, exchanging fear for fatalism.

The morning arrives. Goodbye to all the children. The journey to the army base is like the cutting of an umbilical cord, disconnecting from mother-society. A journey away from life, towards the confined world of army and war. My wife is the only connection with ordinary existence that still remains, and then she disappears as well when we separate in front of the gate.

Getting into uniform takes place in silence and with hitherto unknown efficiency. A striking contrast to the usual chaotic atmosphere of shouting, friends meeting again, excitement, exchange of experiences. So different this time! Not even the ruminations of two years ago – should we demonstrate before we go to Lebanon, or when, hopefully, we come back? Usually the duffel bags that were handed in to be stored at the end of the previous stint of reserve duty are opened and turned upside down with loud complaints that things are missing, that nothing fits. This time everything is there, everything fits. Civilian clothes and identities are silently exchanged for army uniforms. Those who did not find a way out of reserve service resign themselves to the speedy transformation from civilian to soldier. Amazingly, it takes only an hour.

Then, we speed away for intensive pre-Lebanon training in the Judean hills. As the sun sets after a day of target practice, a young corporal mechanically repeats the cold, metallic facts about the rifle. It is no more than an iron tube encircling a hollow space; as colorless and empty as a cannon in a rainy day military parade, filmed in black and gray. Not even the dazzling light of the sun setting behind the hills can make it shine. It is a dead piece of iron with tremendous martial power, a contrast hardly noticed in the corporal's monotonous repetition of the standardized instruction. Relations among nations are sometimes determined by inducing dead matter with lethal spirit.

If the journey to the army base is like holding on to a slender guyrope before being thrown into outer space, the journey to Lebanon is just the reverse. What seemed like outer space now narrows down into the imprisonment of uniform, duffel bag, rifle, and the bus from which there is no escape hurtling towards war. The landscape is strikingly familiar, yet remote and inaccessible.   In the faint, awakening light of early morning, the barren scenery does not tell on which side of the green line, between Israel and the occupied territories, that we actually are. A need for orientation. At a roadblock, a truck is kept waiting while our seemingly civilian bus passes by. Should the truck-driver raise his bent-down head – but he doesn't – he would see the Israelis he has come to know so well in other settings reluctantly being transported to the battlefield. How would he react were he aware of the absurdity of this existential non-encounter? Perhaps it is his *son* that does raise his head, throwing the stones of the Intifada, when at the present crossroads of history it seems obvious who is perpetrator and who is the freedom fighter – at *this* particular crossroads of history.

Inside the bus – silence. No one asleep, no one awake. A collective tremor, shared reluctance and unshared fear. Senses are sharpened and every perception becomes an event. Like the two horses in the grassy island dividing the highway. One, confident and fearless, advances to cross between the cars rushing by. The other one hesitant and indecisive, pulls back. Different in temperament, still they form a unit, belong together. They reflect the journey from Israel to Lebanon, from civilian life to war. Hesitation, apprehension and a feeling of defeat merge with anger and a need to rush forth and get it done with.

The bus heads north, rushes by my hometown of Ra'anana. I can almost see the house I left just a few days ago, a lifetime ago. Only a few hundred meters away the family is waking up. The double life of Israel. One reality, chaotic enough in itself, in which life proceeds – work, family, outings, mortgage, bureaucracy, crowded hospitals, etc. The other reality with the very same roads and buildings, but observed from within the imprisoned distance of an army bus on the way to Lebanon. The essence of life seems so simple and obvious, but then the physical image disappears, the streets and houses – *home* – vanish beyond reach.

The internal tremor continues to build up until it is time for a rest stop. Last chance to phone home. No answer. Five years you had to wait for a phone (in those days), and now there's no answer. Onward, north to the border town of Kiryat Shemona.   We arrive at the transport base close to the border and unload the bags from the bus, realizing there is nothing to do but wait. This time we will not enter Lebanon by *Safari,* the half open trucks with pointed guns, but in an old army ambulance, six men to a group. It takes a couple of hours to negotiate the few kilometers – looking for gas, changing a tire. A fantasy of freedom, a self-produced delusion, even though we inevitably approach the fateful crossing. Just like the two horses some hours ago. The war zone is just across the border, minutes away. Ostensibly we are angry that nothing works, but with mixed feelings we play chess with fate by trying to repair a tire that cannot be repaired, until we succumb to the destiny we have chosen not to escape. A sudden, non-verbal decision terminates the game. The ambulance makes a U-turn. We arrive at the border, rush into the army base at full speed, into no man's land. The point of no return. The tempo accelerates. Filling in necessary forms for entering Israeli-occupied Lebanon, the war-zone; receiving battle-grade; putting on helmet, splinter goggles, protective clothing, loading a gun. The fear intensifies. It climaxes and is transformed into heightened activity – everyone is hurrying to do something. It becomes unbearable to remain between the lines; there must be movement, forward. We get into place, the old ambulance accelerates toward the last barrier – and that's it. Entering Lebanon. Mines, ambushes, RPG's – and family at home.

Then the last trace of fear vanishes. It has all been channeled into sharpened awareness, vigilance, intense concentration on the breathtaking landscape, and on the figures walking along the road side, whose every movement becomes suspicious. Everything triggers the drive to release energy, to find an enemy. There is a frightening instinctual need for the enemy. The super-ego comes forth to reign in the instincts. There is something to fear around every corner, and yet, a fatalistic calm affords plenty of time to take in the harsh scenery.

As we pass by the Beaufort fortress, time is condensed with hallucinatory clarity, and I see the commando soldiers advancing, crawling silently up the steep hillside, their hearts pounding in the darkness, moments before they are killed. I see them fall for a purpose that many of them rejected. I see then Prime Minister Menachem Begin on top of the mountain, leaning on his cane, talking to then Defense Minister Ariel Sharon. "The country will be calm for forty years," he quotes the Judges, and he declares that the Beaufort was taken without any losses; maybe he has not even been informed about the facts. Two and a half years have passed since, and like madmen we now force our way forward in the gray army ambulance, threatened by every peasant and shepherd along the roadside, forcing every car to hastily pull aside by our wild driving. Forward, through fear, in order to stay a month in a confiscated house turned medical clinic, hardly providing even an illusion of protection from the seductive beauty and brutal tragedy of this torn country. There is no protection, just the close proximity of life and death.

On *Tu b'Shevat* – Arbor Day – Israeli television shows children singing to the trees, the "beautiful Israel." In the operating room next door, Israeli physicians and medics treat a severely wounded Palestinian militant, shot while planting a bomb. Outside a member of the Lebanese Phalange in high boots and gold chains tries to force his way in to settle accounts with the Palestinian, thwarted only by a young Israeli officer, dressed in a PLO shirt. The dangerous narrow roads, the mountains and canyons, the houses that are either unfinished or bombed-out, the smiling children and the suspicious villagers who always shower their new occupiers with rice; the interconnectedness of scenery, people, and events that make up Lebanese and Middle East reality – all of it seems reflected in this absurd scene of contradictions.

An army at war is like any closed and totalitarian system. It represses individuality and independence, yet fuels the drive for stamina and self-reliance. When the routine is suddenly interrupted and I have the possibility to take off by helicopter for a day back home – an opportunity not to be missed! – the reality of war loses all its strength and impact within a matter of minutes. But there are those who don't survive, physically or psychologically, and as I return the following morning, the sense of freedom is wiped out. Two soldiers have been killed at that very spot, an hour earlier.

There are those who turn to me in my capacity as front-line psychologist. They have internalized the outside threat, and fear they will explode. And there are those who externalize their internal fear and rage, and then panic when they confront them in external reality. For some the external and the internal are one, with only self-inflicted harm, a scratch of the knife, as a masochistic way of knowing that one is still alive (cf. Joseph 1982). Is it a mere coincidence that three soldiers from one particular unit turned to me for help, struggling with their anxiety, desperate to get away, only a couple of weeks before their unit lost twelve men and had scores of wounded? Feeling the pain of the tragedy, I am thankful I sent them home, even though at the time I did not really understand why I did it. I wonder what their feelings may be, wherever they are right now, wondering what it was that surfaced by means of their anxiety, driving them to survival. And

I wonder if maybe I could have understood something more, just the way we reflect on those hints that were there but which we do not notice until afterwards, the hints we often grasp only too late, for instance after someone has died.

When I cross the border back to Israel my personal duress comes to an end. Stepping out from the shadow of war, I mourn the killed and weep for the wounded. I feel thankful, and perhaps ontological guilt, for being alive and unhurt. I feel a profound appreciation for the time still available. Then comes anger, fury at those that imposed this maddening reality upon us; that made us seem to be only tin soldiers and tin civilians.

The prophet Jeremiah was regarded a pacifist and accused of being a traitor, demoralizing the army. He was enraged by the broken word, as when the king, threatened by enemy forces, made a covenant to release all Hebrew slaves but enslaved them again. War as a means to fuel the perpetual projection onto the enemy, promises to fuel the inflation of power and the illusion of strength. "When will they ever learn?"

The anxiety that for weeks superstitiously has not been put into words, relaxes its grip and fades away. Asleep on the bus-ride home a dream comes to me with unusual clarity. I am riding on a skateboard at astonishing speed, feeling joy and fear, as I skillfully maneuver the curves into an increasingly deep, green landscape. It is dawn, just that very tiny crack between darkness and light. The dark green is half covered by grayish blue; as if spirit and matter try to reach out to each other. A simultaneous inner and outer journey in which life and death merge, become one, a reflection of each other.

As I step off the bus, dirty boots to be put away unpolished for another year, the intimate connection between one's individual life and one's collective responsibility is more apparent than ever. Especially, maybe, here in Israel where individual and collective processes overlap, the existential questions of responsibility, meaning, and death are constantly present.

Several years later. Friday, January 11, 1991. By emergency order our medical unit is ordered to stay on after a week of regular training. If scud missiles hit the Haifa area, we are at the front. The front is here, right here. Or at home. Home is the front. And if missiles equipped with unconventional warheads will hit, it will be difficult to know who is chemically wounded and who *thinks* and *feels* he is. The distinction between health and illness becomes increasingly diffuse.

Neither external borders nor internal boundaries provide a barrier for the anxiety that Saddam Hussein spreads.   Just like West Bank Palestinians were not given gas masks when Jewish settlers were, so the Muslim preacher asks Saddam Hussein to particularly protect Muslims in the area and only hit the Jews. It appears neither they nor we understand that it is not at all certain evil will make those fine distinctions.

What will be, will be evident only in retrospect. Yet, could we have used the intervening years differently?   Can we care better for the future?

February 28, 1991. Purim.   Seven in the morning, Israeli time. As far as the Gulf War is concerned, we have come to the time for retrospection. The war ended this morning. Six weeks of anxiety, threat, attacks, killed and wounded, and destruction caused by thirty-nine missiles launched against Israel. For us, the Gulf War was the Missile War, and wearing gas masks as we entered sealed rooms, it became the *Sealed Room War.*

I'layah will soon turn eleven, and No'ah turned eight at the outbreak of the war. It was a strange birthday, the streets were completely empty, and we seemed to be entirely alone out there in the tense, thick air. Unlike older Israelis, they had not experienced the Yom Kippur War, or the War of Attrition, or the Six Day War, or the Sinai War, or the War of Independence, or the Second World War and the Holocaust – except through our collective memory, that as is said on Passover, is told by every generation to the next. But the other day, while she was taking off the gas mask after still another missile attack, I'layah asked when had there been peaceful years in her life. The sharp contours of a child's question. The somewhat peaceful years, though perhaps just an illusion, were those relatively calm times in the wake of the peace agreement with Egypt. Since then, war in Lebanon, years of Intifada, their older brother Lawrence serving three years in a parachute commando unit and living with the constant fear that evokes; and now the Missile War, during which they, their parents and grandparents sit at home – at the front. If Israel is meant to be our future and not only our past, the time has come to radically revise our thinking, so that we shall not have to live solely by the sword.

September 13, 1993. Again, one of those strange turnarounds. The White House: Peres, Rabin, Arafat and Clinton.   Perhaps less dramatic, but nearly as implausible as Sadat's arrival in Israel sixteen years earlier. Rabin hesitates as he shakes Arafat's hand. Hesitates, but doesn't hold it back. The boyish, shy hesitancy seems to reflect what many Israelis feel. There is no real sense of euphoria, rather a tentative effort to come to grips with the inevitable obligation to turn the wheel and break out of the vicious cycle of animosity. I am impressed by the lack of euphoria. It reflects maturity. Hardships lie ahead. Extremism, violence, hatred, fear and anger are all the unavoidable shadow of peace.

November 4, 1995 ... yes, shadow of peace. The Peace Process as guiding myth had suppressed the former myth, the *Whole, Greater Israel*, into the shadow. But the spirit had evaporated from the peace process. While the collective ego, represented by the politicians, was busy doing, what was taking place backstage went unnoticed.

Myths, however, do not die when dethroned from the collective ego's consciousness. Spirit searches for a dwelling place. Not finding one among the supporters of peace, the winds swept across the country and settled with those who grieved the loss of the defeated guiding myth of Greater Israel. In the constant sliding between words and deeds, they aimed at dethroning the myth of Peace, de-legitimizing its proponents. The right-wing claimed that "the government has no mandate," and later-to-become Minister of Justice, Zachi Hanegbi silenced Prime Minister Rabin by disconnecting the loudspeakers during a public speech, diverting them to an outpour of foul talk. And Benjamin Netanyahu could speak in front of a crowd waving posters of Rabin in a Nazi uniform, as if the Nazi shadow had been introjected, and again he could claim he did not see, and he did not see, because to see means to carry the yoke of consciousness.

Unfortunately, the collective ego psychologically denied what was there to be seen and sensed, and repressed the feelings of fear and darkness spreading across the country. So, the man who brought the new myth – its hero in the psychological sense – walked down the stairs backstage, after a huge rally in support of peace and against the mounting violence, directly into the evil eye and pointed gun of the assassin who lingered in the shadow-less shadow. A shadow-less shadow because the murderer stood there as if he were simply one of the drivers, or policemen, or security agents. Not a stranger, not an enemy, not an easy target for projections.

It is disturbing that it was so banal. The lack of subjectivity, of a psychological attitude, blinds us so that we see solely with our all too empirical eyes, unable to perceive even what stands out in the light of day. Without the psychological, we don't see. We don't look behind us, we don't see in the dark, we don't see that in our very backyard the murderer is twelve times hero: in promotion pamphlets of the Bar-Ilan University, the picture of Yigal Amir appeared no less than twelve times as the ideal student, representative of the university. After the murder, the administration embarrassingly 'forgot' to delete the photos.

And we let the murderer vote, a decisive vote because the judicial ego-system does not see things more clearly than the rest of us. The Ministry of Justice rejected a proposal that would ensure the murderer would serve his entire life-sentence, stating that every one's life is equally dear, including that of Rabin. True, the life of Yitzhak Rabin as an individual is neither more nor less valuable than that of any one else. But this was an assassination of democracy and society as well. Such blindness is mad, suicidal and sociopathic. Winnicott (1965, pp. 157-59) says democracy implies that

> there is sufficient maturity in the emotional development of a sufficient proportion of the individuals that comprise it for there to exist an innate [natural] tendency towards the creation and re-creation and maintenance of the democratic machinery.

The murder of Prime Minister Rabin was not simply the murder of a living person, terrible enough in and of itself. The fact that the murderer was narcissistically and archetypally invested in a grandiose myth, which was suppressed during the Rabin-Peres era, must not be apologized by being pathologized into the particular individual. The madness is that he became the hero-ideal of some, and blindness is the guilt. He then reflects rather than individual pathology.

March, 1996. It would be equally wrong to emphasize the individual distress of the suicide-bomber and define his desire to enter Paradise along the road of evil merely in terms of individual pathology. What a sign of collective pathology that *terrorists* are going to determine the outcome of the forthcoming elections between Peres and Netanyahu! It is frightening to quote the words of my daughter, who told me – the day before she knew she would attend yet another funeral, of a young girl killed by a terrorist in Tel Aviv – that when she rides on the bus, she always puts her school bag in front of her, so that if there is an explosion her body parts won't fly in all directions, for her to remain identifiable. This is the collective vulnerability and proximity to our psychotic and ontological anxiety that we are forced to face. It becomes worse in the guise of denial and inflation, as was the case following the triumphant Six Day War – in the infamous words of General Shmuel Gonen (Gorodish), "We looked Death straight in the eye, and Death lowered its gaze."

May 27, 1998. There are too many signs. Violence against judges, provocations by extremist Jews, the regime hitting back at journalists, and more. Netanyahu declares the time has come to replace the former elites by new ones, made up of those who previously belonged to the fringes of society – it rings a gloomy bell of history. It almost seems to confirm the thesis that he is driven to correct a kind of family complex of being outsiders, which in fact may have been what drove the family to leave the country for America. And he refuses to talk to the Chief-of-Staff. And the tactics of delay in the peace talks make the water in the kettle boil under the still closed lid. Now even his Minister of Defense, Yitzhak Mordechai, who will later leave the government, says openly that without progress and constructive action, disaster may lie ahead.

But there are not only the outer signs, picked up by plain extraspection. I have all too many times experienced the lucid truth that ascends from the soul of those sensitive enough to turn to therapy and analysis. They tell us, as Rollo May says, where and what society is heading for. And the apocalyptic dreams, images and fears are all too abundant. Too many bring the very same image – the coastline crowded by people trying to get on the ships. The core anxiety of being thrown into the sea reemerges, and as I hear the song from the 1960's, *Distant Drums*, the words of the prophet Jeremiah come to mind,

Why is my pain unceasing, my wound incurable, refusing to be healed? (Jer. 15:18); My anguish! My anguish! I writhe in pain! Oh the walls of my heart! My heart is beating wildly; I cannot keep silent; for I hear the sound of the trumpet, the alarm of war (Jer. 4:19)

Jeremiah was an outsider, torn by conflict. He was not a man of simple solutions, nor did he gain peace of mind. His is the anguish of a heart that can not be deceived into putting its faith in the mirage of a future Golden Age, and the words of a voice that hears the alarm, rather than sounding the trumpets of glory.

May 17, 1999. The virtuality of Netanyahu is reflected in his speedy resignation just minutes after polls close, even before the counting of the votes has even started. As his rule comes to an end, people pour in to celebrate at Tel Aviv city hall's renamed Rabin Square. Many feel the curtain of incitement and animosity has been lifted to let in light. In a last desperate act he nearly set Jerusalem on fire by looking for, as his own Minister of Internal Security says, a "filmed invasion of the Palestinian Orient House," which would let loose the forces of rage and violence, shattering the fragile glass vessel within which they are barely contained. Though hardships lie ahead, this time the consciousness of concerned citizens changed the course of events. The turbulence of the years ahead is hard to predict. The road to peace seems to lie open; Barak promises to turn every stone along the road. He conceptualizes a formula that will enable him to explore possibilities that no previous Israeli leader has dared to venture, "nothing is agreed upon until everything is agreed upon," thus looking into far-reaching options that remain theoretical until the other side is willing to come to terms with the existence of the Jewish state. But as so often we will find out that there are ever so many unforeseen obstacles ahead.

May, 2003. Behind the Veils of Deception.

The *war of terror* that has been raging against us since the failed Camp David talks in 2000 has caused severe national and existential crisis. As we face it, history and our Jewish thought tradition oblige us to look into the mirror of moral and ethical reflection. We must examine our actions, contemplate our shortcomings and question our motives.

We need to bear to listen to the accusations from the Arab world, however outrageous and anti-Semitic many of them are, for instance,

> The Jews of yesterday are the evil fathers of the Jews of today, who are evil offspring ... the scum of the human race 'whom Allah cursed and turned into apes and pigs...' These are the Jews, an ongoing continuum of deceit, obstinacy, licentiousness, evil, and corruption... (The Imam of the Al-Haraam mosque in Mecca; the same words of incitement repeated time and again in the mosques of Gaza and Ramallah.)

And we cannot disregard the outcries from the West about crimes of war, even when they reverberate with cynicism, such as "the shitty little country" that French ambassador Bernard nonchalantly throws out together with the remainders on his dinner plate, and hostess Amiel has the chutzpah of picking up from the garbage – "in violation of protocol," to the dismay of the diplomatically correct.

And we cannot ignore the criticism and the contempt from intellectuals, even when far too many have a pervert and shameful affaire de coeur with, as Oriana Fallaci says, "the assassins of those in

Jerusalem who cannot go to eat a pizza or buy some eggs without being blown up."

And we must put up with the condemnations of the United Nations, even when the voice of moral stature and integrity has been silenced by the ferocious screaming of nations united in Durbanian scapegoating – more reminiscent of the ancient custom of throwing stones at the envoys of Satan (and, as Sheikh Abdul Halim Mahmoud, rector of Cairo's Al-Azhar University, says; "Allah commands Muslims to fight the friends of Satan wherever they are … among the foremost friends of Satan in the present age are the Jews," *Holy War and Victory*, quoted in Wistrich 2002) than a civilized gathering examining and condemning racism in the world.

And we must listen to the Palestinians, even when they rejoice in the killing of civilians, when their school books incite against the "tricky, greedy and barbarian" Jews, and their mosques and their media pour out incitement calling for the murder of Jews and the destruction of Israel, and their TV 'documentaries' intend to 'prove' there never was a Jewish connection to the Holy Land. We have to see through the deceptions and lay bare the lies, yet, we must see the Palestinian in his and her suffering with the clarity of compassion when attacked by settlers during olive harvest, when intimidated and violated by soldiers at roadblocks, when there is curfew, arrests and house demolitions – and we must respect and recognize their national aspirations.

While distinguishing between anti-Semitic projection and genuine criticism – a razor-sharp difference, yet far too often blurred by indistinguishable tincture – we must listen and we must look and we must ask, "What have we become?" and we must contemplate our gloomy silhouette, reflected back on us by the soiled earth of occupation and disgrace.

Beyond the material welfare of Palestinians and many Israelis, we must be concerned with how well or how bad we fare humanely and democratically.

Pogrom-like attacks on innocent Palestinians, and settlers' violence against soldiers evacuating illegal settlements, and soldiers firing at the innocent – they are all unbearable and devastating.

Worse, the silence of the regime becomes a call to crime.

So I look in the mirror, and the deformations in my reflected image compel me to ask, 'What have we become? Barbarians? Fascists? Indifferent to the suffering and the misery of the *Other*?'

Fascism stares at us around the corner, stretching its threatening shadow in front of us. Social breakdown quakes the earth. The malaise of poverty spreads epidemically. There is despair and demoralization. The internal threats and conflicts are such that only by recruiting the forces of reason, wisdom, judgment and integrity, as well as endurance and compassion, can Israel survive. (In parenthesis one may wonder if Israel's existence, however legitimate in itself, carries any real importance for the Jewish people. Ironically, I assume that as long as Israel *does* exist, its existence for the bulk of world Jewry is fairly insignificant.)

The War of Deception
The above said, it needs to be considered within its true context, and truth and honesty should be spoken, particularly when they are at odds with one's Weltanschauung. And the context of our national crisis is the present war. As has happened in the past, this war has brought to the surface our ancient feelings of existential vulnerability; fears that are deeply rooted, yet barely covered by the unsettled sand of the desert. Linking up with the apocalyptic fears of death and destruction, the threat of impermanence and becoming refugees again sweeps over Israel, carried by the evil Pneuma, the harsh desert wind that brings overwhelming danger from the East.

Hardly anything new, not to be blamed solely on our enemies' cruel intentions (though their guilt must not be ignored), but entrenched in the horrors of our own memory. As Chaim Potok says, "To be a Jew in this century is to understand fully the possibility of the end of mankind, while at the same time believing with certain faith that we will survive." (I am confident Potok intentionally choose the ambiguous word *certain*.)

This war has, however, brought to the surface one further sinister dimension (though neither novel nor unique in our history) – deception. This is a *war of terror and deception*. It has been compared with the first Intifada, the uprising that began in 1987, when young Palestinians took to stones against our occupation of their land, breaking the passivity and the compliance of the oppressed (though let us not forget – Palestinian terrorism, despicable in every sense, has a long record, and was a co-habitant also before and during that uprising).

But everything, *everything*, is different as regards the cause, the means and the aims between then and now:

The Cause of the War. The cause of the Intifada was Israel's intransigent refusal to consider Palestinian national claims. The cause of *this* war, however, has been the Palestinian refusal to end the conflict by peaceful means. Among others, PNA Minister Imad Falouji (as reported in the Palestinian daily *Al-Ayyam*, December 6, 2000) has confirmed the war was planned, by instruction from Arafat, immediately at the conclusion of the Camp David talks – Arafat rejecting the Clinton proposal; Barak returning in defeat, Arafat waving in victory from the plane-window having "survived the trap" of Camp David, where the Palestinians had not intended to make concessions (Abu Mazen, in *Al-Ayyam*, July 29, 2001). And now Premier Abu Mazen has said that the Oslo accords have been Israel's greatest historical mistake, by handing over territories in exchange for nothing.

Yes, our desire for peace is enormous, and we did hope and believe it would not be cynically related to as an act of weakness, with dishonesty and deception in return.

And the war had been given its name before it started, *Intifada Al-Aqsa*. It even started a few days *before* Sharon's provocative Temple Mount visit; by an act of treachery when a Palestinian policeman killed his Israeli counterpart on joint patrol – intended to ensure that the swords on either side let the ink of Oslo speak.

The Oslo agreements entailed Arafat's commitment to refrain from terror, and to resolve all future conflict between the parties by peaceful means. By reverting to violence, Arafat undermined the foundation of the peace process.

And Yitzhak Rabin declared that if the PLO (Palestine Liberation Organization, headed by Arafat) charter not be revised, the Oslo accords would collapse. And promises were made and letters written that the charter will be changed, paragraphs deleted, the text revised:

December 14, 1998, in the presence of President Bill Clinton, members of the Palestinian National Council (PNC) and other personalities convened a meeting in Gaza. The participants reaffirmed the decisions of the Executive Committee and the Central Council to reaffirm Arafat's letter to Clinton, January 22, 1998, concerning the results of the PNC decision to abrogate the provisions of the PLO charter that contradict Arafat's letters to PM Rabin, September 9, 1993 and May 4, 1994, and to mandate the legislative committee of the PLO to present a new text of the charter. According to the original agreement, "within two months of the date of the inauguration of the Council, the Palestinian National Council will convene and formally approve the necessary changes in regard to the Palestinian Covenant, as undertaken in the letters signed by the Chairman of the PLO and addressed to the Prime Minister of Israel, dated September 9, 1993 and May 4, 1994."

That is, the Palestinian National Council agreed to agree to agree with what was agreed upon but never implemented – to present a new text of the charter within two months of the Council's inauguration. However, the charter remains unchanged and in force (as for instance stated by the Council's Chairman Salim Za'anoun in Palestinian Authority daily Al-Hayat Al-Jadida, February 3, 2001). And you need just to go to the official Palestinian website at the United Nations, and there it is, aiming at "the elimination of Zionism in Palestine," i.e., calling for the destruction of Israel.

It is the deceptive, archetypal fantasy expressed in the charter that should be of greatest concern. The killing and the cleansing of the Jews from the land "will provide the Holy Land with an atmosphere of safety and tranquility, and guarantee freedom of worship without discrimination of race, color, language, or religion" (article 16). Where there are no Jews, there will be no discrimination. Without Jews, the Holy Land will be a Paradise of safety and tranquility.

While many of us – and many of them – wanted to speak and to hear the words of peace, in the backyard Arafat called for the elimination of Israel. We tried to be blind when at the signing ceremony, May 1994, Arafat put his pen to the paper pretending to sign, but to Rabin's and other participants' astonishment, he left the agreement unsigned. Already in 1993, after the initial Oslo accords, Arafat compared them to the *Treaty of Hudaibiya* – signed, only to be broken when conditions permit.

And it is far too easy for a peace-loving Europe to play the same accord; "Israel simply has no right to exist," says an opinion piece in the Guardian (Jan 3, 2001) – a fact which, says the author, he always has "considered central to any genuine peace formula."

Genuine peace – did we hear the refrain of the PLO charter? – means Israel will be laid to rest in peace. Yet, the dead have a tendency to come back as haunting ghosts, disrupting the peace and tranquility even of such ingenious peace formulae. That may be the reason for a deplorable Jewish quality of being an eternally wandering nuisance, defying the yearning of some to cut off the Jewish branch from the Tree of Nations.

The Means of the War. And the means of this war are different: The Palestinian hero of the Intifada was the stone-throwing youth; the insignia of this war are carried by the suicide- (or rather, homicide) bomber, who is deceived to believe in the perfect *selection* – he (or she) to heaven, the monstrous *other* to hell.

But a suicide bomber has nothing to do with suicide. This is a deceptive term, sometimes leading to the "clarifying" statement that the Koran forbids suicide. Hardly ever a mentioning of "casting terror into the hearts of those who disbelieve" – perhaps a significant idea within a web of sacred imagination, but in the hands of fundamentalists, it becomes a grenade in the market-place.

"They want to impose the term 'suicide' on them, but they are not suicides," says Dr. 'Adel Sadeq, chairman of the Arab Psychiatrists Association, and he is right. When the bomber blows himself up, he "senses himself flying, because he knows for certain that he is not dead... It is a transition to another, more beautiful world, because he knows very well that within seconds he will see the light of the Creator. He will be at the closest possible point to Allah," says Dr. Sadeq. The homicide bomber acts out of hope no less than out of despair; a flight of hope on the wings of the archetypal fantasy of 'peace' through destruction that we also find in the PLO charter. A sensible view implies that behind suicide there is depression and despair. But, as Dr. Sadeq says, these are not suicides, and the Islamic Jihad movement emphasizes in its recruitment campaign that the female suicide bombers "were not ugly or unlucky, as the Zionist slanderers try to say. They were top university students who had a good living." The fact that some of the now all too many suicide-bombers are poor is no more conspicious than some being rich and many highly educated; and some suffer from personal distress and psychopathology, whereas others do not. Islamic fundamentalist terror, says French philosopher Bernard-Henri Levy, has nothing to do with post-colonial poverty. Terrorism has little to do with personal pathology and more with collective ideology, norms and morals, which in the eyes of the beholder may be considered pathological.

And in this war, the moral message of terrorism has been condensed into nuclear clarity. They target shops and restaurants, schools, buses and market places, beaches and synagogues, the elderly playing chess in the park, the young trying to live a normal life, children sleeping in their beds, and their mothers who in vain try to protect them from their barbaric executioners. The silence of the barren skeleton of a burned bus, the dismembered bodies and sometimes unidentifiable corpses, shattered lives and destroyed families – and heroic struggles – are the remains after the terrorist minds have engineered the slaughter of men rather than the building of bridges. Suicide- (or, again, homicide) belts and bombs are smuggled in baby prams and ambulances – and so we become satanically inhuman when blocking the road, checking the ambulance for explosives, and hindering its free movement. The Hamas organization has expressed a desire to achieve a balance of "one to three" between Israelis and Palestinians, i.e., one Israeli killed for every three Palestinians. Together with their fellow organizations, such as Islamic Jihad and Al Fatah in its different denominations, they have in fact fared somewhat 'better' – but statistics speak a very partial truth. Four fifths of Israelis killed are non-combatants killed by Palestinians, of whom 40% are female. More than one out of every thousand Israelis has been killed or injured, which compares to more than a quarter of a million in the USA, or three hundred and fifty thousand in the European Union. One third of the Palestinians are non-combatants (of whom 9% are female) killed by Israel – itself terrible enough. In the statistics, Palestinian death-toll includes suicide/homicide bombers as well as the innocent, and several hundred whom the Palestinians themselves have killed (either suspecting collaboration or mistaking them for Jews). While the non-combatant Palestinians have not been intentionally targeted, in contrast to the Israeli civilian, there is no difference in the tragedy of lost lives.

And along with amoral statistics in which the suicide-bomber counts like his victim, the media is easily (self-) seduced into distortion and deception. Fierce battle against terrorists barricaded with enormous amounts of accumulated explosives is called "the massacre of the 21st Century" and compared to the "killing fields" of Cambodia where millions were slaughtered. Houses trapped with bombs on ground floor, civilians on the second, and snipers on the third. Bombs and weapons stored in civilian houses, explosives, suicide-belts and fighters hidden in ambulances. Besides twenty-three Israeli casualties, fifty-two Palestinians were killed, almost all combatants, says the UN report that investigated the "massacre" – rather, the exploitation of United Nations (UNWRA) facilities, equipment and vehicles, to give cover and transport terrorists and weapons, is giving rise to concern. Fifteen thousand (!) explosive devices, including suicide belts ready for use against civilians, were seized in Jenin.

There was no massacre in Jenin. There was no Holocaust there either, and to insinuate that the destruction in Jenin was 'almost a Holocaust,' as a number of European papers hinted, amounts to Holocaust denial. And when Saramago compares Ramallah to Auschwitz, that is Holocaust denial as well, not unlike his once blindfolded straying the streets of Stalin. Ramallah is *not* Auschwitz. And the silence of the European media-witness, at place, who revealingly pronounces "every one knows there was no massacre in Jenin, but you can't write that," becomes megaphone for the homicide-bomber who blames his victims for the death he has brought upon himself.

And how easily we forget, whereby we become participators in denial. The faked, staged funerals that were to increase the number of 'dead' in preparation for the UN fact-finding mission served as reminder of the uncanny *poisoning of Jenin;*

> In 1983, almost a thousand school girls in and around Jenin reported fainting, headache, stomach pain, and dizziness. Israel was blamed for either having poisoned the water, or having gassed the classrooms. Scenes of hundreds taken to hospital swamped the media, and the UN was called into action. In a letter (31 March 1983, UN document A/38/128 S/15667) to the Secretary-General, the "Chairman of the Committee on the Exercise of the Inalienable Rights of the Palestinian People," Massamba Sarre, expressed his concern about "this deplorable event ... in the occupied territories that has served to exacerbate tension in the region still further and, by extension, threaten world peace." Prior to "pending results of any investigation that might be carried out," the honourable chairman expressed his devastation that it is "the young people in the occupied territories that have taken the brunt of those acts of repression and violation of human rights."

Medical tests proved negative. There had been no poisoning and no gassing, and the symptoms soon receded. After foreign media left, pictures showed some of the girls, who had been brought by trucks to the hospital, getting out of bed making V-signs.

While the symptoms receded, the accusations continue, and so lies are repeated, such as "intensive daily use of poison gas by the Israeli forces" (Suha Arafat), or that Israel uses depleted uranium against Palestinians (Arafat, over and over again, e.g. February 21, 2002, l'Humanite).

Occupation poisons, but so does incitement and blood libeling.

The Goals of the War. And what about the goals of this war? In the first Intifada, the Palestinians fought against Israel's occupation. This war, paradoxical as it seems, was initiated when Israel was willing to withdraw from the remaining occupation (unless by occupation is meant the very existence of the State of Israel, which several Palestinian groups in fact do mean), and to recognize a Palestinian state with Jerusalem as shared capital. But at the moment of truth, the Palestinian leadership disclosed its strategic goal, aiming at the sociocide of Israel, destroying its vulnerable social fabric, expecting disintegration, death and emigration, convinced and determined that Israel shall be a temporary phenomenon.

In order to make peace, one must be willing to concede one's grand fantasies, while paying respect, indeed, to *the other's* all-embracing belief, as reflected notably in his/her religious belief and worship.

Identification with and self-imposed engulfment in an archetypal image – whether Greater Israel or Greater Palestine, PLO's "safety and tranquility" without the Jews; transfer of the Arabs or throwing the Jews in the sea, or the suicide-martyr's 'heavenly marriage' to the seventy-two virgins – such celestial desires inevitably bring earthly disaster. While taking off toward his heavenly fulfillment, the suicide bomber physically blows the innocent in pieces, aiming at the disintegration of the other's sense of identity, expecting his holy war will bring divine purity by exterminating the evil shadow – as carried by that other/enemy/ Zionist/Jew.

In the course of history, the symbolic element comes to supercede the physical reality upon which it is based. *Representative* meaning replaces its *concrete* manifestation. However, fundamentalism destroys images by making them graven. The Passover massacre, in which twenty-nine were killed and hundreds wounded, became particularly significant not only because it was yet another act of terrorism in this war of terror, but because it became another Passover pogrom in the history of the Jews. Carried by the winds of renewed anti-Semitic defamation, Arab media (and leaders such as the Syrian Minister of Defense) keep repeating the ancient allegation of ritual slaughter of non-Jewish children for the Passover meal – blood libels that then justify, as it were, the terrorist's slaughtering of the Jews and their rituals. Arafat builds upon the same distortion and deceit when he tries to tear down the link between the Jews and the Temple – "There was no Temple in Jerusalem," he repeats (e.g., Dennis Ross, Aug. 8, 2001), in an attempt to build his own myth by the denial of history.

By terrorizing another people's religious observance and tradition and cultural body of imagery, the Palestinian terrorist and those behind him and her, destroy not only the fragile fabric of dialogue, but their own human and ideational foundation; the account of Muhammad's night journey, in which he ascends through the seven heavens from the Temple Mount, arouse from recognition of the Mount's sanctity to the Jews, but now, under the present Muslim rule of the Mount, invaluable – primarily Islamic – archeological treasures are just dumped at the dunghill.

A Second Look. And as I again gaze into the mirror, I see Europe throwing stones from within a glass-cage; and I see the spirit of evil released from the bottle by the very one together with whom we were to prevent it from shattering; and I see the hunger and humiliation of the other.

And I look at myself, at my own contours of cruelty, rage and evil – and I see how I have been seriously wounded and deformed by the scars that come from wrestling with evil, forcing the ghost back into the bottle, struggling against the seemingly all too convenient "genuine peace" of annihilation.

The struggle has not come to an end, and perhaps it never will. In lieu of being confronted with hatred, incitement and deceit, fantasies of ethnic cleansing and genocidal aspirations, I, we, Israel and possibly the Jewish People will pay dearly – physically and morally. Simultaneously, I would see it as a moral obligation of honest intellectuals to unveil the veils of deception. But as Saul Bellow has remarked, "A great deal of intelligence can be invested in ignorance when the need for illusion is deep."

Perhaps in greatest need of illusion and deception, and yet with what I feel profound kinship, is the spirit of the enlightened Jewish intellectual; a spirit distilled from the grapes of Europe's bitter-sweet soil, a spirit simultaneously wearing the garment of universalism and stained by the concentrated stripes of particularistic history. Always on the side of Isaac against Abraham's credulous obedience to an authoritarian Father, some liberal and leftist European Jews turn to the sacrifice of Israel (son of Isaac), pleading exculpation by Isaacian submission at the altar of Bon Ton. "It is not me, I have nothing to do with those savages," some say.

The essence and beauty of liberalism is the capacity to live with ambiguity, to tolerate conflicting views of the world, and to respect the other. Freedom cannot thrive where the other is bound by chains.

In a liberal mind the other is my worthy equal, and my heart relates to him or her as I, myself, want to be related to. In difference, I see similarity. Yet, the very aesthetics of liberalism may turn into escapism. By seeing similarity, I might be blind to difference. When failing to recognize Islamic fundamentalism and deception as radically different from European liberalism, the latter becomes foolish and hypocritical. Foolishly blind by looking where there is light rather than in darkness, hypocritical in defense of evil and in Chiracian intolerance of those (Eastern European countries) that do not share his worldview about *the other*, onto whom he therefore bestows the 'freedom of silence,' and demands they behave like subjugated children who have "just arrived in the neighbourhood." This is the perverted logic of brotherhood of those in the West who felt justification and compassion for the terrorists who crashed into the World Trade Center, giving us a preview and an example of what World War Three will look like. In every twinship, however identical, resides not only the mirror of narcissistic similarity, but a shadow of the dissimilar as well. And in every towerful of hubris, the shadow of downfall threatens arrogance with disaster. The World Trade Center symbolized world trade according to capitalism, which casts its inevitable shadow. And shadows must be related to. But Islamic fundamentalism seems neither the right judge, nor the good enough mechanic to repair the wrongs of the West.

I am obliged to hear the Palestinian's cry of suffering, and the liberal and intellectual is obliged to see beyond the superficial bombardment of deceptive media-images, and hear the screams of anti-Semitic incitement in a mixture of Nazi language and the Koran (as Holocaust historian Yehuda Bauer has said) that resounds through the Wadis of the Middle East, and you must ask what freedom can a nation build on the piles of dismembered bodies, of infants, of the young and of the elderly who can no longer weep.

Sometimes I am bewildered by the bizarre tolerance of the most horrendous acts of terror, as if justified for instance by Israel's demolition of (terrorists') houses (which *follows* upon the acts of terror). If the Palestinians were to destroy houses (and honestly, I'd prefer they did *that*) – would that justify targeting and killing the innocent? I hope the answer would be an outrageous "NO!" Yet, this is the distorted moral correlation between condemnation and tolerance that comes out of the call for "cultural and scientific" boycott of Israel, while not protesting the Palestinian Authority, which said no to peace, planned the war, and instigated to terrorism. Mrs. Duisenberg, well-known European Central Bank's President's wife, is a spokesman of this inverted ethics – "not even the Nazis demolished houses," she says, meaning our crimes are worse than Nazi atrocities, simultaneously expressing her understanding for terror (against Israel). The voices of ambivalence vis-à-vis the Jews and the Holocaust are again heard in Europe, where sometimes projected condemnation replaces necessary introspection. Passionate conviction of Israel's crime seems to exculpate for being bystander to Hitler's camps.

Incidentally, I can somehow understand the urge of some to be 'human shields,' protecting demolition of terrorists' houses, but I wonder why not a single 'human shield' has offered protection against terrorism by riding on a Jerusalem bus or guarding a kindergarten? I feel great admiration for those who courageously *do* raise their voice against the hypocritical approval of sociocide and ethnic cleansing by terror. The magnitude and brutality of the onslaught would have been undeniable, were Israel unable to fight back. I confess feeling contempt for the compassion that comes alive only when the land has been cleansed, and the Jew has regained his classical role.

Terror is a weapon in the hands of someone whose hand you cannot shake. Peace and dialogue, agreement and disagreement, fury and embrace, lamb and lion cannot dwell together under such circumstances.

The work of repair and re-civilization can only take place when the painful cry for life as living reality, rather than the archetypal flight to divinity by destruction of the enemy, is heard from within the suicide bomber's killing womb.

Aware of the Palestinians' anger and despair and our mutual mistrust, and even if still bleeding and restraining my narcissistic – no, existential – rage, I will then again stretch out my hand to the Palestinian in an effort at appeasement. Familiar with the tides and turns of Middle Eastern politics and states of mind, I know that not only does despair replace desire, but sometimes new possibilities arise from the anguish.

December 17, 2011. ... Hope and possibilities alternate with anguish and despair, as a year of protesters' spring and danger of nuclear winter comes to an end. Sophia, the Wisdom born out of the secrets of the Night and the reflection in Depth, seemed to have abandoned the streets and the places of concourse (Prov. 1:20-32). Then, in an era in which all seemed to dwell in the self-imposed solitary confinement of virtual reality, life in vitro behind the screen, the young take to the streets and gather in the squares. Attempting to break the bonds of oppressive regimes and cold-hearted mammonism, they have raised their voice across the globe, demanding freedom, solidarity and justice. Will these voices persevere to withstand the strong, silencing forces of darkness, of ruthlessness and oppression? Will the Voice of Wisdom be listened to, so that we may "dwell safely, without fear of evil" (Prov. 1:33).

Chapter 3

From Dream to Reality

The Dream of Redemption

Modern Israel is based on an idea:

> The idea which I have developed in this pamphlet is a very old one: it is the restoration of the Jewish State (Theodor Herzl 1946, p. 7).

The idea was a dream:

> I have been occupied for some time past with a work which is of immeasurable greatness. I cannot tell today whether I shall bring it to a close. It has the appearance of a gigantic dream. But for days and weeks it has filled me, saturated even my subconsciousness; it accompanies me wherever I go, ... disturbs me, and intoxicates me.
> What it will lead to it is impossible to surmise as yet. But my experience tells me that it is something marvelous, even as a dream, and that I should write it down – if not as a memorial for mankind, then for my own delight or meditation in later years. And perhaps for something between both these possibilities: for the enrichment of literature. If the romance does not become a fact, at least the fact can become a romance. Title: The Promised Land!
> (First entry, Herzl's Diary, 1895)

The dream was one of redemption, of promise and hope:

> The King-Messiah came, a glorious and majestic old man, took me in his arms, and swept off with me on the wings of the wind. On one of the

iridescent clouds we encountered the figure of Moses. The features were those familiar to me out of my childhood in the statue by Michelangelo. The Messiah called to Moses: It is for this child that I have prayed. But to me he said: Go, declare to the Jews that I shall come soon and perform great wonders and great deeds for my people and for the whole world.

This was the dream of 12 year old Theodor Herzl, the founder of political Zionism. A person who acts out such a dream is archetypally possessed. Herzl was captured by the *Grand Idea*, which would serve as his guiding spirit. Archetypal possession may cause a sensation of triumph and glory, of energy, euphoria and narcissism, but also death or psychosis. Herzl died at the age of forty-four, heavily overworked, consumed by his life project.

Redemption originates in death and destruction. Legend says that on the day the Temple in Jerusalem was destroyed, the Redeemer was born. In the words of Gershom Scholem (1974 p. 246), Zionism is the Jewish people's dreamed-of return to its own history, directed at the past as well as the future. Redemption is a search for restitution of the destroyed center (Kluger 1976), whether personal or collective. It is a dream of discovering the hidden treasure that lies dormant within oneself, reflecting something greater than one's own individual consciousness. Redemption means unearthing the soul that has sunk into barrenness, an end to wandering and homelessness. The Zionist dream of redemption was to materialize by laboring Mother Earth. A.D. Gordon, an early pioneer, wrote (as quoted in Hertzberg 1969, p. 371):

> And when, O Man, you return to Nature – on that day your eyes will open, you will gaze straight into the eyes of Nature, and in its mirror you will see your own image. You will know that you have returned to yourself, that when you hid from Nature, you hid from yourself.

It is the dream of Jerusalem – the Whole Center, the One – a spiritual and emotional affinity to something greater than one's conscious identity, either within or outside oneself, as in the following dream by a middle-aged, secular man in search of himself.

> I am looking for a wounded man that I am supposed to treat. I inquire with a clerk at the post office. He tells me I can get help in Jerusalem. I'm surprised when he says it will only cost thirty-six (I don't know of what). I thought it would cost a thousand. 'But,' he says, 'I have to go and look, myself.' As I wake up I notice the double connotation of 'to look, myself' – '*by* myself' and 'for my *self*.'

This man is called to treat his wounded shadow. The humble

clerk directs him to heal the shadow by coming to himself, to his inner wholeness, as symbolized by Jerusalem. The price is not high, but it is significant: thirty-six (in Hebrew ל"ו, 'lamed vav') righteous men who, according to legend, are present at all times in the world, humble and unknown to others as well as to themselves. The dream makes a point of the tedious and lonely task of uniting the opposites of *shadow* and *wholeness*, through man's search for him/her self, by oneself. The shadow has a place in Jerusalem – that is, within the idea of peace and wholeness. However, the means of getting there are humble (thirty-six) rather than grandiose and absolute (a thousand). Most important, man is to consciously search along the painful road of individuation, rather than being deceived into believing that the goal, individual or collective, whether Peace or the Messiah, can be attained and fulfilled as an eternal, paradisiacal condition. As Jung (1966b, p. 200) says,

> The goal is important only as an idea; the essential thing is the opus /the work/ which leads to the goal; that is the goal of a lifetime.

Dreams of Jerusalem are frequent and profoundly symbolic for the individual as well as for the collective Jewish psyche. But Jerusalem can be divided and the dream of the *Whole Center* shattered; a sharp line of red across the night sky drips blood on the crumbling houses reminiscent of the exodus from Egypt, as in one man's dream. While *Heavenly Jerusalem* constitutes an image of wholeness, *Earthly Jerusalem* entails a reality of conflict.

Thus, the idea of redemption and rebirth means to find one's way home to an inner sense of a cue or a key. On the collective level, the Land is home. To sink into its ancestral earth, its fields and valleys, to feel embraced by and in communion with Mother Earth, is to find *home*. To destroy it, to handle it carelessly by wasting its modest resources or polluting its water, for example, is to destroy one's *Self*, one's sense of wholeness, by the arrogant creation of a toxic carcinogenic shadow that monstrously grows beyond the point of no return.

Since redemption grows out of death and destruction, Zionist redemption has always carried a dark shadow of death and madness, despair and alienation. The *second a'liyah*, the consequential wave of immigration between 1904 and 1914, suffered massive remigration and numerous suicides. While the early plays and dramas about settling the Land depicted the pioneer in accordance with the collective idea as a giant, "sunburnt as the earth with which he identified," the so called *theater of doubt* had him appear as a weakling, "pale and out of place in nature" (Ofrat 1979, p. 46). The pioneer who redeemed the land and felt at one with it, who built the new national home, was portrayed as a collective being, representing the collective's ego-ideal. However, in the more pessimistic, skeptical plays of the period, "he dissociates himself from his people" (ibid., p. 46). In these dramas we find the loneliness and estrangement of the individual who felt he or she did not belong, or who was unable to fit into the collective ego-ideal. Underneath the hope for the future, there was despair of the day, as expressed, for example, by the characters in Orlov's *Alla Karim*, written in 1912:

> I ask, is there a reason why we are wallowing in the filth here in blessed Palestine, suffering hunger and sinking from day to day?... We are lost, all of us, lost ... with no path ... where are we going?

Madness lurks in the background of redemption, as told by the narrator in a story by Yehuda Ya'ari from 1934:

> In their souls there was a striving for redemption, redemption of the entire people and redemption of the individual human being. And, I'll tell you a secret: this striving was greater than they could sustain or even comprehend. Too great a soul's desire ... can drive a person out of his mind.

The individual's identification with the archetypal idea of redemption threatens him with madness. Behind the notion of home, we find displacement; behind redemption linger death and madness; and behind the dreams we are ridden by the mares of the night. The dialectic was and is inescapable. However, if the collective dream accounts for its nightmarish aspects, not letting the outsider and the outcast be sole carriers of the entire burden, society stands a better chance not to fall victim to its own split-off shadow, or misled by false conceptions (such as the fallacious self-perception leading up to the Yom Kippur War).

Eros and Mars, Alienation and Aggression

Eros, the life instinct, is necessary for both the establishment and preservation of relationships and to enable rebirth and redemption. Eros is the principle of unification. Freud (1949, p. 379) says,

> The aim of [Eros] is to establish ever greater unities and to preserve them thus - in short, to bind together.

The sexual act, behind which we find Eros, is based on the tension that causes union, which enables the creation of life. Relatedness partakes in love, which can be sexual and spiritual, but fundamentally is a way of feeling for *the other*. It is the capacity to surpass one's restricted ego and relate to the other, the 'not-I.' Inwardly, Eros enables a relationship between one's ego-identity and those layers of the soul that are outside the domain of the ego, or of which one is not conscious, such as one's complexes (cf. Shalit 2002). Eros therefore makes it possible to feel at home within oneself. Outwardly, it provides the possibility to relate to others. Without Eros, the world is lifeless, cold and alienated, rather than warm, loving, containing and nurturing. *Eros* is antithetical to the need for power, hatred, envy, and greed. It is the opposite of *Thanatos*, the death instinct, and to *Mars*, the god of war (ibid., p. 48ff.). Jung (1969a, p. 28) defines libido as a hypothetical life energy resulting from the tension of the opposing life and death forces. So in fact, Eros, the life principle, needs Thanatos, death and the death instinct, for its existence. There can also be no Eros without Mars, since Mars, the warrior, is necessary to establish, define, and defend one's identity, distinct from others. However, being permanently in a situation of battle and strife, identity becomes increasingly restricted, and relatedness to others impaired. The ego soon dries up and becomes lifeless without the relatedness of Eros (e.g. Gath 1983, p. 3). Under such circumstances, *I* eventually find *the other*, the despised one, *inside myself*, as a cancerous enemy to be exorcised. Infected by *the other*, *I* find *myself* contaminated by the shadow, in constant need of purification.

Israel is the constant wavering back and forth of Eros, Mars, and Thanatos; between life and relatedness, death and aggression. At times one triumphs over the other, at times they blend together:

> As Israeli parachutists approached the Western Wall in the Old City of Jerusalem, June 1967, they heard a woman screaming in labor-pains. In the midst of battle, the physician did not hesitate. While he was later killed in the 1973 Yom Kippur War, the baby he had delivered turned out to be Jewish, her mother having stayed on in the Old City, which was seized by the Jordanians in the war of 1948. Twenty years later, the girl serves in the Israel Defense Forces.

> Israel is also the story of the only family to remain in an Arab village that was annexed to a Jewish town. The children went to a (Jewish) religious school, the son converted, served in the army, and was killed in the Lebanon War. And so the mourners on Remembrance Day for the fallen soldiers are, paradoxically, mostly Palestinians.

Israel is also the heart of a dead Jewish soldier, transplanted into the body of a Palestinian man. Jewish extremists calling themselves Sicarii, borrowing their name from the ancient sect, threaten the surgeon by placing explosives at his door. The surgeon and his operating team knew what the Arab woman in the hospital expressed, as she simply stated that the heart was given from one human being to another human being. A simple truth that becomes exceptional under the vicious circumstances of the Middle East.

All too few are those who follow the *law* of integrity and the *voice* of the self, but under the sinister circumstances in which Israelis and Palestinians find themselves those who do, become particularly notable. It may be the orthodox Jewish woman who saves a terrorist from being lynched, or the Arab man killed with the young woman he tried to protect from a terrorist. In fact, as time goes by, I see and admire the not so few, and many of the young, who are able to rise above uncompromising animosity and account for the complexity that comes from living in constant danger.

The spiral of confusion invades every organ of the body, making it difficult to retain integrity in circumstances that hold so much conflict and so many dilemmas. A psychiatrist confesses that he has learned to play two different roles with different sets of rules. One as a civilian, the other in uniform. One in peace, one in war. One at home, another one out there. One role with *Us*, another one with *Them*. Split behavior and separate norms, an uncanny balance that affects all.

Israel is a country in which each life has paramount value – yet with almost no geographical distance between us, *the other* may be killed or wounded, arrested and under curfew – and we don't always manage to see.

Personal responsibility, the ability to respond, weakens as Eros, integrity and conscience are tarnished. When the enemy is nameless, "an Arab was killed ...," we become faceless as well, apathy creeps in, and we may become bystanders. However, even with the pain, frustration and anger that came out of the war of terror that the Palestinians brought upon Israel in 2000, the years of rapprochement affected the capacity to see the other, and something may have softened in the previously so characteristically aggressive Israeli way. This may have been what Arafat mistakenly understood as weakness, which he believed he could exploit to damage the vulnerable fabric of Israeli society.

And Israel is a country where peace activist Abie Nathan, at the time, was sentenced to eighteen months for speaking to the enemy, according to the (later annulled) law against terrorism, while the extremist Rabbi Levinger was released after three months in prison, having killed "someone he didn't see." And he also didn't see, because the person a few meters away from him did not really exist. In his boundariless world, Arabs are an obstruction. In his world, shared with other ideologically motivated settlers, of archetypal identification with the myth of Greater Israel, violence against shopkeepers and going berserk in Arab quarters become legitimate. The viewpoint of the judicial system can also become obstructed. And perhaps it cannot be otherwise, since the judicial system represents the conscious ego of the collective, of society – its laws, norms, and values. A (female) lawyer with the West Bank Civil Administration could, as long as occupation was barely questioned, argue that the husband of a killed Arab woman in fact benefited from her death, since if alive, he would have had to provide for her; thus, the inflicted harm is at most zero.

When Eros, the cement of relatedness that was once so characteristic of Israel is lost, the societal web draws to itself an overload of aggression, brutality, apathy and lack of concern. These are all features of fragmentation that threaten to break the fragile web with the result that "we're all here on the verge of departure," many of the young intending to leave. The desire or intention to leave is a sign of the lost sense of belonging and direction that a living guiding myth brings. This brings fear and estrangement that result in abandonment (e.g. leaving the country), aggression (e.g. inconsiderate traffic behavior and, often domestic, violence), and self-destruction (such as the myth of Masada, or the suicidal soldier).

Without Eros, relatedness, the boundaries between *I* and *Thou* become harsh and tense, without an intermediary space to soften the encounter. We blow our horns if the car in front of us does not move practically before the light has turned to green. Bureaucracy seems often not to serve the citizen, but becomes a Kafkaistic ordeal (cf. Reich 1972). While there are subtle changes toward an increasing gentleness, for instance in public services, the once socialist principles of caring for society's weak, of which kibbutz ideology was a prominent manifestation, have seemed to be declining – possibly until the point when enantiodromia makes the swing back, and the voices of Eros rise again.

Lacking in Eros and without a firm collective conscience, society does not provide the necessary protection. Feeling exposed, unprotected against external threats, like the mythical child placed outside the city boundaries (e.g. Oedipus), society's weaker layers readily ask for the strong leader.

The soldiers of the Intifada, starting in 1987, were exposed to violence for which they had not been prepared, and so they were told to "break the bones" of the Palestinians. And the concentration camp survivor who during the Gulf War of 1991 had to stay, passively, in the sealed room felt exposed, threatened by German-Iraqi gas. Looking through the gas mask at his or her children and grandchildren, Israel no longer provided a safe and protective haven.

And Israel is also the triumph of Mars in his assertive capacity as guardian. In May of 1991, a brief moment of accomplishment and euphoria, as fourteen thousand Ethiopian Jews were airlifted in one day, taking advantage of the thin crack between two shaky regimes. "Once Jews were shuffled in for transportation to the death camps, while this time they were rushed onto the planes to safety," was the thought that went through the mind of one of the participating physicians.

But these are the very same Ethiopian Jews, stuck together in caravan encampments, abandoned in neglected areas of the country. These are the Ethiopians that protested when their blood contributions were rejected because of the incidence of AIDS among them. They protested because they know that blood is soul and blood is *Eros*, relatedness. By blood we are related. When blood is purely "a red liquid circulating in veins of higher animals," as the dictionary tells us, then we extract anorectic sterility and take away the *Blood,* the *Flesh,* the *Soul* and the *Eros* from blood.

And then there are the unlikely scenes of Rabin meeting Arafat, of Israeli officers suddenly discussing security matters with their Palestinian counterparts, the former enemy. And Nabil Sha'at of the PLO, the long-time Palestinian enemy, wishing "Good Morning Israel" on the radio. The Prime Minster in Arab lands, open meetings with the Jordanians and other Arab leaders. And the Palestinian flag, so unbearable to the authorities during the Intifada, suddenly becoming acceptable. What had been the utopian hopes for one sector of the population became political reality 'over-Oslo-night.' But simultaneously, these are the doomsday fears of another segment of the population that comes to feel robbed of its guiding myth. And so it wavers back and forth like unruly winds. Middle Eastern reality remains unsettled and unpredictable.

The electronic media cause us to adapt with unprecedented speed. There is no digestion, so indifference sometimes becomes the defense of choice. There is a false, artificial sense of nearness (proximity) in time and space to events, which turns them into pseudo-events, and leaves us untouched. In effect, the artificial nearness creates distance, alienates. Reality itself becomes artificial and simulated, computer-animated; it becomes soulless and often meaningless. Could this be the background to the clockwork-orange violence of killing out of boredom, as part of the increasing violence? Is such senseless cruelty worse than medieval burning of witches or Holy Wars? How does it compare to terrorism or ideological murder and political assassination? There are perhaps no precise or definite answers, but the questions must be asked. If we do not ask questions, how can we find meaning?

Israel is an incessant stream of events – terror, retaliation, festivity and commemoration, search for peace and holding on to war. We need the capacity to imagine peace so that the future will not merely replicate the past, and we need the capacity to imagine war, so that its horrors not be acted out.

De-Narcisstification of the Relationship between Individual and Collective

Israel is going through a process of de-Zionization, or de-narcisstification, i.e., a change in the close relationship between the individual and the collective, between the individual's personal identity and his extended identification with the collective, with society. The process has been going on since the 1970's. It is reflected, for example, in the increased vote for ultra-Orthodox, non-Zionist political parties, and the phenomenon of *yerida* ("descent"), emigration from Israel. Both these phenomena reflect a decrease in the individual's sense of commitment to the collective, to Zionist ideology, and to society in Israel. Almog (1993) found these changes empirically expressed as a shift from group culture to individual culture, and as a move from ethnocentrism to egocentrism. The 1992 election results, Labor with Rabin regaining power, also reflected people's withdrawal of narcissistic energy from the myth of Greater Israel. The Likud headed by Netanyahu was back in power in 1996, because the Labor government was in denial of the fear, insecurity and violence, caused by horrendous terrorist bombings that preceded the elections – *the shadows of peace* were repressed behind the naive image of peace as archetypal harmony and wholeness.

Thus, in general there is a withdrawal of the State as a

narcissistically invested self-object.

Narcissism and Self-Object
Narcissism usually carries negative connotations. We describe as narcissistic a person who is exaggeratedly self-involved, who behaves as if superior, and who relates to others not as individuals in their own right but rather as parts or extensions of the narcissistic person himself. However, narcissism can be a healthy involvement in oneself, for example through creativity and sound self-esteem, which are necessary for one's capacity to relate to others.

A self-object is a term that relates to those objects (persons) who supply functions and fulfill needs for the self (child). This takes place prior to the differentiation of the self from the object, i.e., before the child understands others as not part of himself. Because of a fundamental identification with the collective idea, the individual has related to (Israeli) society as a self-object, the individual and the collective being woven into each other. As differentiation and ego-self separation takes place, the collective becomes objectified and serves less as a self-object. Individual and collective then become less intertwined.

Since a self-object is part of the self, the self's (individual's) investment of energy into the self-object (collective) is not object-related or altruistic but essentially narcissistic.

The 'withdrawal of the state as a narcissistically invested self-object' is a process of deflation, and may lead to loneliness and alienation as well as depression. Mainly, it is a normal and healthy development and leads to differentiation and individuation. Applied to the present Israeli condition, however, it is also a dialectical consequence of the collective consciousness, to the process whereby the expanded geo-political borders of the 1967 Six Day War were "filled out" by settling the occupied territories. The expanded borders came to define the identity of the collective group-self in terms of historical as well as military and psychological security, leaving little room for deviance. In the wake of the first Intifada in the late 1980's, there has however been a return to excluding the occupied territories from the general public's collective identity, reflected in statements such as "Why should we assume the burden of Gaza?" This gradual change laid the basis for what was once a most unlikely option, the withdrawal from "Gaza and Jericho first," which was the beginning phase of the Oslo accords. While this was once a minority position, it eventually became recognized and readily accepted by practically all segments of the Israeli population. Prime Minister Sharon can therefore in 2003 conveniently declare that occupation is bad for both Israelis and Palestinians, relying on the support of the majority even of his right-wing supporters.

A return to religion and emigration are expressions of de-Zionization, of the withdrawal of narcissistic energy from a collective based on the Zionist idea – which does not necessarily mean Israel is becoming a non-Zionist country. Various defenses have at times been implemented against this painful process of de-narcisstification, or ego-self separation, for instance an excessive need for *wholeness* (expressed by consensus and national unity government), for *purity* (such as the idea, expressed by extremist groups, of ethnic transfer), and for *grandiosity* (e.g. inflated schemes and projects).

These defenses reflect the difficulty in coming to terms with conscious, individuated living on archetypal ground.

Chapter 4

Origins and Myths

Close Proximity

There is a unique quality to the relationship between the individual and the national and social collective in Israel, or between what may be termed the personal and the extended national self (Group for the Advancement of Psychiatry [GAP] 1978).

The relationship between the individual and the collective is characterized by a particularly close proximity, which is understandable, considering the fact that most Israelis have actively participated in or been exposed to profound collective military, social and historical processes. The Holocaust, mass-immigration, state-building, and several wars have all contributed to the oscillation between extremes of darkness and light, euphoria and depression. Throughout the history of so called practical Zionism, a high degree of identification – too high for many – has been quintessential to its implementation.

Close proximity emanates from the exceptional fact that modern Israel owes its very existence to the not so many, but still enough number of revolutionaries, willing to turn the abstract idea into concrete reality. Additionally, the proximity to geo-political borders causes immediacy between the boundaries of the individual and the borders of the collective; the capital of Israel has in the past been divided by a concrete border, and West- and East-Jerusalem remain de facto separated; the very center of Israel is a brief strip of fourteen kilometers between the sea and the Palestinian areas.

The individual's identification with the collective, as expressed by the particularly close proximity between them, has been fundamental to the realization of the Zionist venture. The words of a contemporary Israeli folk song, "I built a house, a road, a bridge, and planted a tree in the Land of Israel" reflect how the yearnings of the traditional Jewish prayer, "Next year in Jerusalem," were turned into tangible reality.

The transformation of idea into concrete, geo-political reality meant a collective change of emphasis, exchanging spirit for matter, thinking for doing. This remains a principal conflict between Ultra-Orthodox Judaism and modern Zionism.

Origins

Detached from the Earth

As the Jews dispersed in foreign lands, they became detached from the earth, from the material, tangible aspects of existence. Removed from the geographical, earth-related prerogative of defining a territory, they could not set an actual boundary that would define their existence as a nation and a people. In the Diaspora, unlike olden times, the Jews could no longer draw their own geo-political map;

> And the east border was the Sea of Salt, to the end of the Jordan... And the border went up by the valley of the son of Hinnom to the south side of the Jebusite; that is Jerusalem; and the border went up to the top of the mountain that lies before the valley of Hinnom westward, which is at the end of the valley of the Refaim northward; And the border was drawn from the top of the hill to the fountain of the water of Nephtoah,... westward to Mount Seir, and .. along to the side of Mount Jearim,... And the west border was the Great Sea. (Joshua 15: 1-12)

Biblical geography became religious sentiment rather than living reality, a process that Zionism set out to reverse.

Spiritual affinity

During their long history in the Diaspora, Jews developed a unique quality of spiritual survival. A handful of religious objects served as concrete expressions of spiritual affinity:

The *Book* as source of wisdom and sustenance of life, but also the Book of Life from which the enemy should be "blotted out" (Psalm 69:29);

the *mezuzah*, the parchment scroll at the doorpost as divine protection and affirmation of Jewish identity;

the *menorah*, the candelabrum, and the *candlesticks* as life and light, soul and remembrance, "the spirit of man is the candle of God" (Proverbs 20:27);

the *bread*, which God "has brought forth from the earth," without which there is no Torah;

and *wine*, the grapes of joy and the grapes of wrath, the blessing and the offering, the spirit that arises from the body.

Simultaneously, an elaborate codex of beliefs and regulations formed the main body of Judaism. Compulsive adherence to laws and rules may have served as substitute for an actual, natural relationship to the soil and to nature, to a place and to a home. The seemingly exaggerated arguments about minor details of this or that *should*, "an equal emphasis on the great and the trivial," sometimes perhaps at the expense of an inner relatedness to God and spirituality, provides a geography of logos rather than of Gaia, the Earth. In the course of Jewish history, *place* increasingly became a *sanctified abstraction*. *Heavenly* Jerusalem disconnected from *Earthly* Jerusalem, spirit was removed from matter, whereby only the idea remained – an idea that could be endlessly purified and refined.

As the Jew wandered, he brought his few belongings with him. External characteristics such as clothes and side-locks were added to the religious objects, and set him apart from his neighbors in the host country. Occasionally these attributes were acquired or adapted from the local inhabitants, and only the Jews' perseverance, wearing the same costume for centuries, set him aside.

And wherever the Jew migrated or fled, he brought with him the worn and tattered carpet. When unrolling it, a lifelong pattern of woven and torn web unfolded, enabling him to set off a bit of territory, a tangible ancestral connection with which to create a *place of his own*, even though there was no ground underneath. Also, as a reminder of Jerusalem, destroyed and in ruins, a corner of the wall in every new home was to be left unfinished.

Carpet, candles and book were tiny objects of great magnitude, giving matter to an identity which relied on historical fate and ancient scriptures. Clinging to a detailed belief system and an elaborate codex enabled a living connection to the past. It also held a promise for a better future, a longing for a paradisiacal time when relief would be found and the Messiah would arrive. It was all held together in the prayer "Next year in Jerusalem," wherein *next year* was as much an abstraction of *Time* as *Jerusalem* an abstraction of *Place*.

As the luminous spirit of the Enlightenment spread over the European continent, it cast a stark shadow of nationalism and a search for particularism. While opening the window to the modern world, the philosophical and existential winds of the Enlightenment in the West further disconnected the Jew from his roots in the ancient tribal soul. Not only was the Jew land-less and nation-less, but as the Enlightenment came to see the Jew as solely a follower of Mosaic law, he was losing the connection to his peoplehood. Judaism, so it claimed, was to become the "true religion of Moses" (Ettinger 1979, p. 224), based strictly on reason rather than on emotion (cf. Schulman 1963, p. 27). The feeling that unites and keeps together, was threatened.

While these progressive changes in relating to the world and to the group-self (and to the God-image and the Torah) were not widespread among nineteenth century Jews, the shadow cast by the Enlightenment was unmistakably sharp. If the spiritual affinity of the Jew was to be based increasingly on reason, then beyond a certain point, the soul would be lost. And "Next year in Jerusalem" without even the small material objects that one can touch, see or smell, cannot maintain its own image of Heavenly Jerusalem, of a greater Self. There is an inevitable need for transitional objects to uphold the link between the individual and the archetypal images of wholeness. Feeling without reason may lead to being inundated, and reason without feeling may lead to alienation. Yet, the essence – that is, the idea, the image, the abstraction, the spirit – dries up when all that matters are external formalities such as customs, clothing, outward appearance and rules, laws and regulations. Archetypal energy is extinguished in the grip of collective consciousness, and the soul shrinks when imprisoned by obsessive litany and compulsive decree.

From Spiritual Idea to Concrete Matter

Practical Zionism became the way by means of which the idea was transformed into concrete, earth-bound reality. Spirit was to be reconnected with matter (material, mater, mother-land), which constituted a momentous challenge to the abstract belief-system of Judaism. Ultra-Orthodox Jewry violently opposed Zionism, and Basel became the location of the first Zionist congress in 1897 instead of Munich, due to local Jewish opposition.

The very idea of reconnecting spirit with matter, with earth and earth-bound instinctuality, of providing the ideational with concrete contours, literally the ground under one's feet – territory, and eventually boundaries as the state was established – was revolutionary. From its inception, Zionism's striking feature of pouring spirit into matter in an attempt to unite them, and of transforming an idea into concrete reality, has been not only its unique and grand aim but also its great difficulty and weakness. An idea is not easily forged into a concrete mold, yet, if it is not to dissipate, it needs this very transformation. Implementation is the essence of the Zionist idea, though for a large part of the Jewish people it remains an abstraction similar to the yearly repetition of "Next year in Jerusalem." In order to materialize, the idea needed people who were willing to carry it to fulfillment, willing to have their individual life merge with the idea. In this way, the idea was energized, libidinized, filled with narcissistic energy. Close proximity between the personal and the extended self, between the ideational and the concrete, has been manifest since the birth of practical Zionism in the late nineteenth century. Close proximity expresses the specific bond that enabled the implementation of Zionism.

The personal ego of some individuals merged, so to speak, with the idea. Initially there were those, such as Moses Hess and Theodor Herzl, who wrote about it, dreaming of its practical implementation. They did so quite often in a fantastic, grandiose way. Herzl, for instance, called the Zionist weekly he founded *Die Welt*, "The World." Another example of Herzl's hubris, and his doubts, is his diary entry which says,

> The difference between Sabbatai Tzevi and myself is that he made himself great to be like the great ones of the world, whereas I find the great just as small as I am. (Herzl 1961, p 82)

Herzl's doubts about his life project were profound. As reflected in this entry, he felt the need to differentiate himself from Sabbatai Sevi, the seventeen century false Messiah.

Then there were those who merged with Zionism by uniting their own physical and psychological destiny and sense of self-fulfillment with its implementation, such as the early pioneers (in the 1880's) of *Hovevei Zion* and the *Bilu* movement. The common practice of changing one's name also reflected this merger of personal identity with the collective enterprise. In addition to simple Hebraization, names were often chosen to be "strong, biblical, heroic, royal, independent" or those of ancient heroes (Falk 1975, p. 653). For example, in the early days of Tel Aviv, one girl was named "Ahuzat Bayit" (Homestead – one of the city's first neighborhoods) and another, "Ivrit Safa Hayah" (the Hebrew language lives). Thus the Zionist project was narcissistically invested.

Individual and Collective – Gratification and Disappointment
The so called *magshimim* ("materializers"), though few in numbers, took it upon themselves to implement and actualize the idea. Individual ego and personal identity merged with the collective idea of realizing the Zionist credo, of a return to Mother Earth in the land of the Fathers. In the face of historical and psychological circumstances, it was an enormous enterprise. For many, it was too burdensome an undertaking. The idea was perhaps admirable but its realization was questionable. There were serious doubts about the possibility of its fulfillment, and failure seemed more certain than its future. It required a readiness for sacrifice, since the social and physical conditions of the *Yishuv* (the Jewish community in the Land of Israel/Palestine) were extremely severe. As Sachar (1958 p. 268) writes,

Exhausting physical labor under the blistering sun, years of crop failures and illness destroyed their illusions. Some of the Biluim died of malaria; some returned to Russia; and some severed their contact with their fellows and strayed off into limbo.

The narcissistic gratification of taking part in a great idea, the inner sense of grandeur and excitement, vitality and energy, easily lost its colors, becoming pale and unappealing in confrontation with the harsh reality. The Land of Israel was never marked by green rolling hills, by an abundance of streaming, bubbling water and soft riverbeds, a sun that rises and sets gradually. There are no four seasons that unfold one into the other, in a calm cycle of nature that man can easily move along with. On the contrary, the harsh, unprotected encounters that characterize almost every aspect of collective behavior and social interaction are already present in the harshness of the earth and the sharpness of the sun. This is the blazing sun of which *Psyche*, the human soul in the tale by Apuleius, is warned, because it maddens the golden sheep who "vent their fury in the destruction of men" (Neumann 1971, p. 43).

Many of those rather few who were drawn to the emerging idea that was beginning to take shape at the shores of the Eastern Mediterranean, could not bear the burden of frustration as they encountered the reality of pain and suffering. Reality looked more like the poverty and the neglect of the old, pre-Zionist Jewish Yishuv than the utopia that Herzl dreamed of. In the very merger between individual and collective, which requires identification, lie the seeds of disillusion and abandonment. The fact is that while the legendary second a'liyah (the wave of immigration, 1904-1914) brought forty thousand newcomers to the land, almost the same number of people left the country during that period (Greenberg 1979, p. 46). It is noteworthy as well, that Jewish immigration, however small and struggling, not only planted the seeds of the future state, but did bring a sense of prosperity, with Arab immigration in its wake. As the sparsely populated coastal plain, which makes up the bulk of the state of Israel, was slowly coming alive, Arabs from neighboring countries and other areas of Palestine (such as what is now called the West Bank, and [Trans-] Jordan, then part of Palestine) were drawn there in search for work. For example, in 1889 the 40 Jewish families in Rishon l'Zion had been followed by more than four hundred Arab families from Egypt and elsewhere.

A Brief Outline of the Myths

The molding process of Zionism and the subsequent birth of the State proceeded through the unfolding of a number of key myths (for *myth*, see glossary). These myths became the leitmotifs or guiding principles, which enabled the individual to be committed to the Idea of the *Return to Zion*, to give it body and soul through the merger of his/her private life with the collective idea. These guiding myths will here be briefly outlined, and further elaborated in the following chapter.

The *Idea* of the Return to Zion takes its origin in the primary *myth of redemption*. Substituting the experience of weakness for an identity based on strength and self-determination was axiomatic to the Zionist conception of redemption. This required splitting-off the collective self-experience and identity of Jews in Exile where "the Jew suffered a soul-crippling sense of inferiority because he was a man without a native country" (Schulman 1963, p. 123). The Zionists, who perceived their people in this light and actively sought to alter the destiny of their nation, were guided by the myth of revolt against the Father's way.

Redemption
The longing for redemption is based on the messianic idea. It implies a deep yearning for home and home-coming, in contrast to the experience of homelessness, of being in exile. Homelessness and exile served as Kabbalistic symbols for the soul's exile (Scholem 1974, p. 250). It pertained to a God having become divided from His feminine element, the *Shekhinah*. Whereas the conventional religious messianic idea saw "[r]edemption as a confrontation between the Jew and God" (Hertzberg 1969, p. 17), Zionism concretized redemption by turning to Mother Earth rather than the Heavenly Father. To be redeemed, to come home, means an end to wandering (see Hesse 1975), an end to being homeless and rootless (Gath 1983, p. 4). It is the attainment of belongingness by immersion in the ancestral earth, to stand on the archetypal ground of the Jewish people's origin. The search was back to the earthly womb by actively attaching to the Mother and the Feminine, in absolute contrast to the foundation on Father and the masculine emphasis of Orthodox Judaism.

Revolt
Cut off from the earthly, feminine side, the Jewish people developed in the direction of spirituality and a stern patriarchal/father code. The struggle of the masculine principle against the goddess is, in fact, a founding pillar of Yahweh (Kluger 1999). Early Zionist pioneering entailed an act of aggression and revolt against the ways, norms, traditions and life structure of the Father. In Oedipal opposition, the early Zionists left home in order to find a way to work the ancient Motherland and, filled with romantic fever, dig into her earth and farm her fields (e.g., Falk 1974; Hazelton 1977). Those who actually set out for Zion, mainly from Eastern Europe, revolted "against their pious parents" and fought against "the old values of the ghetto" (Hertzberg 1969, p. 74).

Thus, practical Zionism was a revolt against the Spiritual Father, and it entailed a return to the Great Mother, Mother Earth, who had been buried in the ground of the unconscious. In fact, the hero's task was to redeem the very myth of redemption, to raise the soul out of the barren earth, to free the spirit that had stiffened in the conventions of and adherence to the way of the fathers.

Identity Change – Exchanging Weakness for Strength
Zionism carried a message of identity change for the Jews. Ahad Ha'Am (1856-1927; cf. 1962, p. 171-194), emphasized regeneration through cultural work and spiritual freedom, in contrast to what he

considered to be the moral and intellectual slavery that the Jew suffered. While settling in Tel Aviv, he remained skeptical and doubtful to Herzl's grand scheme. Practical Zionism set out to replace what was seen as weakness and helplessness for an ideology of strength and courage. There were those who saw the Jew himself as responsible for his tragic fate. The Hebrew writer Perez Smolenskin (1842-1845; as quoted in Hertzberg 1969, p. 150) says,

Why are we treated like this? Because we have sunk so low that our self-respect has died ... If we really want to help the victims of the pogroms, we must first proclaim unceasingly that we ourselves are responsible for our own inner weakness.

The proud Jew would rely on himself rather than "rejoicing when ... granted a favor and exulting when ... tolerated and befriended" (ibid., p. 150).

The aim of Zionism was emancipation and self-determination in view of weakness and dependency. In revolt against the Father's Way, the return to Mother Earth was an effort at uniting spirit and matter.

The profound relationship between spirit and matter in the entire Zionist project is evident in Israel's Declaration of Independence. In the first paragraph, the connection between the Jewish people's spiritual identity and the land is established. More striking, however, is the wording of the third paragraph, which deals with the revival of the Hebrew language and the building of the land. The English translation of this part speaks about the pioneers who have "made deserts bloom," which is usually taken for granted to be the formulation in Hebrew as well. However, the Hebrew original has a dramatically different wording (Shachar 1999). Either because of a very small but significant typing error, or due to Ben-Gurion's profound knowledge of the Bible, the night before the signing ceremony, Friday May 14, 1948, the draft which did say "make deserts bloom" ("lehafriach shmamot," להפריח שממות) became in the official version "make the souls (or spirits) blossom" ("lehafriach neshamot," להפריח נשמות). This remarkable interchange between soul/spirit and land/desert has its source in the Bible, e.g. Ezekiel 36: 35.

Chapter 5

From Redemption to Shadow

Redemption

The Search for Mother Earth
The implementation of Zionism was the outcome of a search for individual and collective redemption: a new myth for the Jew and for the Jewish people. The individual who chose to merge with the idea could proceed only by taking part in collective ventures such as establishing a kibbutz, state-building and national defense. The initial stage of redemption aimed at creating "a new man," complex-free and self-reliant, in whom spirit and matter were joined together. It was to be accomplished by integrating into a self larger than the individual, "the renewal of the true self in reverent harmony with the cosmos" (Hertzberg 1969, p. 371). The new Jew would not turn to the Father for redemption, but rather embrace the ancient Earth of the Motherland.

The Individual and the Group
At its inception, the rather insignificant number of pioneers (*halutzim*) rendered the implementation of the Zionist idea frail and vulnerable. Thus, the group (*kvutzah*) soon emerged, at the beginning of the twentieth century, as a means of channeling the instinctual and psychic energy necessary to cope with the hardships. Mother Earth was harsh and, as Erich Neumann says, she creates madness and behind her "looms the experience of death" (1970, p. 58). Setting out alone to deal with the barren soil was beyond the capacity of the

individual. He needed the group, the collective *kvutzah*, to direct energy (libido) to the task.

During the early stages of Zionism, three different causes seem to have converged to bring about the many group undertakings and collective enterprises such as the kibbutz and worker-consumer co-operatives. One was political-ideological. Another was the practical need to join forces in order to struggle with the inhospitable earth and cope with hard social conditions. Given that the ego of the single individual could not alone carry the burden, there was a need for an ego-strengthening collective. In addition to these ideological and pragmatic causes, the third reason was psychological. Since the implementation of Zionism depended, in part, on the individual joining, or merging, with the collective idea, the group constituted and fulfilled an intermediary, linking function. It protected against despair and alienation; it enabled a sense of belongingness. The group was greater than the individual. It provided a vessel in which the collective myth could be contained and merged with. In the framework of the group, individual ego and collective self found a viable meeting ground. The group libido was indispensable in absorbing the individual ego into the collective self in the process of Zionist implementation, quite similar to the spring-ritual described by Jung (see above, p. 5). From the early kibbutz settlements there are stories of hard work during the day and dancing through the night, communal libido and free sexuality; as well as a shadow of despair, departure and suicide. At the early commune of Beitania, for example, settling the land was described as an act of engagement with the earth, and sitting in a circle around the fire was a covenant of passion. The digging of the well was an erotic act, with its tragic side of not bringing enough life-giving water to all. One member describes "the heat that streams from flesh to flesh and from soul to soul, the stroke from hand to hand and from dream to dream, the kiss from lips to lips and from undertaking to undertaking." This, however, meant a blurring of boundaries between individuals and between the individual and the collective, the extent of which depended upon the particular person, the climate of the group, and its structure. The kvutzah, the group, often came to take over functions and fulfill needs that traditionally were carried for instance by the family. As the first children were born, the lack of grandmothers who could instruct in child-rearing was a major reason why mothering was turned over to the collective.

This blurring of individual boundaries and merger with a self greater than oneself, particularly in the context of the return to Mother

Earth, can be explored from the perspective of its roots in the yearning for the archetypal primal relationship, in which the infant has not yet separated from the mother.

The Primal Relationship

At birth, the infant physically separates from the mother. Psychologically, however, the infant is not yet 'born' (Mahler, Pine, & Bergman 1975, p. 3; Neumann 1973, p. 7). In fact, it takes years during which the infant passes through various stages of maturity and separation, until the human individual can be considered to be psychologically born.

If the ego is understood as the seat of our consciousness and the self is the totality of the psyche, then it may be said that "the self is born, but the ego is made" (Edinger 1973, p. 7). Initially, the infant's ego rests passively, as "not yet awakened ego nuclei" (Samuels 1985, p. 156). The baby cannot separate or distinguish its own body from the environment; it is not aware that "this is *my* hand, foot, etc." The pre-conscious body experience dwells in a dual union in which "child and mother are still so intermeshed as to be one" (Neumann 1973, p. 12). The child thrives in "symbiotic fusion with the mother" (Mahler et al. 1975, p. 4). At this early stage, mother and infant function as one psychological unit. They thus form a primal relationship (Neumann 1973) in which the mother carries the baby's self. 'Mother' does not refer strictly to the biological mother but to *mothering*, which can be carried by her, by the father, or by some other person. Furthermore, when primarily carried by the biological mother, the father can, as well, be part of the mothering in addition to fulfilling his fatherly task of protecting the dual union from outside intrusion (e.g. Davis & Wallbridge 1981, p. 134).

Actually, this is "the original state of unconscious wholeness and perfection" (Edinger 1973, p. 7) which is depicted in the paradise myths of the Garden of Eden. All through life there is a "perpetual longing of the human being for reunion with the erstwhile symbiotic mother" (Mahler et al. 1975, p. 290), for the paradisiacal state of the primal relationship. This longing for what has been may cause regression and threaten individual identity and independence. Therefore it must be held at bay; indeed this is the purpose of the fear of regression (Mahler et al. 1975, p. 290). This barrier has been broken through in psychosis; either the ego has not developed well enough, or has been injured and sinks back into the unconscious, into the original or primary self. Thus, coupled with the fear of engulfment there is a longing for what has been, for regression into a state of unconsciousness, for slumbering peacefully in the primal relationship. As Neumann (1973, p. 17) says,

> The primal relationship is the foundation of all subsequent dependencies, relatedness and relationships. Whereas dual union is guaranteed by nature in the uterine embryonic phase, it emerges after birth as the first need of the mammal and especially of the human child. That is why in all living creatures who come into being inside a mother, the dependency of the small and infantile on the large containing vessel stands at the beginning of all existence.

This is a longing back to a state of total union and merger with the mother who embraces, nurtures, holds and completely cares for the infant. It is the divine paradisiacal state of merger with the gods, before the birth of a differentiating consciousness. Developmentally it is an initial stage necessary to build the very basis of one's post-uterine existence and basic trust in the world and in oneself (cf. Erikson 1968, p. 96 ff.). Longing back is natural, but remaining there becomes psychotic; identification with it characterizes the *puer aeternus*, the eternal youth, who is "all promises and no fulfillment" (Edinger 1973, p. 14). The puer's identification with original wholeness disables him, in as much as actual work and accomplishments necessarily entail the giving up of other potential possibilities.

The primal relationship is necessary for the infant's psychological birth, and the longing for it is expressed by archetypal images such as Peace, Wholeness, the Golden Age, the Good Old Days, and the projection into the future of the coming of the Messiah. To remain in this stage, however, means severe disturbance, and to identify with it sometimes carries a flavor of youthful charm, but inhibits maturation.

Investing the Idea with Narcissistic Energy
Aspects of the primal relationship remain with the individual and are carried throughout life, sometimes with ache, often with desire and longing for 'home.' Many expect their spouses to meet a need for a primal rather than an adult relationship.

It was this longing back that guided a segment of the Jewish people to return to the ancient homeland. Without the particularly close relationship between individual and collective, evolving out of psychological and historical circumstances, the sense of liberation on a national scale would not have been possible. It brings about periods of euphoria that alternate with depression, feelings of hubris that turn into the aches of inferiority.

The intensity of this close relationship between individual and collective, in the past so essential and uncompromising, is now declining. The personal and private ego in today's Israeli society has more space and freedom to differentiate from its dwelling in and merger with the grand collective self. This constitutes a healthy development, but when unconscious, easily becomes acted out. The process of separation between the individual and the collective then takes the form, for instance, of unrestrained privatization of limited land and natural resources. Mother Earth, whom the early pioneers set out to revive, is now being dismembered, not only as mythological metaphor of a psychological process, but actually split up and divided by real estate speculators.

In the process of Zionist development, certain projects carried particularly redeeming qualities. Foremost among these was cultivating the land, draining the malaria-infected swamps, and the planting of trees in a land without forests (coniunctio, purification, fructification). While Israel is a society that came into existence thanks to the tilling of the soil, working the earth is no longer so highly valued. Soil and soul again part. Agricultural settlements, moshavim and kibbutzim, struggle with financial, ideological, social and inter-personal problems. Society's natural bond to Mother Earth is strained. Present collective consciousness turns away from digging down into the ground, turning towards hi-tech, seemingly unable to hold the balance between the two.

Likewise, water, the source of life, was once related to in a respectful, perhaps sacred way. The scarce resources had to be strenuously searched for. Often in the early collectives there was not enough water for all. The digging of the well enabled the early settlers to connect with the "domain of the earth mother" (Neumann 1963, p. 48). The careless draining of the earth and the one sea (of Galilee), implies neglecting the feminine principle, as so often was the case in Biblical times as well. Israel is a land in which rivers turn into wilderness and springs of water into dry ground (Psalms 107:33). A fruitful land that becomes barren. We must keep in mind, though, as the Psalms say, that it is the "wickedness of its inhabitants" (107:34) that causes barrenness; often the wickedness of draining Mother Earth of her milk without considering her need for rest.

Biblical Naomi (which means 'my pleasure'), for instance, was married to an inflated masculine principle, Elimelech ('my God is

King'), with two debilitated sons, Mahlon and Chilion (both names meaning 'sickly') constellating in the shadow. They were married to two Moabite women, Ruth (meaning 'beloved') and Orpah (meaning 'neck'). Domination of the masculine principle was too strong and oppressive, the earth dried up and there was famine. The family left for the land of Moab, east of the Jordan River (today's Jordan), to regain the soul of fertility. The Biblical land of Moab originates in the feminine, since in Hebrew legend it descends from the incestuous relationship of Lot's daughters with their father (see Kluger 1999). The dominant masculine principle had to be replaced by feminine loyalty and Eros, as represented by the beloved Ruth, who followed her mother-in-law back to the land of Canaan (while Orpah 'turned her neck;' she followed Ruth and Naomi on the way, but did not object when Naomi told her to return to her own country). Back in Canaan, in Bethlehem, she met the more earthly connected Boaz (meaning 'strength'), significantly spending their first night together at the threshing-floor. Their great-grandson was King David. That is, the roots of the Hebrew kings can be traced to the re-fertilized earthly meeting-ground of protective strength and loyal love – however, as is well known, history eventually, and necessarily, corrupts archetypal blueprints.

A shadow-side of loneliness, alienation and homelessness, abandonment and sometimes aggression against the collective, accompanied the "ingathering of the exiles" as the guiding myth of redemption, which was intended to create a sense of home (and, to a large extent, succeeded). As has been mentioned (p. 36), the feeling of being "Aliens in the Homeland" (as Boshes 1988) titles her review of Nathan Shaham's *The Rosendorf Quartet*), has recurrently been part of the modern Hebrew narrative. The immigrant narrator in Shaham's (1988) story considers Palestine, the Land of Israel, a transitory, "godforsaken place" (p. 32) of utter hopelessness. Poetically, he expresses the difficulty of the outsider, saying,

> In the divine score everything is written: how the oboe will wail, what the first violin will say to the second, when the viola will sob, when the ram's horn will sound its blast, how far the Jew will wonder, what exile he will call his motherland, in what language he will sing his despair.
> On the island where I was cast ashore there are many beautiful birds, but I can't understand their language. (p. 333)

Revolt

Redemption could take place only by revolt against the Father's way. Transforming myth and religion into political reality, and concretizing the Father's repeated "Next year in Jerusalem," violated an elaborated codex and belief system. The impact is evident by the intense opposition that Zionism evoked among the ultra-Orthodox. The young pioneer who revolted against his father, broke away from convention and challenged the old way. The archetypal relationship of *father and son* is not to be understood solely in its interpersonal aspect. It serves, as well, as a model for the struggle between control (father) and instinctual energy (son), as Jung (1966, p. 157) has described. As carrier of the *Father's way*, the renowned Rabbi Eliezer Shach (who was head of the world's most important Lithuanian yeshiva [academy for the study of Talmud, the body of Jewish law], the Ponevich Yeshiva in B'nei Brak; a crowd of four hundred thousand took part in the funeral procession when he died in 2001, supposedly at the age of 103) cast the blame on the kibbutzim. The kibbutz connected man to Mother Earth rather than to God. The kibbutz was the most prominent conceptual implementation of a collective and of a (certainly not uncomplicated) relationship between individual and collective, which enabled the libidinization of an alternative to the Father's way. (The Father's way itself demands a very close proximity between the individual and the extended self, often at the expense of a differentiated personal identity.) In the kibbutz, the Father's way of authority and command was replaced by the effort to enliven the forsaken ground, to make earth matter.

The pioneer broke off from the Father's way, from being the son who walks in the footsteps of his father, and then becomes the same father himself. He left to search for the abandoned *Great Mother* in the *Old Homeland*, libidinizing her, bringing her back to life in hard labor. Initially the pioneers were like struggling son-lovers. Then, as the earth slowly gave in, they exchanged the religious idea of Jerusalem as the earthly dwelling of the Shekhinah, God's feminine aspect, and made the "Zionist project" their bride, in perhaps an equally religious fervor. Their devotion to the collective was unconditional, often to the neglect of their personal families. In fact, the sons (and daughters) of these fathers often had a difficult time establishing their own separate identity, finding their own place. With reference to the pioneering collective, Zvi Luz (1988), the son of a founding father, claims that the sons are inferior to the fathers, who had to undergo severe ideological and psychological ordeals to survive. Only by separating the parents (see Neumann 1970) and finding an opening between them, can the ego and a separate identity develop. The myth of the World Parents, according to which the sky originally rested so close to the earth's surface that man could not stand upright, is replicated ontogenetically in the child's struggle to establish a separate ego (cf. Shalit, 2002).

If, however, the father is "married" to the project this may become difficult. There may not be an opening for the son (or daughter) to establish himself in the extra-familial world, since the father has already been there. Society becomes part of a father-dominated family. For example, the son of an army officer whose caring father has already contacted the commander of every army base the son arrives at, may find no alternative than, as one such man described it, to "get into trouble so I can get myself out," in order to be someone for and by himself.

The revolt against the Father's ways meant suppressing into the unconscious major features of the old way, such as religious customs, spiritual principles, the old language.

The author Micah Joseph Berdichevski (1865-1921), who "saw only tension and affirmed only revolt" (Hertzberg 1969, p. 291) compared the Jewish condition to that of an ailing old man,

> The entire Israelite nation resembled an old, white-haired man. His legs are swollen from so much wandering, his bones are thin and his skin is covered in sores, his back is bent and all his vertebrae have collapsed. And the small and injured body has a big head, ... and this wounded thinker from head to toe is standing in a narrow trench, shallow and poor, from which he can deviate neither to the right nor to the left ... and the old man's head and most of himself is sunken in a pile of books heaped up and lying before him.

And Uri Avnery (1968, p. 155) observed,

> The difference between Jewish fathers anywhere in the world and Israeli sons is much more than the usual contradiction between generations; it is a mutation. A different mode of life, nutrition, climate, political reality and social environment could not but make the Palestinian-born son vastly unlike his ghetto-born father.

The old way, then, was discarded, rejected into the shadow, in spite of the words of the poet Natan Alterman that "The new Jew shall never forget his debt to the Jew of 'old'." But like anything repressed, it finds its ways to re-appear, often as a consequence of guilt-feelings.

There is, for instance, a return to Orthodox Judaism and a revival of the Yiddish language. Referring to Hebrew literature, Gershon Shaked (1988, p. 12) says that

> young people with the hunched back of exile are certainly less attractive than the tall, clear-eyed youths of whom their fathers dreamed ... Nevertheless the portrait of the new Hebrew as an old Jew is perhaps far more authentic than the portrait of the Israeli as a young non-Jew.

When consciously related to, returning shadows become treasures.

Identity

Strength

Zionism offered the Jew a new identity in a number of ways. As has often been described (cf. Elon 1981; Gonen 1978; Talmon 1970), the emphasis in Zionism on an identity of strength, courage and the mystique of violence was a response to persecution and threats of annihilation. Or, as Erikson (1977, p. 26) puts it, to "the Jew's special fate in the face of anger and violence." By exchanging what was seen as weakness and helplessness for determination, strength and self-defense, Zionism carried a message of identity change for the Jew. This was the case as regards the early Guards, the *Shomrim*, who, as Abba Eban (1968, p. 385) says, "saw their work as a personal mission undertaken for the benefit of an entire nation. Their example was to inspire the Yishuv with courage and self-reliance." The aim was to be a Hebrew, not a Jew. *Hebrew* designates someone at home in the land of Israel; the word Hebrew originally meant someone who had entered the land from the East 'beyond the river.' The Jew, on the other hand, as the designation indicates, is 'led by God.'

The struggle for self-determination was carried out in a triangular context that consisted of Zionist Jew, Palestinian Arab, and Ottoman or British ruler (see Cohen 1970). The coalitions varied somewhat, but the similar claims of Jew and Arab separated rather than united them. Eventually, the latter came to see himself as victim of the victim-turned-aggressor, which is how the Arab – now Palestinian – came to view the Zionist Jew – who previously was called Palestinian.

Practical Zionism in the Yishuv – the pre-state Jewish community in Palestine – came to rely on strength and force. This was not only the result of prevailing circumstances but also the polar opposite of, and compensation for, historical fears of destruction and ultimate loss. It was highly purposeful, enabling a process of national independence and actualization to take place. In fact, any national movement's struggle for independence entails an act of aggression. The claim for territory and territorial boundaries, within which the evolving nation becomes defined in contrast to and differentiated from what is considered foreign rule (see Koestler 1949), relies on aggression, even if not necessarily by means of violence. An independence movement will view aggression as life ensuring, since it is essential for the establishment of ego-boundaries, while the object of the aggression naturally sees it as destructive. This, for instance, is how Israelis and Palestinians respectively view the first Intifada, the Palestinian uprising that began in Israeli occupied territory in December 1987. Yet, in the course of time, most Israelis have come to recognize that uprising as a catalyst for the withdrawal from territories occupied following the 1967 War.

Because of changes in identity, aggression and strength, force and power became central features of Zionism. However, the tension between aggression and the fear of annihilation became unbearable prior to and following the events of the Six Day War in 1967 because of the intensification of these opposites. In the period just before the war, Israelis felt their very existence threatened, whereas victory paved the way for an exalted sense of strength and power. As a consequence, aggression eventually came to assume a life of its own. Its underlying connection to fear was commonly denied. Fear was split-off from the collective consciousness. The underlying connection between aggression and fear had originally enabled a process of collective actualization, of nation building. Now this connection weakened, and "free-floating aggression" became apparent (cf. Moses 1983), with a concomitant grandiose self-perception. At the extreme, aggression disconnected from fear actually evokes the very existential anxiety it is supposed to protect and defend against, since the divested fear is projected onto and fuses with the actual threat posed by the enemy.

Significantly, the myth of Masada has become a national symbol of Israel. The myth tells about the Zealots, who after the destruction of Jerusalem by the Romans escaped to Masada, the desert mountain fortress. Besieged, Masada became the center of rebellion against the Romans, the heroic Zealots holding out for about two years. When defeat was imminent, they chose suicide rather than capitulation, slavery or death by the hand of the enemy.

The narrative of this myth was developed by secular Zionism at the turn of the last century. Historically, according to the accounts of the

Jewish defender of the Galilee Joseph son of Matthias, who became Roman historian Josephus Flavius, the siege was significantly shorter than the myth tells us, and the rebels at Masada belonged to the considerably more extreme Sicarii sect than the Zealots.

In the myth, heroism is emphasized, and suicide becomes an expression of courage. The defeatist implication of suicide – rather than, say, diverting the Roman legion's attention so that women and children could escape – has been repressed. The myth served the purpose of inspiring the modern Hebrews to self-sacrifice, to fight till the bitter end, if need be. It seems far from incidental that suicide is part of the hero-myth, since it thrives in the Zionist shadow.

Without resemblance, particularly since 2000 suicide became the principal characteristic of the Palestinians in their war against Israel. While homicide more accurately depicts both the terrorist's intention and his self-perception than suicide, there evidently is a prominent self-defeating feature in the martyr's willingness of sacrifice.

Developmental Aspects of Fear, Aggression and Boundaries

Fear and Aggression

Although the belief that ontogeny recapitulates phylogeny, i.e. the notion that the development of the individual mirrors the evolution of the species, has been reassessed, parallel development and characteristics of the individual and of the species, or the single person and the larger group, may be observed (cf. Neumann 1970, p. xvi, pp. 266-275). An examination of the relationship between fear and aggression in the child's early development might contribute to our understanding of the Israeli collective's psychological development.

In the newborn, biological as well as psychological life functions have not yet stabilized; they are in the process of taking shape. Therefore, the infant experiences the ultimate anxiety inherent in being at the edge of existence. The neonate finds him- or herself at the crossroads of not-being-into-being (Shalit 1994). The very proximity to not-life constitutes a threat, with a consequent fear of annihilation. This is symbolically repeated in the adult fear of being devoured by the unconscious, by the negative pole of the Great Mother archetype, by the dark and unknown, "the world of the dead" (Jung 1968, p. 82). This death instinct is partly deflected into aggression (e.g. Segal 1974, p. 25), which enables the infant to "pull away" from the threat. Basic aggression can be found in the child's very first movements; in fact, Winnicott (1958, p. 204), sees the origin of aggressiveness as "almost synonymous with activity," and as the life force instrumental in ensuring "movement rather than stillness" (Winnicott 1980). Aggression as such is thus not necessarily destructive. As an archetypal energy it is bipolar, and a powerful drive for existence. Initially, however, there may be a fear that the energy of the life force will not be strong enough to combat and pull away from the threat of darkness and the void of nothingness. This is a fear of not being sufficiently strong to arrive safely into the harbor of symbiotic protection. This fear increases or decreases depending on the environment's capacity for holding (Winnicott 1980), of providing appropriate safety, and its tolerance for being intruded upon.

According to Kleinian theory, the primary fear of the death instinct is partly "changed into a fear of a persecutor" (Segal 1974, p. 25). That is, it is projected (primarily) onto the mother's breast (which is simultaneously libidinally invested). The infant's aggression is directed against the persecutor. The capacity to annihilate is thus projected onto and consequently acquired by the external object. If the environment is able to cope, a possibility is provided for the life force (aggression) to deal with the fear of annihilation. The child will then be better able to encompass both aggression and libido, thereby expanding and developing the self. If the environment's aggressive response, which has been evoked by the child's aggression, is strong, then the child's fears of persecution and annihilation are likely to be intense. The child's aggression thus bounces back, since aggression is, as Guntrip (1977, p. 37) says, a "defensive anger in a situation in which the menace is not too great for us to cope with. Otherwise aggression changes into frustrated rage, hate, fear, and flight." That is, in normal development the external object is impacted on by aggressive and persecutory elements. However, if the external object is hostile, the child's aggression may become one-sided and undifferentiated.

An external enemy may evoke this early fear of annihilation and aggression.

Aggression is dialectically related both to the original fear of annihilation and to the various parts of the external object (projected persecutor as well as real frustrations). Under favorable circumstances, aggression is a life force that enables the integration of the basic fear of annihilation into the self without being overwhelmed by it. When the direction and the intensity of aggression are appropriate, it serves the child's constructive development. Aggression, movement and activity compel us to encounter the world. Psychologically and in terms of motor skills, aggression enables the child to establish territory and delineate boundaries (cf. Mahler et al. 1975), to develop a secure identity and become an independent individual capable of mastering life. Aggression is instrumental in the child's activity, body control, will, initiative and self-reliance. As the child encounters external physical and psychological boundaries, when "falling and knocking against unyielding objects," it "seems to augment his feeling (the cathexis) of his body-self boundaries" (Mahler et al. 1975, p. 222). There must be an appropriate sense of pain and vulnerability not to purposelessly 'fall and knock,' and enough aggression to try again. The child needs a holding environment that helps him become aware of his capacities so that he does not trespass boundaries to the extent that he runs too far, getting lost in a boundary-less space of anxiety, finding himself outside his own territory and borders, as if "outside himself."

Even when constructive, aggression implies a violation of or intrusion upon the environment. The healthy adolescent, for instance, experiences a fusion of erotic and destructive drives in the process of his identity formation (Winnicott 1980, p. 82). He gains increasing control of internalization (forming internal images of external objects) and externalization (perceiving internal objects externally). Aggression as part of this growth process implies violation of and separation from parental images or, as Winnicott (1980, p. 170) says, "the death of someone."

The inability to be aggressive impedes the child's development, establishing his identity and boundaries, and claiming necessary space for himself. Temperamentally, this may be found in the "slow-to-warm-up child" (Chess & Thomas 1978), and in dysthymic disorder. Even slight amounts of frustration or fear can sometimes severely inhibit the person who lacks appropriate aggression and vigor, affecting his curiosity, will and activity.

Inhibited aggression aggravates the fear of annihilation, whether from within or from projection onto the external object, and the individual consequently feels engulfed or impinged upon (Laing 1971).

If the basic fear and threat of annihilation are too strong, or the outside threat too great, the self may disintegrate or withdraw, meaning death, autism, psychosis or depression. The result can also be frustrated rage and uncontrolled violence (see Guntrip 1977). In such a case two possibilities exist. One is that the tremendous release of aggression and unfocused rage comes to a breaking point, and there follows a phase of self-blame, guilt, and feelings of being flooded by death-anxiety. This is repeated over and over again. The other possibility is that the intensive aggression becomes seemingly autonomous, as if disconnected from the underlying (internal or external) fear and threat. The uncontrolled rage will then intrude indiscriminately and violently on the environment (including the persecutor) in a way that is strikingly different from constructive aggression. Often the (projected as well as real) power of the persecutor is denied, though paradoxically recognized by being acted upon. Thus the (seemingly autonomous) aggression may actually evoke the very fear and threat of annihilation whose existence the self tried to repress and deny.

The Relationship between Fear and Aggression during Israel's First Years

As described earlier, by the latter part of the 19th century, Zionism offered an alternative Jewish identity of strength. This took on a new and dramatic dimension in the shadow of the Nazi Holocaust during which the ultimate threat and fear of annihilation became reality. A third of world Jewry was extinguished, and entire Jewish communities were physically, socially and spiritually annihilated. Individual and collective encounter with death created a condition of annihilatory and ontological anxiety, the deflection of which may have been the catalyst that enabled the enormous release of strength and aggressive energy during Israel's War of Independence. This was very different to the psychic numbing, "constriction of the self and diminished capacity for experience" (Lifton 1983b, p. 43) characteristic of many survivors. Conviction and determination to establish a viable and independent nation enabled the small Jewish community in Israel to stand firm against the invading Arab armies. Geopolitical borders, which were to encompass the national self and the national identity, could thus come into existence (Shalit 1987). The deeply rooted fear of annihilation, which during the Holocaust more than ever turned into evil reality, was externalized onto the identifiable outside persecutor. The internal Zionist struggle to pull away from death and ensure life did not take place in a holding environment. The enemy was not merely an innocent object of persecutory fantasies. Having been attacked by Arab nations in 1948, the Israelis were further convinced of the justness of their cause, and that strength and force had been applied as a defense in order to secure independence. Tens of thousands of Arabs became refugees, leaving entire villages – some old, others having been recently settled. There was a general feeling of contempt for those instances, such as Deir Yassin, Kibieh, and Kafr Kassem, in which violence had been exercised against Arab civilians. In those early years of statehood, Israelis related ambivalently to weakness and fear of annihilation, which were largely separated from the national identity. The determination to survive, whether peacefully or by means of Mars, was cynically contrasted to what many at the time considered to have been the Jews' lack of resistance against Nazi atrocities. Simultaneously, in the relationship between strength and weakness, aggression and fear, the Israeli compared his character to the Sabra, the fruit of the cactus plant, "hard and thorny on the outside, but soft and tender in the center" (Spiro 1969, p. 442).

Boundaries
Birth, borders and boundaries are bound together. When the child is born, he becomes a physically (though far from psychologically) separate being, with distinct body boundaries (though he himself is not yet aware of them). When the State was born, Israel's borders were established, within which the governing and regulating (ego) functions could take place.

The Development of Personal Boundaries
The relationship between the development of the child and the establishment of internal boundaries has been extensively dealt with in psychological and psychoanalytic literature (e.g., Laing 1971; Lichtenberg 1978; Mahler et. al. 1975; Winnicott 1965b). The development of psychic and bodily ego-boundaries is essential for healthy movement through the stages of development. Winnicott (1965b) says, "there comes into existence ... a limiting membrane, which to some extent (in health) is equated with the surface of the skin, and has a position between the infant's 'me' and his 'not-me'."

Mahler emphasizes experiences of boundary-formation in the processes of individuation and separation, and observes it already in the stage of symbiosis "much before the baby's earliest approach and distancing behaviors in space would occur" (Mahler et. al. 1975).

During the second phase of separation and individuation, in adolescence, when "all samenesses and continuities relied on earlier are more or less questioned again" (Erikson 1968), i.e., during the later process of differentiation and identity-formation, the youth must redraw the internal boundaries. A secure identity and a mature self necessitate appropriately established mental, emotional, and body boundaries (e.g. Bowen 1985) that differentiate between inside and outside (Lichtenberg 1978), and that are adequately permeable, as well as neither excessively constrictive nor too expansive. This amounts to a sense of self-cohesion, the threat or loss of which can be found in borderline and narcissistic personality disorders (Kernberg 1975; Kohut 1971; Lichtenberg 1978).

If the ego-boundary becomes too *constrictive*, it will not only differentiate between inside and outside, but cause "diminished capacity for experience" (Lifton 1983b) or, as Rank (quoted in Lifton 1983b, p. 42) said, the neurotic's "constant restriction of life." On the other hand, if the ego-boundary is inappropriately expansive, either narcissistic projections (Masterson 1981) or psychopathy (Davis & Wallbridge 1981) may be detected. The narcissistic person is not able to "establish and slowly dissolve the requisite narcissistic self-object configurations which ... generate healthy structures within the self" (Greenberg & Mitchell 1983), while the antisocial individual "cannot make use of boundaries in the world of shared reality ... because control has not yet become internalized" (Davis & Wallbridge 1981).

Not only is the position and outline (along the axis constrictive - expansive) of the ego-boundary important, but also its *permeability*. An impermeable boundary is *rigid*, characterized by a lack of flow and of give and take, a lack of mutuality. It *separates* the inside from the outside rather than merely differentiating between them. A rigid ego-boundary exerts control at the expense of expressiveness (Rycroft 1983), and determines autonomy by letter rather than by spirit (Erikson 1977). Many obsessive and compulsive traits with concomitant lack of libido, impulsiveness, and emotionalism (Rycroft 1983) are connected with a rigid ego-boundary (see Lichtenberg 1978; Perls, Hefferline & Goodman 1973).

The same may be true for certain psychosomatic symptoms, for example amenorrhoea (absence of menstruation). Anorexia nervosa may be seen partly as an attempt at constricting and rigidifying the psychological and body boundaries in order to avoid being penetrated from the outside (unconsciously, by the mother; see for instance Selzer 1984). The adolescent (girl) closes off, refuses to take in, keeps herself internally pure in order to ward off the intrusion, for instance of mother's food or feminine identity.

The lack of control of certain body functions, e.g. enuresis and encopresis, signifies a problem of autonomy (Erikson 1977, pp. 50, 72) and independence. The ego is not adequately differentiated and the internal boundary is excessively permeable. If the boundary is too permeable from the outside, the individual may feel overwhelmed or engulfed. Sometimes in enuresis the child is unable to withstand parental over-involvement (penetration from the outside), related to a difficulty in expressing anger (emotionally rigid boundary), leading to a porous boundary. Several symptoms of panic and anxiety disorder indicate excessive permeability of the ego-boundary from the inside out, as well as from the outside in.

The Psychological Meaning of Geopolitical Borders
It is possible to relate the basic axes of viewing boundaries, that is, constriction/expansion and rigidity/permeability, to Israel's geopolitical borders. These boundary-issues are constantly present: geographically because of the country's (small) size, historically and politically because of internal and external disagreements about the borders and their past and future changes. There is, as well, the element of close proximity between individual and collective processes in Israel. In addition to collective, social processes mentioned earlier, the unique border situation influences the individual, his comprehension and conceptualization of reality, and the interrelationship between individual and collective.

It seems significant that some of those who have written on the psychological aspects of geopolitical borders have written out of their personal experience. Avner Falk (1974) relates his interest in borders to having grown up in Israel, and Vamik Volkan deals extensively with his experience in Cyprus (Volkan 1972, 1985). Both Falk (1974) and Moses (1983) quote experiences related to the border that divided Jerusalem until 1967. By enabling a group or a nation to differentiate, geopolitical borders provide a sense of identity (Erikson 1968, 1985); they are needed to create a feeling of "being there, to overcome the panic of the symbiotic loss of ego boundaries" (Falk 1983, p. 218).

The two sides of a border may represent archetypal parental images. Crossing an international border may thus, occasionally, imply the desire to cross into the archetype of the Great Mother and regression into a lower level of consciousness, into which one is drawn by fascination, seduction, and a search for unconditional acceptance. Simultaneously, however, there is also fear of engulfment and being devoured by the unknown across the border, outside the ego. Babineau (1972) holds the view that the individual's way of perceiving a nation is partly "a projection of fantasies about parenting figures." Falk (1974) mentions the border's splitting and projective functions, and Volkan (1985) speaks of "drawing lines between *them* and *us*" in the strengthening of positive self-representations.

Babineau (1972) stresses the polarizing quality of the new (good) country that one might have arrived to, versus the old (bad) one that one leaves behind. The values ascribed may of course sometimes be the reverse, for instance when the new country is experienced as a harsh struggle for survival, and the old land is remembered as an idealization of a happy childhood.

The new country may provide a possibility to escape from intimacy (or incest, or symbiosis, or too close proximity in relationship to the *Father's Way*, or alternatively, to the *Mother's Land*) and to search for a personal identity, separate from the collective. Many Israelis, who have chosen to emigrate, have felt a need to escape the overwhelming sense of intimacy and the strong demand on identification. Emigrants are disparagingly known as *yordim*, meaning those who descend, in contrast to *olim*, those who ascend, the term used for immigrants to Israel. (Originally from Ezra 2:1: "And these are the people of the province who *went up* from the captivity, of those exiles whom Nebuchadnezzar the king of Babylon had carried away to Babylon, and returned to Jerusalem and Judah, every one to his city.")

To immigrate to Israel often stands for, or is considered as, the personal ego's *ascendance*, connecting with the greater Self, while emigration reflects the ego's need or desire to separate from that overpowering Self, and become independent from a too harsh collective, archetypal and cultural Father, and a sometimes too nurturing and suffocating Mother. For many it is easier to identify with Israel, with the carrier of the projected self, from far away rather than remaining at home and pay the price of war, aggression, instability and normativeness. To dwell in the vicinity of a projected self, which often manifests as a punitive super-ego of the collective consciousness, may not leave enough space for ego development.

Furthermore, when most violently exposed to physical and psychological border situations, face to face with the enemy at war, Moses (1984) asks if the soldier must not "identify ... with the enemy ... And then, ... disidentify in order to be able to aim and kill?" That is, internal boundaries come under severe stress. When departing for war, it is obvious who the enemy is. At the very moment of confrontation, there might be confusion between *Us* and *Them*. If this confusion in battle is not overcome rapidly, the enemy will likely strike first. And if identification remains afterwards, conscience is likely to be in agony.

The boundaries and border situations of society provide a context and a framework for individual and collective psychological processes. Due to historical, geographical, military and political reasons, borders and psyche are particularly intertwined in Israel.

The War of Independence and Its Aftermath

Birth and Boundaries

The State of Israel was born after a long and painful pregnancy, as Gonen (1978) says. The birth was violent, traumatized by war, and few expected it to survive infancy. However, the state was established within defined boundaries, which is crucial to the essence of statehood. Since the neighboring Arab states did not recognize Israel, its borders were closed. Indeed, Israel became hermetically sealed with cease-fire lines to be as impenetrable as possible. For security reasons, Arab villages within the state were under military administration for many years (until the mid-sixties), whereby freedom of movement for Israel's Arabs was limited. The only crossing point to an Arab country (Jordan) was the Mandelbaum Gate in Jerusalem which, of course, Israelis were not permitted to pass through. Only a few, stationed at the Hebrew University on Mount Scopus, which remained an Israeli enclave, were permitted through Jordanian controlled territory, in closed vehicles with Jordanian guards. The borders of Israel were firm, severe and closed. They were restrictive and almost impermeable in either direction. They brought about a sense of claustrophobia, feelings of being locked in and isolated. This reinforced a concomitant need to unite within and to "belong" – to a political party, an army unit, a youth movement. Under such circumstances, travel abroad may be an effort to expand boundaries, to breathe, to escape from intimacy and over-identity. Leaving the country in the early years of statehood was similar to abandoning the mother (cf. Falk 1983), with concurrent feelings of guilt. It was often an effort at escaping the restrictive, ideological framework with its demands on conformity. The need to draw borders was sometimes acted out with great passion. For example, in the early 1950's the major kibbutz movement split over ideological matters (ironically, the newly separated movements carried the names of 'Unity of Kibbutzim' and 'United Kibbutz,' respectively). In some kibbutzim, members who belonged to different political groupings refused to talk to each other, and in some a physical boundary actually divided the communal dining room.

For some, *Mother* Israel and *Father* Ben-Gurion were simply too demanding.

Crossing the border was an immoral act. To physically do so was not only to move into the unknown, it was dangerous and forbidden. There were some for whom simply escaping the severe super-ego by leaving the country was insufficient, they needed to tempt and provoke it. The tight, rigid border spawned a playing ground for fantasy and mystique, and there were those who actually crossed the border to act out the forbidden. What lies buried in the earth across the border is fascinating and attractive, frightening and unknown, which can compound in the psyche as the archetypal image of the Great Mother, projected onto geo-political reality.

During the 1950's, the ancient town of Petra in Jordan became the target of adventurous Israelis who endangered their lives as myth, projection, and reality merged. A powerful song about the Red Rock of Petra was once forbidden (in order not to encourage the young and daring), but this chapter now belongs to history, since Israeli tourists following the peace treaty with Jordan freely can "invade" Petra. While the beauty of Petra remains, the special mystique it carried to Israelis has faded. Prior to the opening of the border, there were claims made of an important Jewish burial site at Petra. Now that Petra can be accessed, there is no longer a similar need to search for the hidden treasure.

Splitting of Fear and Aggression
The firm and restrictive boundary between the known and the unknown does not only cause the projection of fantasies of mystique across the border. The rigid and constrictive boundary becomes restrictive and punitive, and causes a split between *Us* and *Them*, in which the *Us* (in Israel) represents isolation from the outside and unity within. *They* are perceived as carriers of threat and aggression, both real and projected, followed by fear. In Israeli reality this amounts to the fear of annihilation, of losing one's boundaries and disintegrating (Lifton 1983b), i.e., a loss of ego. The rigid, constrictive boundary may evoke memories of the ghettos and the Holocaust, and of the besieged at Masada who ultimately committed group suicide. However, in the early years of statehood, there was a strong tendency to repress the questions of loss, fear and weakness. The Jewish victim of the Holocaust became the one to carry the shadow of the arrogant Zionist, of the "New Jew." As Davidson (1987, p. 29) emphasized,

A further important element in the social climate of the new State was the denial and repudiation of vulnerability and passivity which were associated with the overwhelming confrontation with the mass violent death of the Holocaust, both at individual and societal levels. The Israeli new-born generation with its (Sabra) self-image of mastery, action and invincibility replaced the stereotype of the vulnerable, persecuted and disdained Diaspora Jew, powerless and helpless in the face of persecution and genocide. This image of the Israeli became the idealized model for a new identity for the immigrants and especially for their children.

Yet, by comparing his own character to the Sabra-fruit – hard (tough) on the outside, soft (weak) on the inside – the Israeli subtly recognized the inevitable relationship between strength and weakness, aggression and fear.

The struggle between aggression and fear, and the drive to separate them and increasingly deny fear, continued to be a dominant feature in Israel's psychopolitical development. The Sinai War of 1956 was possibly an early expression of 'strength and force' becoming autonomous and assuming a life of its own. In that war, force was applied not only to counteract murderous Fedayeen terror attacks (in which approximately 1300 Israelis had been killed and wounded), but also to achieve political gains. The delicate tension and balance between strength and power versus fear of annihilation and historical loss were not yet completely interrupted, but there may have been a beginning sense of *the strength of strength.*

Projects of Redemption
In the early years of statehood there were many opportunities for object-cathexis, or the merger of one's personal ego with the national venture, "the project." The infant state provided an overwhelming number of needs that required caring for, plenty of room for an upsurge of collective energy. The draining of the Hula Lake, in order to combat malaria and turn the swamp into fertile land, is one example. Ecologists today re-evaluate the importance of that endeavor, and part of the lake has been re-flooded, but the project was an expression of nation-building, as were similar enterprises such as construction of the national water carrier and the revitalization of the Negev desert. Collective energy was released "to make deserts bloom," which also meant, as in Ezekiel 36:35 and in the Declaration of Independence, to "make the souls (or spirits) blossom" (see above, p. 53).

The Six Day War and its Aftermath

From Fear of Annihilation to Crossing the Borders

Great anxiety was felt in Israel during the weeks preceding the 1967 Six Day War. The threat of annihilation was experienced as very real, evoking images of the Holocaust (e.g. Elon 1981, p. 216) and genuine anxiety that the trauma would be repeated. The strong and self-reliant hero as a manifestation of national identity was threatened. However, the fear of annihilation, with its concomitant death anxiety, was diverted into the will for survival, thereby serving as a catalyst for the release of tremendous force (see also Lifton 1983a, chap. 12). In the perspective of a threatened repetition of the Holocaust, this release of aggressive, Martian energy was understood as ensuring the safety of the nation and its citizens. However, the extremes of fear and the subsequent release of strength severed the tension between these forces and upset their polar balance. This was a consequence of triumphant aggression that had successfully repelled the sense of impending disaster, but which became inflated and as if self-sufficient. In the aftermath of the Six Day War, the dialectical movement that had existed between strength and force versus loss and fear of annihilation come to a turning point.

The pre-war fears of catastrophe gave way to relief and triumph as Israel crossed its borders and defeated enemy armies. As a result, Israel conquered the Gaza Strip and Sinai Peninsula from Egypt, the Golan Heights from Syria, and the West Bank from Jordan. Greater physical space created the temporary illusion of open borders and the end of isolation. The pre-war border was crossed. Israelis gained access to places in the land that had hitherto been beyond the border and which they only had dreamed of, and which had been unreachable, since independence nineteen years earlier – most significantly the Western Wall. Israelis could actually see the object of their fears and tread the realm of their fantasies. Greater space provided, again temporarily, a decrease in feelings of claustrophobia, as Israelis could go traveling to exotic places, such as the Bedouin villages in Sinai. The enemy, now under control within the expanded collective ego-boundaries, was weakened and defeated, which caused relief and reduction of the previously felt anxiety.

The military operations of the Six Day War thus precipitated the expansion of Israel's previously constricted borders, as well as making them permeable (from inside out) in place of their prior rigidity. However, this was possible only as a temporary phenomenon. In the course of time, political and psychological reality caused the borders to again become constricted. The borders were geographically expanded, but they remained as closed as before the war. Open borders signify a state of normality, which is not the case following aggressive, even if defensive, expansion of borders. A pseudo-realization of this was expressed as the major political focus changed from peace to security. Peace is a concept of mutuality based on agreement, dialogue and exchange. Without such prospects, security becomes the objective as a desire to reduce the experience of threat.

Confusion
Initially, there was relief, euphoria and hope in the air following the Six Day War, with concomitant feelings of grandiosity and omnipotence (e.g., Gonen 1978; Moses 1983), all of which served to repress fear. In the youthful glamour of heroism, death was denied. The fear of loss and annihilation was replaced by a reliance on strength, force and power. The latter position, disconnected from the fear, causes hubris and a sense that *the other* need not be accounted for. Repressed fear, however, tends to attract the very calamities, the fear of which was the very cause of repression. And the means applied to maintain the illusion of strength are themselves signs of underlying fear. From the vantage point of ego-consciousness the increased production of weapons, intensified military training and fortification of lines (such as the Bar-Lev Line that was built along the Suez Canal) all seem to express strength and mastery. However, walls are built by fear, and they may blind those who construct them rather than prevent the enemy from attacking. The Bar-Lev Line did not obstruct the Egyptians in the Yom Kippur War of 1973 but rather prevented the Israeli collective from seeing them, psychologically as well as militarily. The security fence erected by Israel in the wake of the literally thousands of terror attacks, following the failed Camp David talks in 2000, is a manifestation of fear, mistrust and tangible threats. In contrast to the Bar-Lev line at the time, there is, however, no denial that the fence is constructed out of fear – in the hope that fences may make good neighbors. The fence is, as well, a recognition of the need for borders, and materializes externally because boundaries have psychologically become conceptualized. Journalist and author Ari Shavit (2003) calls the fence repulsive and ruthless, yet a "definition fence," defining dimensions of identity in the absence of peace, rather than the borders that will be implemented when the times are ripe.

Mistaking expanded borders for open borders and permitting the temporary to become permanent, causes ambivalence and confusion. In the sense that what had been a firm, rigid and closed boundary was crossed and became permeable from the inside out, the pre-1967 border (the so-called Green Line) was opened. Prior to that war, the border had provided a clear separation between *Us* and *Them*, between the known and the unknown. The new expanded border, which included the occupied territories *and* the enemy (the object of projection), provided an illusion of limitlessness. However, the new border was as closed as the old one, since an open border is characterized by appropriate permeability, based on an inner sense of cohesion and identity, and on mutuality in the interaction between *Us* and *Them*. Eventually, the border became permeable in the opposite direction. Long before the onset of the Intifada in December 1987, fear kept most Israelis away from crossing into the West Bank and Gaza (Shalit 1987, p. 370). Simultaneously, Palestinians in increasing numbers entered Israel from the occupied territories seeking employment, becoming familiar with Israeli towns, restaurants and factories, and becoming fluent in Hebrew. Hundreds of thousands of Palestinians in fact settled – legally as well as illegally – in Israel proper.

Following the Six Day War, the expanded border provided the framework for narcissistic self-aggrandizement, self-reliance and omnipotence. It was related to as a 'secure' border that provided 'strategic depth.' However, even before Arab armies crossed the border in 1973, the self-sufficient conceptualization of reality had been challenged by enemy violence. On the Egyptian front, the War of Attrition (1967-1970) took a heavy toll in dead and wounded in a slow, non-glamorous way. Terrorism gathered momentum in 1968 with bombings, hijackings, and attacks on civilians. But in spite of its dramatic, anxiety-provoking character it was met with "resigned acceptance" (GAP 1978). In the national atmosphere that prevailed at the time, the emotional impact of such incidents was repressed. It was not allowed to disrupt the collective self-image; it had no bearing on collective consciousness. Those who did sense the threat and feel the anxiety could easily be dismissed as weak and neurotic, due to the discrepancy between their personal sense of insecurity and the national self-perception of security and strength. The more sensitive individuals may easily feel invaded by anxiety from the outside, since they are not deluded by the false safety provided by the 'parental' border. Acts of terror during a right-wing regime, non-reconciliatory toward a clearly defined *Other* who is not considered to be a possible partner, only seen as *Enemy*, enable splitting between anger and fear. During a process of reconciliation, fear and anger fuse internally, which requires a great degree of integrity.

Not only in order to reduce the confusion of having two borders, but also as an expression of an inflated extended self, the Green Line ceased to be drawn on maps or marked on roads. Young Israelis growing up after the Six Day War did not see a map that showed the borders of Israel proper until the onset of the Intifada in 1987. Since then, the cognitive boundary between Israel and occupied territory has been reestablished. Ongoing occupation came to influence norms, attitudes and behavior inside Israel in a slow and subtle manner long before the more blatant expressions in the wake of the Intifada. Yet, the very Arab enemy who had to be controlled *outside* the Green Line was, in increasing numbers, being brought *inside* the boundary, working in industry and construction. Though Arabs from the occupied territories were not legally permitted to remain in Israel proper overnight (a subtle recognition of boundaries), Palestinians have throughout the years been sleeping in storerooms, orange groves, and other primitive lodgings on the margin of society, often without essential facilities. Fear and aggression, however, forced the need to reestablish the border, and the Israeli government came to take increasing measurements to prevent Palestinian terrorists from entering Israel proper. Closure of the border between Israel and occupied Gaza and the West Bank – the Green Line – was initially highly unusual. It contradicted the cognitive map, but in the course of time, the Green Line came to receive renewed geo-psychological recognition by the Israeli collective.

The mutual Israeli-Arab denial of boundaries creates confusion, and threatens the sense of self-cohesion. This increases adherence to the collective world-view, and augmented sensitivity to deviation from it. Moreover, in order to reduce the confusion, the expanded Israeli boundaries needed to be 'filled out,' concretely by being built up. In spite of official ambivalence in the aftermath of the Six Day War, this enabled ideologically motivated Israelis to settle in the occupied territories. Although initially they were only a handful of activists, they became the means by which the change from *security concerns* to *historical rights* as the rationale for prolonged occupation could take place. Historical rights imply the expansion of collective identity (see Erikson 1985 on *pseudospecies*) to the entire area within the expanded boundary. Dissonance between the psychological sense of collective identity and its physical, geo-political manifestation is consequently reduced, as the occupied territories become narcissistically cathected, for instance by renaming them Judea and Samaria – names rooted in ancient Jewish history rather than the *West Bank*, the name given by Jordan when annexing the area after the 1948 War.

Inflated Strength and Denial of Fear

Illusions of safety and self-sufficiency were the result of excessive reliance on strength with concomitant denial of fear following the Six Day War. President Sadat's attempt to initiate negotiations in 1971-72 did not elicit an unambiguous Israeli response, because there was no real feeling of need. The psychological frame of mind was such that no one seemed able to pose a threat to Israel, or even evoke fear. Thus, despite Sadat's repeated declarations that the coming year would be one of either war or peace, the warnings were foregone and the 1973 Yom Kippur War erupted in complete surprise to the Israelis. As a consequence of such an illusion of self-sufficiency and invulnerability, Israel's leadership was unable to correctly interpret the intelligence at hand about imminent attack. Like the entire Israeli collective, the leadership was caught in the dangerous psychological condition of fusion between the individual ego and the extended national or collective self. Personal and collective identities had merged, they were as if inseparable. The individual could (and, in fact, social undercurrents encouraged him to) identify with the national image of strength, omnipotence and fearlessness. Even death was challenged. Nothing could inflict harm or injury. This state of psychological inflation affected the entire nation, including the political leadership, which was unable to differentiate itself from the collective process. The leadership had fallen victim to the collective self-image of invincibility, and was therefore unable to prevent the war. In striking contrast, following the Declaration of Independence, May 14, 1948, when the people rejoiced and danced in the streets, Ben-Gurion was gravely concerned with what lie ahead, contemplating the possibility of the Arab nations' forthcoming attack. In 1973, however, the process of redemption, of the individual ego merging with the collective self, had attained its tragic peak.

The position of strength, force, and power, disconnected from its opposite pole of loss and fear of annihilation, collapsed following the Yom Kippur War. Since any trace of weakness might have threatened the sense of hubris, and therefore had been denied, the gap between reality and self-perception had reached unhealthy proportions. With devastating clarity, the Yom Kippur War brought to light the weakness that lingered in the shadow behind the persona of strength and self-sufficiency, by which the collective ego had become possessed. The war brought forth the sense of loss and – again – the deeply rooted fear of ultimate destruction. This, in turn, generated the release of strength and the will to survive. The Yom Kippur War was the tragic outcome of a complex having taken possession of a nation's collective consciousness.

The Yom Kippur War and Its Aftermath

From Ambivalence to Unconditional Ideology
The mood in the wake of the Yom Kippur War was entirely different than the triumph and euphoria that had followed upon the Six Day War. Israelis now found themselves depressed and in grief, the narcissistic illusion of grandiosity and invulnerability had shattered. Ego-consciousness had been possessed by a hubris complex, leading to denial of the enemy's strength and potency, which otherwise is a pivotal feature of projection onto an enemy. Thus, the war came as a devastating surprise, in contradiction to what has been called the collective "conception" of invincibility and immortality. The collective ego was assaulted. It was like the Sphinx who killed the inhabitants of Thebes, who did not understand and could not answer its existential riddle that man goes through a life cycle and therefore, unlike the gods, is mortal. This did not, however, lead to serious reconsideration or to an active search for new solutions. The belief that the enemy eventually would agree to Israel's holding on to the occupied territories was not reexamined. Certain compromises were made and parts of Sinai and the Golan Heights were returned, but until Sadat's peace initiative the prevailing attitude was characterized by "more of the same" (Watzlawick, Weakland, & Fish 1974). The Agranat Commission of Inquiry into the war unjustly focused blame on then Chief-of-Staff David Elazar, which led to his resignation. Instead of terminating settlement activity in occupied territories, it was intensified. In the 1977 elections Labor lost power, having formed every government since independence. The Likud party under Menachem Begin came into power, whereby previously marginal settlement groups such as Gush Emunim ("the Bloc of Faith"), came to embody government policy. Increasingly influential, the settlers' ranks soon included ordinary citizens, drawn to live in the West Bank

because of the promise of cheap housing, rather than being committed to nationalist ideology. Labor had been divided over the issue of peace versus territory. The Likud party was much clearer, offering an unconditional, uncompromising ideology. In the elections of 1977, when many felt a need for authority and "strong leadership" as a way out of confusion and ambivalence, which had intensified by the events of the 1973 Yom Kippur War, Labor was dethroned.

Thus it was Menachem Begin, a political right-winger, who came to return Sinai. As opposition leader, it is doubtful whether he would have supported similar concessions by a Labor-led (in itself ambivalent) government. Consequently, when in opposition, the Likud vehemently objected the negotiations with the Palestinians conducted by Rabin's Labor government 1993-1995. Withdrawal from territory, however, and constriction of the border (even though its character changed from rigid to appropriately permeable in both directions) constituted a narcissistic loss (Falk 1983). The Israeli-built town of Yamit, in northeastern Sinai, could psychologically not be handed over as a good-will gesture to the Egyptians, when Israel withdrew from Sinai. The Israeli government destroyed it, when then Minister of Defense Ariel Sharon had given the green light to evacuate. When the dream of an Israeli Sinai proved an illusion, nothing of the collective self could remain outside and yet so close to the state's body-boundary. This narcissistic act of self-destruction recalls the suicide at Masada, where capitulation to the enemy was intolerable to the self. Compensating for the Sinai withdrawal, west of Israel, Begin expanded in the east by increasing settlement activity in the West Bank.

From Security to Historical Rights
Security concerns served as the transition to demands based on historical rights. *Historical rights* implied ideas, images, attachments, symbols and signs dating back to Biblical times with which there was a desire to reconnect. For Gush Emunim and the ideologically motivated settlers, Palestinian presence was and remains an obstacle to their ideational world, which they attempt to consolidate concretely in physical reality.

To in-*spire* matter and awaken the earth is justifiable both psychologically and politically, on condition that the equilibrium between spiritual yearning and geographical reality is kept. Israel, with Gush Emunim as its spearhead, could not endure the geo-psychologically expanded boundaries without concretizing the ideational.

Historical rights came to represent the view of the government, that is, of the nation's conscious attitude. Historical rights thus provided the ideational basis for expanding the collective self into the occupied territories.

Proceeding in this direction, more and more individuals settled in the territories. Similar to the beginning stages of Zionism, individual egos merged with the geo-historical self. Although there was never a consensus, this stance increasingly became the accepted, concrete manifestation of the collective consciousness, and the settlers became the carriers of the redemption motive of Zionism. No account was taken of the fact that this individual merger was made with a greatly inflated expression of the collective self.

The Shadow of Collective Consciousness

The process of expanding the collective self into the occupied territories cast a dark shadow, to which the political leadership (which as executive and legislative authority serves the ego-function of the collective) was blind. Many of those who felt that Israel and Zionism had gone astray could no longer see a value in personal sacrifice and began to "drop out." Two paths that after the wars of 1967 and 1973 became major avenues were emigration and (sometimes anti-Zionist) religion. In increasing numbers, many of the younger generation turned to these options in response to collective social processes.

There had always been those who felt the burden of close proximity between the individual and the collective to be too heavy a load to carry, and therefore left the country. Most had gone to the United States, where the collective myth, in contrast to the Israeli guiding myth, emphasizes individualism. This phenomenon became more pronounced after 1973, reflecting an increasing separation, and alienation, between the personal ego and the collective Idea.

The Lebanon War

Rigidity of Aggression

With a policy of "more of the same" rather than political and psychological change, Israel moved one step further in the unfortunate process of extremism and rigidity. Strength, force and power continued to be emphasized, blinding the nation to alternative solutions to fundamental questions of survival. The disastrous 1982

Lebanon War was the direct outcome of this collective process. Its futile logic was reflected in then Prime Minister Begin's declaration at the outset of the war that he had now "erased" the trauma of Yom Kippur. "There will be no more terrorism and no one will dare to wage war against us," he said. Presumably, the use of force would not only neutralize and frighten the enemy, but it would also restore self-confidence and eliminate fear, loss and trauma. This position was expressed in statements such as, "The country will be calm for forty years" (Judges 3:11), and "There will be no more rockets and no more fear in Kiryat Shemona," (cf. Jansen 1987, p. 66). This reflects how the leadership remained possessed by a grandiose position, a belief in invincible strength and force – that is, hubris. This is a position of Mars, force and aggression, without Eros, without a need to relate to the other.

The Lebanon War was waged on the basis of a rigid, extreme stance of (false) power, a position, which deceived its adherents into believing that the exercise of strength can prevent loss. It was blatantly expressed in an interview that Israeli author Amos Oz (1984, p. 89) conducted with a right-wing extremist:

> Maybe the world will finally begin to fear me instead of feeling sorry for me ... quaking in fear of my whims instead of admiring my nobility ... Let them quake. And let them call us a mad-dog nation. Let them realize that we're a wild country, deadly and dangerous to everyone around, awful, crazy, capable of suddenly going nuts because they murdered one of our kids – even one! – and running wild and burning up all the oil fields in the Middle East.

The 1982 Lebanon War was the result of the position of strength and power having been disconnected from its opposite pole of fear and loss. It had taken on a life of its own. The balance and interaction between the opposing poles are thus disrupted, and energy is directed towards reinforcing and rigidifying the extreme position. Paradoxically, this can produce violent repercussions in the opposite direction. The development of Israel's arms industry may serve as an illustration. Following the Six Day War, when France placed an arms embargo on Israel, a decision was made that to the greatest degree possible, Israel must become independent in terms of its militarily needs. In this way, the supply of necessary weapons would be ensured in case of future war or attack on Israel. As the military industry expanded, the problem of product application arose. In fact, prior to the Lebanon War, it was actually suggested that Israeli weapons must not fall into disuse. There was a psycho-military need to find an outlet. The energy accumulated by an extreme position of strength and power may create the need to act it out, which not surprisingly opens the way in the opposite direction, toward the abyss of fear and loss.

By nature, the collective fantasy of being invulnerable and of triumphant strength must periodically be reaffirmed in confrontation with the enemy – or relinquished. If not exposed to external reality, the repressed fear may invade the fantasy. This grandiose position was, however, challenged by the Israeli collective itself during the Lebanon War. An omnipotent position of strength and self-sufficiency requires a constantly threatening externalized persecutor in order to be reaffirmed, and is therefore essentially paranoid. Indeed, weapons that had been marked for use in an emergency situation were squandered in Lebanon on Syrian missiles (which the Syrians quickly replaced with more advanced ones). Such manifestation of power derives from an internal need to maintain the repression of fear of annihilation, rather than accounting for outer reality. Ironically, this strengthens both the external threat and the underlying fears it was meant to ward off. Complexes have this very capacity to drive us down the very road we did not want to take (cf. Shalit 2002).

Denial of Fear

The Yom Kippur War was an outcome of the illusions of grandiosity and the denial of death that followed the Six Day War. As a result of the war, the fears resurfaced with awesome strength. The Lebanon War became, psychologically, a compensatory effort to re-repress the underlying fear of annihilation. As echoed in Begin's statements, it served the need to ensure reliance on one's own strength, without a need to account for the Other. The Yom Kippur War had brought on a traumatic resurgence of the fear of annihilation. Due to the Yom Kippur War, the deep-seated fear of annihilation had resurfaced. Subsequent negotiations and peace agreement with Egypt were based on a mutual renunciation of archetypal fantasies. Sadat's recognition of Israel's existence meant relinquishing the hope of destroying the Jewish State, and Israel began a process of abandoning the dream of Biblical borders.

Mutuality between self and object is concomitant to negotiations and agreement, and implies *seeing* the other, whereby both become personalized and projections are withdrawn. This challenges a position based entirely on strength and self-reliance, and therefore inflicts a narcissistic wound that needs to be cared for by mourning the loss. Otherwise, the lost narcissistic position will thrive in the shadow, and is likely to be acted out. It is noteworthy that for eleven months prior to Israel's invasion of Lebanon, the Israeli-Lebanese border was quiet, following a meticulously kept cease-fire agreement with the PLO, which had been mediated by American envoy Philip Habib in 1981 (cf. Jansen 1987, p. 62; Yitzhak Rabin 1989). The agreement could have reduced the fear along Israel's northern border, which stemmed from the frequent rocket attacks over the years on civilian towns and villages. However, interdependency with the enemy seemed to contradict the prevalent self-perception.

The northern border town of Kiryat Shemona provides an interesting case. Since its foundation in 1949, the town has suffered social and other internal problems. In 1971, the author Carl Alpert called it "the city that needs a psychiatrist," writing about a neglected, dead town without a future. All through the 1970's the town, with an already low self-image, had suffered severely from Katyusha rockets. Since the cease-fire agreement did not gain psychological backing, the fear of the citizens was not alleviated. Consequently, even when no rockets were fired, the fear of rocket attacks was retained from the preceding years, while rockets that were fired and hit Israel's northern region *following* the invasion of Lebanon, for a long period of time did not appear to cause a similar level of anxiety. As long as there was substantial belief in the myth of strength, whether corresponding to empirical reality or not, fear could be repressed.

The Lebanon War was embarked upon by conscious decision. However, the leadership was probably unaware of their motives from a psychological point of view. The attack on the enemy (real and projected) was across the border, on the other side of a well-defined boundary. Israeli political leaders argued whether the attack should be limited to forty kilometers north of Israel's border, or continue beyond that point. As this became the case, some of them would feel deceived. For some, forty kilometers was enough to control the projection onto the other, while for others the abolition of the projected enemy-shadow required boundless belligerence.

The Intifada

The Palestinian uprising, the Intifada, began in the occupied territories in December 1987. Even though Israel under PM Shimon Peres had unilaterally withdrawn most of the troops two years earlier, in 1985,

Israel kept a fifteen km security zone to prevent terror attacks, until PM Ehud Barak withdrew completely from Lebanon in 2000. The Intifada constituted a further step in an enantiodromic process, whereby everything turns into its opposite. It was the very negative of the Lebanon venture, in which Israel tried to fight against large-scale terrorism by conventional military means. No longer was the enemy a well-defined terrorist group, but the entire Palestinian population under occupation. Nor was the enemy across the border, but barely across the Green Line that supposedly had been erased. Advanced war strategies and weaponry were futile, and as the Palestinians turned to stones, the Israelis turned to sticks. Israel did not know how to handle the situation of fighting a civilian uprising. Mere reliance on force became inappropriate. Except for soldiers and settlers, fewer Israelis crossed the Green Line. This process had on a moderate scale begun already before the onset of the Intifada. It is noteworthy that already in 1981-1982 there was increased unrest in the occupied territories, which waned at the onset of the Lebanon War. However, that war and the Palestinian uprising became overtly interconnected when in May 1985 more than a thousand Palestinian security prisoners were exchanged for three Israeli soldiers captured in Lebanon. The Palestinians were brought in buses and released beyond the Green Line. For Israel, this was a subtle but definite recognition that the occupied territories were Palestinian, not Israeli (cf. Volkan 1988), in contradiction to official policy at the time, which was ambivalent on the question whether to hold on to the territories for security reasons or because of historical rights. Eventually, many of the released prisoners became leaders of the Intifada.

The Missile War

From an Israeli political perspective, there was a certain absurdity to the Gulf War. Israel occupied the West Bank as a result of Arab hostilities, while Iraq invaded Kuwait claiming historical rights. As occupation became permanent, official Israeli policy changed from retaining the West Bank for security reasons to claiming historical rights. The prolonged occupation has, naturally, evoked the anger of the world community and is unacceptable to the Palestinians, claiming their right to independence. However, from an Israeli perspective, it seemed all too easy for the Palestinians to accept Saddam Hussein's claim of historical rights to legitimatize the invasion and occupation of Kuwait.

The close proximity between individual and collective was strongly felt during the war. Iraq declared its intention to destroy Israel and launched thirty-nine missile attacks against the country. As a consequence, eight people were killed, close to eight hundred casualties were evacuated to hospital (Bleich, Dycian, Koslowsky, Solomon & Wiener 1992), and more than five thousand houses and apartments were damaged. Fear of the missiles, and especially the possibility that they would be equipped with chemical or biological warheads, kept Israel in a state of siege. During the first days, except for emergency personnel and those involved in essential military and civilian functions, people did not leave their homes, and generally felt under siege. For weeks Israel was kept closed after dark, in a kind of self-withdrawal at five or six in the afternoon, closing off from the outside, tensely waiting for the air raid sirens to sound and then retreating further inwards. Families gathered in the womb of the Sealed Room with its as-if protective membrane of plastic sheets that covered the windows as a shield against gas and the air shock of the missile.

Hundreds of thousands sought safe refuge as they escaped from cities under attack, temporarily leaving for a safe haven in the country or abroad. As things became calmer, in an intermediary step before moving back, many left the city at night, returning during the day to work and attend to their homes and property, a phenomenon often observed in the aftermath of catastrophes.

Israelis became accustomed to a sealed room in their homes, masking tape and plastic sheets covering the windows, a stock of closed water-bottles, preserves and crackers in the event of extended stay, transistor radio in case of electricity cuts so that Civil Defense instructions could be followed when the air raid sirens would be activated, towels soaked in a mixture of bicarbonate to cover doorposts against possible gas leaks, and of course the routine of putting on gas masks. This was the shared existential condition of Israel's population during the six weeks of that war.

The Scapegoat Feeling

From an Israeli perspective, Saddam Hussein emerged as an image of evil. On both the personal level (according to numerous accounts) and at the collective level as leader of a nation, his ways were dark, cruel and evil; begetting war, murder and destruction.

With outstanding technological and industrial achievements, the West has come to consolidate itself on the ego-level; that is, on the overt, conscious level. The West has not, so it seems, accounted well enough for the shadow aspects of this ego-development and ego-consolidation, i.e., the negative effects of such developments. Thus, detrimental corollaries come to reside in the unconscious and, unaccounted for, become autonomous. Ecological concern is one important way of trying to account for the shadow. While the conscious ego asserts itself through scientific and technological developments, industrial and other waste constellate a toxic, carcinogenic shadow, which if disregarded becomes destructive to man, world and nature. Man needs to control certain aspects of nature, such as the acculturation of fire, but if he subjugates nature, for instance by destroying rainforests or setting oil wells on fire, severe ecological consequences ensue. As long as Iraq was a split-off, far away shadow that did not threaten the West, Saddam Hussein could be left unattended. While Iraq fought with Khomeini's Iran, in the distant shadow-land, the horrendous consequences of that war could be ignored. Little was it noticed how the Western ego prospered by pouring weapons into the shadow. As the Gulf War broke out, the West was confronted not only with the evil of Saddam Hussein, but with the fact that it had empowered the malignant golem.

In between East and West, Israel found itself caught in the conflict. There was no reason to claim innocence. Israel had learned to thrive on weapon sales to dubious regimes, among them Iran. Furthermore, Israel had not, at the time, been able to sincerely face the challenge of searching for just and peaceful solutions to the Israeli-Palestinian conflict. Israel's very existence was a provocation to Saddam Hussein, who saw the Jewish State as a thorn of the West in the eye of the Arab World. "Strategic defense" against the very existence of the so-called "Zionist entity," served as justification for missile attacks and damaging central population areas inside Israel. The experience evoked in many Israelis the feeling of being scapegoated by Saddam Hussein, and all too easily abandoned by the West, which had let the shadow grow in the dark; "lo, the people shall dwell alone, and shall not be reckoned among the nations" (Numb. 23:9). Particularly vis-à-vis Germany there was the sense that it had not taken notice of its own past in a way that history required. Germany provided gas and expertise to Iraq, which intended to use it against Israel. And then, Germany also exported gas masks to Israel, making many wonder whether Germany was to gain, cynically, from the aggressor as well as from the victim, or if this was an act of atonement.

Saddam Hussein turned Iraq into a dark shadow with the

co-operation of that split-off part of the Western ego, and as ego and shadow came to clash openly, he tried to actuate Israel as his scapegoat by bringing it into the war. While Saddam Hussein's regime did consider equipping missiles against Israel chemically or biologically, the danger was averted. Yet, Israel remains under the threat of being attacked by weapons of mass destruction by other countries as well as by terrorist groups. Every day Israel's neighbors call for its annihilation in mosques and media, in kindergartens, schools and universities. Apocalyptic fears and images of destruction keep flourishing in the collective Israeli psyche. Unresolved conflicts – even if Israel cannot always be blamed – create autonomous shadows.

Talks of Peace and War of Terror

Peace talks between Israel and the Palestinians, represented by the PLO (Palestine Liberation Organization), began in 1993. They nearly failed at the very initial discussions, when the sides approached each other through their respective historical claims and injustices. A decision was taken to put away the past and concentrate on the present and the future. In the words of prominent Israeli negotiator Uri Savir (1998),

> We had arrived at our first understanding. Never again would we argue about the past. This was an important step, for it moved us beyond an endless wrangle over right and wrong. Discussing the future would mean reconciling two rights, not readdressing ancient wrongs.

This approach enabled the parties to carry out fruitful discussions. Intuitively, they had understood that as long as either side sticks to archetypal sentiments, there is no room for realistic deliberations and pragmatic assessment. However, by brushing archetypal concerns off the table, these became displaced entities in the shadow. Consequently, what was not spoken about, gathered strength in respective backyards, particularly so on the Palestinian side, where the peace process was undermined by the worst kind of incitement, even in school books and children's television.

The 1990's had seen horrendous terror attacks against Israel, among others a series of bus bombings in March 1996 in which close to sixty civilians were killed. The Israeli public was divided between right and left. Whereas the right demanded an end to negotiations while terror was raging, the left followed the motto "to fight terror as if there were no negotiations, and to negotiate as if there was no terror." The understanding was that terrorism was carried out by militants who wanted to obstruct the peace process, undermining what Arafat in his double-talk called the "peace of the courageous."

So why was this war, starting after the failed Camp David summit, summer 2000, different from all previous wars between Israel and the Palestinians? In fact, terror had been a means in the struggle for already a century, and Palestinian rejection of the Jewish state had been persistent since the very notion of establishing one state for the Jews and one for the Arabs.

This war was, from the Israeli perspective, different, because it put an end to what had become a widespread conviction – that the former enemies in unending strife with each other had now become, however reluctantly and hesitantly, partners for peace. Generally, it was believed that Arafat, the terrorist of old, had taken on the role of statesman and leader of his nation, committed to finding peaceful solutions. Little attention was paid to his double-talk, to ongoing incitement in schools, mosques and Palestinian media. The war was perceived of as an act of betrayal.

Furthermore, the two-state solution – an Arab State of Palestine alongside the Jewish State of Israel – which once was a marginal position, had by now become embraced by the majority. The realization that *the other*, the very Palestinian leadership with whom Israel negotiated, in fact did not recognize the Jewish State – which has been confirmed for instance by the moderate Palestinian leader Abu Ala; thus Camp David failed – was devastating to those who had favored the building of trust, mutual compromise and peaceful solutions. The barbaric attacks on civilians caused a feeling that not only statehood, but the very core of society was threatened, as it had been in 1948, when armies from several Arab countries invaded Israel. While severely traumatized, it may well be that Israel came out of the war strengthened, having been able to reorganize, adjust and somehow protect a highly developed society in the struggle for survival in lieu of indescribable terror against its civilian population.

Additionally, it was not incidental that the Oslo negotiators had tried to put history behind them, turning to pragmatism. There can be no progress without movement away from archetypal fantasies, toward interpersonal compromise. "We could go back to King David," Uri Savir told Abu Ala, his Palestinian counterpart. That is, the conflict between Jews and Arabs has deep archetypal roots. It has its origin in the pair of brothers, Isaac through whom the Jews and Ishmael through whom the Muslims each see themselves as children of Abraham.

Isaac (Yitzhak) is the son born from the womb of the favored old woman, Sara, who expels her combatant, Hagar, from the land into the desert. And Ishmael is the expelled woman's son, "a wild man; his hand will be against every man, and every man's hand against him," (Gen. 16: 12), yearning to take what he considers belongs to him, and to "live in the presence of all his brothers."

The initial step toward reconciliation is recognition of one's shadow, and in this case, Jews and Arabs serve as mirrors of each other's shadow.

Seeing Ishmael in a dream, says the Talmud, means one's prayer will be heard, which is the very meaning of Ishmael – God hears. And man may not hear the Divine if he doesn't see his shadow. God "heard the voice of the lad" (Gen. 21:17), and saved Ishmael from death in the desert.

But also *the other* must see his shadow. Islam is ambivalent about its Jewish roots. Muhammad's midnight ride on his flying horse *al-Buraq*, which had the face of a woman, the body of a horse and the tail of a peacock, in the 17th Sura (chapter) is described as taking place from the Holy Mosque in Mecca to "the further mosque" *(al-masjid al-Aqsa),* from where he ascends to heaven, together with the angel Gabriel, coming close to Allah. While al-Aqsa has been understood metaphorically, it is considered to be in recognition of Islam's common roots with Judaism that it received its earthly location at the Temple Mount (which in early Islam was recognized as such, having the name *Bayt al-Maqewdis*), the place of Abraham's binding of Isaac.

In a process of reconciliation, archetypal fantasies of wholeness must be renounced (see chapter 9). At the crucial point of decision, whether to remain within the realm of archetypal strife or accept the loss and the mourning of grand archetypal dreams, Arafat broke the premises of his agreement with Yitzhak Rabin. Rabin had demanded Arafat does not return to the use of violence in any matter of dispute, and he had claimed the peace process would break down if the PLO charter were not changed. Rabin seems to have been aware – if in political terms rather than psychological – that violence here means not only terror against civilians, but that this appalling kind of violence is an expression of Palestinian adherence to an archetypal fantasy of harmony that entails ethnic cleansing.

Terrorism is a mindset which has nothing to do with a fight for freedom from foreign or oppressive rule. It has to do, rather, with an archetypal identification that leaves no room for the shadow, which therefore is entirely projected onto the other, who then becomes all bad and a legitimate target. The Palestinian terrorist, when asked, will answer that no Israeli is a civilian. The Israeli and the Jew are the friends of Satan (see above, p. 22), and so naturally they need to be destroyed, even if they pose as playing children or the elderly walking in the park.

Israel has suffered an unprecedented onslaught of literally thousands of terror attacks, more than a thousand mortar and rocket shellings, several hundred suicide/homicide and other bomb attacks, and innumerable preempted or failed attacks, among them some that would have caused major disaster (for instance the attack on the northern Tel Aviv fuel depot Pi-Glilot – since evacuated – which if successful apparently would have caused the death of thousands). Yet, the picture painted by Western media seemed, consciously or unconsciously, distorted to the extreme. Many Israelis would express how they for the first time would grasp the existential condition of the Jews in the Holocaust, and the feelings of abandonment by the nations that stood by. The initial atrocity of this war, September 29, 2000, was an act of betrayal by a Palestinian policeman killing his co-patrol. The following day, September 30, the New York Times and other media published a photo showing an Israeli policeman with raised baton, underneath him a wounded, bleeding man, as if hit by him ("An Israeli policeman and a Palestinian on the Temple Mount," according to the caption). The truth was that the policeman saved the bleeding man (Jewish) from the (Palestinian) mob, which had beaten and stabbed him. These deceptive distortions were to be repeated daily in Western media, the Jenin libel prominent among them, and seem to warrant self-examination, as well as historical and psychopolitical research.

Chapter 6

Wholeness Apart

Close Proximity and de-Narcisstification

More than a hundred and twenty years of practical Zionism have gone by. The Zionist undertaking has thus transcended the individual three-generational life cycle of personal experience. Additionally, more than fifty turbulent years have passed since Israel gained statehood. In the life of the individual, this is already well into midlife. If all has gone relatively well in the first half of life, the person has taken a foothold in society, proven his stamina, and his capacity for coping and living in shared reality. At this stage, natural development requires a degree of settling down, introspection, and coming to terms with one's place in the world, in order to embrace the possibility of renewal during the second half of life.

In Israel, as has been mentioned, a particularly close relationship exists between individual and society. However, at a certain stage, a change would be expected to take place in the relationship between personal identity and identification with the collective self. The differentiated individual does not identify excessively with the projected self as carried by the collective, whether the state, the leader, the collective norm, group ideal or ideology. Idealizations, which beyond their formative role may serve a defensive, splitting function between the good (collective) self and the persecutory other (the enemy), must be renounced. Otherwise the shadow of fascism that such projections embody threatens to spread and plague the collective ego and its governing institutions.

However, the differentiated individual will also not feel alienated or disconnected from the collective self. Beyond the three-generation cycle of parent/child/grandchild, memories become legend and history, and anticipation becomes visions of the future, whether messianic, apocalyptic or science fiction. The memories of ancestors are not personal, but kept alive as traditions, myths and guiding principles. That is, beyond the three-generation cycle, the personal and the archetypal, the material and the spiritual, separate by necessity. A painful illustration has been the trials of Nazi criminals. The Eichmann trial in 1961 provided the personal concretization of the Nazi enemy necessary to tear down the thick walls of silence. However, twenty-five years later, John Demjanjuk's identity as *Ivan the Terrible*, the gas chamber operator at the Treblinka extermination camp, could not be proven. That is, the Nazi Holocaust could no longer be fully personalized. While Ivan the Terrible was sentenced to death because of his crimes against humanity, his personalization (John Demjanjuk) had to be released. The link of identity between the present and the past, the person and the crime could no longer be upheld.

The implementation of Zionism reversed this natural process. The early pioneers sought to merge with the transcendent idea in order to enable its materialization. However, after more than a century of practical Zionism (i.e., the full three-generation life cycle), the more concrete expressions of close proximity should no longer have to be imperative. The boundaries of the collective ego, the state and its institutions, should be sufficiently stable, and the soul of the (Zionist) idea should recede into the background, neither disconnected from nor overpowering, without an incessant need for manifestation. In an increasingly modern society, it is also gradually becoming more difficult to oblige young women for two and men for three or more years of regular army service, and then yearly reserve duty till around the age of fifty. As it turns out, within a few years, nearly half of the young will, for a variety of reasons, be exempted from army service. For this reason, then PM Ehud Barak proposed National Service as an additional option to regular army service. This reflects the intensified differentiation between the individual and the collective that is taking place in Israel.

It is the hero's task, whether as pioneer, warrior or peacemaker, to redeem a myth from the unconscious, to bring it into consciousness for it to become a new guiding principle. When the hero's task has been accomplished, he becomes "part of the establishment," an aspect of the ruling king, a dominant in consciousness. At that stage, holding on to the image of the hero turns it into an ego-ideal or persona. Having arisen from the depths, the hero may then become a shallow ideal without the depth of shadow. This is the midlife stage in which the ego, the conscious identity, should preferably be well enough integrated for the individual to accept the existence within him or herself of traits undesirable to consciousness. This would amount to recognizing the existence of the shadow, and being in dialogue with it, even though it can never be fully integrated into the ego.

Thus, when the collective ego has been established, a state within defined boundaries, a social system with laws and regulations, with certain basic norms and values, with scientific and cultural achievements, the shadow needs to be accounted for. In the course of time, collective consciousness and the state should less and less be the object and carrier of projections of idealization – and devaluation! – with a decreasing need to project the split-off shadow onto *the other*.

Thus, in an appropriate process of normalization, the collective idea becomes less narcissistically invested. Undoubtedly, there are shared moments of collective joy or anxiety, implying narcissistic empowerment of the collective. However, with greater differentiation the individual partakes in shared reality according to conscious decision and responsibility rather than by symbiotic merger.

The process of narcisstification meant impregnating the cultural images and expressions of the archetypal Mother and Father with great energy. While at the archetypal level the process of de-narcisstification entails a sense of dismemberment, at the conscious level it is expressed by differentiation. The collective's demands on the individual become less harsh, and the union between the individual and the collective is diminished. This may lead to excessive egoism and an emphasis on the private rather than the common and collective, with a possible reduction of social Eros. In the absence of psychological awareness, this process is acted out by indiscriminate privatization of state-owned companies and national resources. The kibbutzim, the prime example of the merger between individual and collective, suffer badly in this process, with excessive search for material benefits of privatization rather than the appropriate differentiation between the individual and the collective.

The individual ego might suffer burnout in excessive sacrifice to the collective venture, prominently discernible in those who have participated in several wars, carrying the scars of multiple traumas. The individual increasingly limits his willingness to sacrifice himself in service of the collective self, and many families are now becoming reluctant to put up with the sacrifice of sons in combat units.

Seen developmentally, it might be said that the first Zionist revolution was *the merger of* the *individual ego with the collective self.* The second revolution was *the establishment of a collective ego*; the state and its formal governing institutions, which control and enable an individual's relationship to the collective self. The third Zionist revolution would be the creation of *a flexible relationship between the individual and the collective,* accommodating for the individual's uniqueness as well as enabling him to take part in joint, collective, humanistic and ecological efforts.

In an adequate developmental process, the individual will be appropriately differentiated from the collective, and the ego-institutions of society would be sufficiently stable to account for the shadow, without an excessive need to project it onto a persecutory other, primarily perceived as *the enemy.* Likewise, the social collective would demand less sacrifice and cathexis of narcissistic investment by the individual.

Why is the process of de-narcisstification so difficult and painful in Israel?

Primarily, ongoing violent confrontation with the enemy reinforces projection of the shadow rather than providing for its eventual withdrawal.

Additionally, the different manifestations of the collective ego remain exposed to danger. A Prime Minister, the foremost representative of the state's governing function, i.e., the collective ego, has been assassinated. The High Court building has been stormed. Legal, constitutional and other collective ego institutions may be threatened and violated. Ministers, even a Minister of Justice, have sometimes evaded resignation when under police investigation for corruption.

Furthermore, with ongoing instability, unrest, and projection onto the enemy, the individual ego is overburdened and becomes a "mass ego." Israel is a fragmented society, with large segments of the population socio-economically weak. There is a distressing demand for the strong leader, and excessive reliance on projective identification. Collective norms and values emphasize wholeness and purity, which inhibits the capacity for separation and differentiation.

Moreover, ultra-Orthodox religion, which has become increasingly influential, is in principal opposition to the collective ego-institutions, primarily taking political advantage of them to strengthen their institutions (which are assumed to serve a transcendent self-principle). For example, a former Interior Minister and leader of the religious Shas party, was found guilty of extortion. He then turned vehemently against "the secular courts" (in spite of the fact that the judge himself was religious).

A confusing and boundariless situation exists that further weakens and undermines the collective ego and the governing functions of society. From a psychological perspective it is a fallacy to believe that geo-political boundaries create protection and security when the needs, motives and aspirations of the other are denied. However, in the short run, it satisfies the weak "mass ego's" need for a clear sense of identity.

Consequences of Close Proximity

Close proximity generates a sense of taking part in a common destiny and a profound feeling of belonging, examples of which abound in Jewish and Israeli history. Link after link, these sensations run like a backbone through all the levels of Israeli communality – from belonging to a particular youth group or army unit, to the total standstill and the shared shiver at the sound of the sirens on Remembrance Day that honor the thousands of soldiers killed in the wars, and the memory of the millions that perished, murdered by the Nazis, on Holocaust Remembrance Day. And there have been moments of intense emotional release at the culmination of dramatic collective events, such as the relief of exchanging gas masks for the masks and costumes of the Purim festival, which remarkably took place the day the Gulf War ended, or the signing of a peace treaty. Close proximity enables the individual to sacrifice his self-centeredness and contribute to the collective. The individual has breathed life into the collective, whereby the latter has become an inspired, living entity. Zionist history is replete with such examples, documented and told in personal histories and biographies, and recorded in vivid descriptions of such undertakings as the pre-state ha'apala (illegal immigration), the establishment of towns and villages, the draining of the swamps, the fertilization of the desert, et cetera.

However, there is a shadow side to this close proximity.

The Pro-Social Personality
When the individual identifies with the collective idea and resigns his individual boundaries, he will (too) easily accept and adapt to the norms and values of collective consciousness. Contemptuously, Jung (1970a, p. 277) characterizes this attitude as

> [w]here the many are, there is security; what the many believe must of course be true; what the many want must be worth striving for, and necessary, and therefore good.

In such a situation there is identification between individual and collective consciousness, with a concomitant tendency to avoid critical thinking and individual differentiation. The more a society emphasizes conformity, the more it invites and encourages the pro-social personality, i.e., someone who reacts to inner and outer insecurity by identifying with authority (see Winnicott 1965a, p. 158). The pro-social personality reduces his inner tension and avoids conflict by "gentle and painless slipping back into the kingdom of childhood, into the paradise of parental care, into happy-go-luckiness and irresponsibility" (Jung 1970a, p. 277). This in contrast to the healthy person, "who is capable of becoming depressed, is able to find the whole conflict within the self as well as being able to see the whole conflict outside the self, in external (shared) reality" (Winnicott 1965a, p. 158). As a common trend in society, conformity greatly increases the risk of producing immature leaders who are steeped in conventions, unable to extract themselves from the crippling grip of mediocrity. Such leaders become a reflection of a collective tendency towards lack of differentiation. They then find it difficult to transcend the prevailing Zeitgeist and Weltanschauung, unlike, for example, Egyptian President Sadat in his peace initiative or Rabin's opening negotiations with the Palestinians.

The Weak Ego
A weakening of individual ego is another consequence of too close proximity since "the more highly charged the collective consciousness, the more the ego forfeits its practical importance" (Jung 1969b, p. 219). The internal organizing aspect of the ego is the function "by which the individual maintains himself as a coherent personality with a sameness and continuity both in his self-experience and in his actuality for others" (Erikson 1968, p. 73). However, social and historical conditions may impede man's "autonomy by precedent, and exploit archaic mechanisms within him, to deny him physical

vitality and ego strength" (Erikson 1968, p. 74). He becomes dependent on the mass, the dominant ideology and the leader, sacrificing his ego and individuality. He is drawn into the mob, overpowered by the "mass psyche" (e.g. Neumann 1970, pp. 436-444), surrendering private ego to the 'Self-fulfillment' of the mass. He comes to act impulsively and instinctively. "The more helpless the 'mass-individual' has become," (Reich 1970, p. 63) the greater his identification with the mass or the leader. This occurs when the ego is weak, whether as a result of a combination of intra-psychic and social reasons, or because of a too great degree of identification between individual and collective. The sense of helplessness and smallness of ego may then intensify when there is a decrease in close proximity. The individual will feel that society provides him with less security than in the past. This is the case, for instance, in times of reconciliation with an enemy, which sometimes causes violent opposition to peace making. The more the individual identifies with society's norms and ideas, clinging to the ruling ideology like a child to its father, the more hurt he will feel when close proximity decreases. A society in transformation, moving in ambiguous directions, creates great distress among many individuals, who might feel orphaned by the archetypal Father, whether as Father Society or Father the Leader. When the enemy intrudes violently in such a social situation, he puts the flashlight on the disparity between a self-image of power and potency, and the underlying sense of fear and weakness (see Adorno, Frenkel-Brunswik, Levinson, & Sanford 1950). He will need to speedily redraw the dividing line between foe and friend, and will identify as enemy whomever he can not safely identify as *"I"* or as *"Us."* After a terror attack he might seek retaliation against Arabs, not necessarily against the terrorist who committed the act. The weak ego is like the weak king who kills the messenger who brings bad tidings, and so the media often becomes identified with the enemy. Since this constitutes a loss of ego-consciousness, there is no capacity of differentiation. The world is, to the weak ego, not made up of individuals but of *masses*, e.g.: "Arabs," "leftists," and "the media," onto whom *the bad* is projected without differentiation. The "ego-weak mass" begs for the strong, authoritarian leader, for an unconditional ideology, and for firm, impulsive measures against those onto whom the enemy-shadow is projected.

Mankind has paid dearly because of the weakness of all too many egos having surrendered to the psyche of the mass. While the above refs to Israeli society, the difficulty of a great many Palestinians to resist collective psychosis is troublesome – and no less so, the ease with which the Western, especially European psyche is captivated.

Inflatedness
The individual who identifies too strongly with the collective and who attains a position of power in the collective structure poses a great risk. He may become inflated by an exaggerated and narcissistic sense of self-importance that sometimes conceals an inner sense of insecurity, which he fears may be exposed behind his social role or political persona. Identifying with the role, with the persona, may render him unaware of whom he is behind the mask he wears, and therefore vulnerable and possibly defensive.

But even more detrimental to the functioning of the collective ego is when an individual in power not only identifies with the collective, but comes to identify the collective as part of himself, whether sociopathically or altruistically. The illness of this power inflation might become visible through corruption. The narcissistic inflation that easily comes with carrying out an important social function leads to a reversal in the relationship between the individual and *the other* – here, his role or position of power. He no longer serves in this or that capacity, but his position becomes part of him, eventually there to serve him. Israel has witnessed, especially since the 1990's, quite a number of police investigations of senior politicians, some whom have been brought to trial for abusing positions of power, including Ministers of Justice, Interior and Defense.

When close proximity and identification are customary, then executive power may often be handed over without essential built-in controls and security mechanisms. During society's formative stages, prior to the establishment of such controls, trust in the individual's devotion to the collective venture is cardinal, but at later stages of collective ego development it may readily be misused, with corruption as a likely consequence.

Over-intimacy
A further outcome of close proximity is the lack of space for individuality, which causes some to leave the country in order to escape the burdensome collective norms, conventions and over-intimacy.

Consider the case of Roni and Sara, a young couple. In the years between the 1967 Six Day War and the 1973 Yom Kippur War they were close to completing their studies, he at medical school, she in

law. Not long before finishing, however, both of them concluded that
they had decided to study only in order to meet the demands and
expectations of their parents and society. Now they no longer wanted
to conform. They stopped at mid-semester and went to Europe "for a
couple of years of freedom, to break away from the chains."
   However, they felt that other Israelis would look at them as
"creatures from outer space, because you have to do exactly what is
expected of you and be like every one else. The usual track of school,
army, studies, profession, family, children and endless reserve duty."
They traveled, and eventually tried their luck at various kinds of small
business. "How do you think people in Israel would look at that?
Dropping out of medical school, just to become a merchant, like the
Jews in the Diaspora?" When the Yom Kippur War broke out, they
considered returning, but decided to stay on. "That was it. after that,
there was nothing to return to any longer. Israel was finished for us.
People would look at us as traitors." They remained abroad. As the
years went by, each of them went through alternating periods of
wanting to "return home," to come back to Israel, but was convinced
by the other to stay in the new country, where "no one watched what
you were doing all the time." Both of them were an only child of
Holocaust survivors, and occasionally felt guilt and anxiety at having
left their aging parents in "the old country," in order to live on "the
bloodstained soil of Europe." Eventually, they cut themselves off
from their Israeli identity. Neither did they mix with other Israelis,
nor did they speak Hebrew to each other. Their only son was brought
up without any connection to Israel. A major crisis occurred when he,
in his teens, got into trouble with the local police, and was sent to
relatives in Israel.
   Abroad is to many Israelis an option to escape and release
themselves from over-intimacy. Even in dreams, abroad is often the
stage on which forbidden instincts and impulses are acted out.

Vulnerability of the Collective
In a situation of close proximity, the collective self inevitably
becomes more vulnerable. The collective is then built on the
identification and the involvement of great numbers of individuals in
national ventures. During transformative stages, during crisis and
under threat, the social collective relies on being narcissistically
cathected. When an individual feels this identification weakening,
when society at large does not provide a good enough mirror,
reflecting back and providing the desired narcissistic gratification,

frustration and rage may ensue. The individual may feel betrayed by the collective, by the country to which he feels he devoted himself. He may feel frustrated in his exaggerated ideas about what the country should be like, e.g. his dream of a childhood paradise or an imperial military power. If his identification with the collective has been strongly inflated, and then collapses, he may experience a sense of loss and abandonment. He may then act out his rage and frustration. Mordechai Vanunu, the technician who photographed installations in the Dimona nuclear power plant, and Victor Ostrowsky who published his experiences in the Mossad, Israel's Intelligence Services, are extreme examples. The latter claimed disappointment with the Mossad at not having been spoken to when he was dismissed. However exceptional, they are not alone. Many others can be found among the yordim, the 'descending' emigrants.

Thus, while close proximity between the individual and the collective in its positive aspects may spur the individual's devotion to common goals, negatively it may influence him to become uncritical, pro-social and conformist. The stricter and the more demanding the social collective is, and the more it requires the commitment of the individual, the more vulnerable it becomes when frustration and disappointment ensue. To many, the tension between the archetypal projection onto Israel as Home, as an embracing, caring and nurturing Mother, and the everyday reality of aggressiveness and forthrightness becomes intolerable.

Consequences of De-Narcisstification of the Extended Self
Withdrawing narcissistic energy from the collective self can lead to greater differentiation of the individual and his personal identity. Undoubtedly, there are also well-differentiated individuals in social situations of close proximity. Such a person can, even in the face of general consensus, stand firm against the majority and hold on to his own independent thinking and perception of reality, as in the examples mentioned above (p. 38). This is the person with integrity, who has the capacity not to be touched by forces from within or from without – forces that seek to capture, seduce and overthrow the authority of one's *Inner Voice* or *Guiding Self* (Neumann 1990). These are the few who were able to resist intense authoritarian pressure in Stanley Milgram's experiments, in which most subjects were – even if reluctantly – willing to dispense severely detrimental, even lethal levels of electric currents. The Israeli army, with all its shortcomings, has a standing order that any illegal order must be

disobeyed.   That is, within collective consciousness there is an authoritative command that commands you not to follow authority blindly.

The loosening of the bond between the individual and the collective may lead to diverse reactions in different individuals, but the particular process of decreasing the proximity between individual and collective reduces the weight of the collective on the individual's personality.   In so far as decreasing proximity leads to increasing differentiation, it reinforces consciousness and the individual's possibilities of choice. However, since the process of decreasing close proximity, i.e., de-narcisstification, is not a slow and gradual process, it is accompanied not only by inevitable pain but by additional difficulties which, in turn, are defended against.

Consequently, the individual who relied heavily on his identification with the collective may find himself in great distress, bewildered and insecure with regard to the relationship between the individual ego and the collective Self.   Trust in the collective is shattered.   When previously stable social institutions collapse, such as a public health care system and in times of social break-down, the socially weak suffer the most, and anxiety and insecurity are natural consequences. Thus, a large segment of the population no longer trusts the judicial system, and the moral standing of politicians, as well as of the religious establishment, has been disputed.

As doubt replaces pride, as intra-social fragmentation and violence take the place of co-operation and belongingness, the sense of a common purpose based on a collectively shared idea dwindles. Fear takes the place of strength.   Alienation follows as the individual feels that a basic sense of security is taken away.   The relationship with the collective breaks down, e.g. among young couples who find themselves unable to afford a home of their own.   The individual is left to cope by himself and carry his individual life, without a sense of being protected by the collective.   In Israel, the state is often accused and blamed even for private misfortunes, in a way that reflects the extent to which it has been narcissistically invested.   Excessive trust in the political and military leadership and in their capacity to protect breaks down.   This is the psychosocial situation in which calls for the "strong leader" arise from the masses, with its inherent fascist danger. (Presumably unaware of or unconcerned with its connotations, "the strong leader" was Netanyahu's dominant slogan in the 1999 elections.)   Coupled with the calls for the strong earthly leader, there is a need for the fetish.   The distribution of talismans has in Israel, as an unstable society in an insecure world, been conveniently politically exploited. A large sector of the population has felt that the amulets of Rabbi Caduri, a more than one-hundred-year old sage, who occasionally has sailed off by boat into the Red Sea to avert earthquakes, carry the spirit of God and can void of evil. The need, in times of fear and great threat, to lay hand on the divine by direct touch is nearly unlimited.

Defenses against De-narcisstification

De-narcisstification is inevitably a painful process. Furthermore, in Israel the withdrawal of narcissism from the projected Self, from the collective as self-object, is strongly defended against, for instance by the yearnings for wholeness and purity, and by narcissistic hubris and grandiosity.

Wholeness
The idea of wholeness serves as a narcissistic defense against the pain of alienation and fragmentation that have come to characterize Israeli society. The search for wholeness is a yearning back to the earliest sense of paradise, the original primal relationship. It is a desire for a conflict-free and harmonious whole which, however, "may constitute a major social sin" (Redfearn 1990, p. 192) since the unrecognized, opposite dark side becomes projected. The desire for wholeness is expressed, for instance, by an emphasis on national unity. Thus, Israel has had periods of National Unity Governments, leaving the country for years in political stalemate and without substantial opposition. Likewise, there is often a desire for consensus, apparently compensating for its characteristic absence, as any political discussion in Israel easily shows. Rather than accounting for difference, there is regression to the illusion of pre-conscious harmony and wholeness. "United Jerusalem, the Eternal Capital" is a common political exclamation, based on the archetypal image of Heavenly Jerusalem rather than Earthly Jerusalem, which is characterized rather by division, conflict and dispute.

Separation, individuation and differentiation, as well as conflict, play a necessary part in the process of growing up, but evoke pangs of loss that are not easily tolerated.

The Need for Purity
Purity is another major defense against de-narcisstification of the collective idea. It may be the nucleus of uniqueness, which stands at

the center of the unity that wholeness tries to preserve. Whereas in the search for wholeness there is an effort to have all fit into the same unified mould, in the quest for purity the boundaries are tightened. From time to time the issue of "Who is a Jew?" sets the emotions on fire in Israel. It is a question of identity. Sometimes the Jewishness of the Ethiopian community is questioned, and the demand has been raised from certain religious circles that Russian immigrants prove they are Jewish over four generations – obviously a reaction to the fact that many non-Jewish newcomers claim rights according to the law of return, which entitles every Jew to immigrate to Israel.

This reflects a paranoid need of some to expel the unfitting, those that are not "genuine" Jews, Zionists, patriots, etc. Thus, *the other*, who can not be trusted, must perpetually be under surveillance. Netanyahu, as Prime Minister and as opposition leader, has deliberately instigated along such lines. In the 1996 election campaign, for instance, he managed to convince a large portion of the voters that "Peres will divide Jerusalem," which to him and the Israeli right-wing has been considered intolerable. Similarly, he whispered (to the aging aforementioned Rabbi Caduri), that the left has forgotten they are Jews. "The Left" stands for him, as he has called it, for "the internal enemy."

Censorship of songs, theater plays (e.g. "Ephraim Returns from the Battlefield" and "O Calcutta") and television programs has been applied on political as well as on moral grounds. Then Prime Minister Shamir refrained from signing a literary prize awarded to authors, whose ideas diverged from his, and a Minister of Housing demanded a page be torn out of an encyclopedia, because the views expressed on Jewish settlements in the West Bank differed from government policy. In general, however, and parallel to changes in public attitude toward peace and reconciliation, the long-term tendency is in the direction of greater tolerance.

The relationship between original, paradisiacal wholeness and purity is apparent in the political party called "Moledet" (*motherland*), whose manifest aim is *transfer* of Arabs. In one of its election campaigns, Palestinian youth were initially shown throwing Molotov cocktails, followed by the young settler dreaming of Palestinian transfer from Israeli-occupied territory. Then, holding his breath, an excited expression over his face, he imagines a future of love, harmony, peacefulness and paradise, which will prevail when the Palestinians have been deported. This notion of ethnic cleansing is similar to that expressed by Palestinian leaders and declarations, prominently the PLO charter.

The need for purity reflects weakness and insecurity as regards boundaries and identity. The bad must be objectified and externalized. But as a consequence of the mere application of this as a dynamic mechanism, the individual will conceive of more and more representations *within himself* as cancerous, threatening and untrustworthy. The bad object must over and over again be externalized, in the hope of achieving the ideal goal of wholeness and harmony. This is what happens to a party like the above-mentioned Moledet, which has suffered continuous internal slander, accusations and expulsions.

The paranoid and obsessive quality of the need for purity is apparent. The national self must be kept, as it were, uncontaminated. Thus, for instance, the extremist Sicarii group threatened the pollster who revealed that more than half of the population was in favor of talks with the PLO, even at the time when this was illegal, before the beginning of the peace process in 1993. The peak, so far, has been the incitement and then assassination of Prime Minister Rabin, who was said to have betrayed the idea of *Whole, Greater Israel*.

Ethnic cleansing is the extreme manifestation of the need for purity. History's extreme example is, of course, Nazi Germany. While there is a constant need to be on guard against such tendencies in Israeli society, especially during difficult times and in relation to an enemy who on a daily basis calls for its destruction, the principles of liberalism seem generally to prevail.

Distorted Grandiosity – "A Light unto the Nations"
An additional defense along narcissistic lines is distorted grandiosity. It is the hubris of triumph, without the old wise man whispering in the ear of the victorious hero that he remains a mortal, as was the custom in ancient Rome when the hero returned in triumph from the battlefield. As long as the Zionist endeavor was developing, grand collective undertakings entailed a portion of healthy, primary narcissism. However, as a defense against the process of ego-self separation, or differentiation between the individual ego and the collective self, the effort to re-invest the latter with narcissistic energy becomes pathological.

The *Med-Dead Project,* the digging of a canal between the Dead Sea and the Mediterranean, is one grandiose idea that did not materialize – so far. It remained an elusive reflection of the national water carrier. Production of the Lavi fighter plane was thought of, among other considerations, as a means to bring back engineers and technicians from Silicone Valley to Israel. The official slogan promised "We shall all take off with the Lavi," an indication of the desire to reinstate national pride on the wings of an airplane. The plane, overburdened by narcissistic fantasies, was grounded after a sole flight-performance on Independence Day. This was not only a symbolic, short-lived narcissistic hope that did not take off, but apparently, many of the engineers and technicians have since left the country.

In some cases history will have to find the answer, whether certain grandiose undertakings were carried out manipulatively, in good intention or by unconscious drives. The Lebanon War began on the day fifteen years after the victorious Six Day War, perhaps with the intention that, magically, similar emotions would be stirred up, erasing the trauma of the Yom Kippur War. When an event takes place immediately prior to elections, such as the dramatic attack on the nuclear reactor in Iraq and the launching of the Ofek-1 satellite the timing seems indicative.

Psychologically, the most pathetic example of being "a light unto the nations" (Isaiah 42:6: "I the Lord...will...give you for a covenant of the people, for a light unto the nations") was the claim by "Financial Super-Minister" (as his inflated title was), Yaacov Meridor, that he was able to illuminate a city of a hundred thousand with the energy of a single light bulb. He spoke of "a chemical process that produces energy, by which oil and coal will become superfluous. The whole world will try to find our secret, a fantastic thing for Israel and the world, including the Third World." He may himself have been fooled by this practical joke, or at least having hoped that others would be, since the "great news" was presented the very eve of elections, 1981.

Return to Religion
The decrease in close proximity between the individual and the collective has taken yet another direction; a return to often anti-Zionist religion. The withdrawal of narcissistic investment in the Zionist endeavor is often coupled with feelings of alienation, vulnerability and meaninglessness. Return to religion may represent an effort at uniting the protection and belongingness pertaining to the Mother, with the spiritual ways of the Father. It may be a way in which the individual ego, weak or burdened by harsh reality, hands itself over to a religious community whose collective consciousness defines the ways of

relating to the transcendent, thereby giving the ego protection and support. Conceding ego-identity for the shared security and conviction that religion may provide in an uncertain and over-rational world is sometimes a comparatively cheap price for the individual to pay.

Chapter 7

Myth, Shadow and Projection

The Shadow of the Myths

Struggling with the de-cathexis of the individual-collective connection, and employing collective defenses against this process, Israel finds itself in a situation where the myths that inspired Zionism with life, to some extent have become repetitive-compulsive. The myths fall into their own shadows.

The Shadow of Redemption
The primary myth of redemption guided the quest home to the earth of the ancient Motherland. However harsh, she did let herself come alive by the pioneers' devoted labor. But she has been drained all too carelessly. Folk dances, characterized by palpable stamping, and going on long tracks, once poured libido into the earth. Urbanization has restrained nature into reserves. The physical aspect of the Motherland is restrained, and the once scarcely populated area (in 1895, the bulk of what is today the State of Israel held less than 155,000 inhabitants: about 60,000 Jews, 56,000 Muslims and 38,000 Christians), has become one of the most densely populated countries.

Not only has the earth suffered. The flames in the hearth of Hestia have always flickered in the Land of Israel, never fully radiating the security of home that the all too powerful archetypal projections have called for. The glue of communality has naturally changed since the early times of small settlements and groups of pioneers. As an urbanized and industrialized society, particularly following the last few decades of intense computerization, Israel does not live up to the projection of an embracing Mother. While in times of crisis solidarity increases, as soon as military and security emergencies recede, social problems resurface. When after a thousand days of terrorism the situation calmed down in July 2003, single mothers started protesting their lot, walking the roads from gloomy desert towns to the capital's treasury, the Ministry of Finance. They followed the custom of olden times to 'walk to Jerusalem.' The power of their outcry echoed through their feet.

From their beginning as farmers, Israelis again turned to become wanderers and travel the world. For many years a travel tax was an undemocratic (and inefficient) attempt to prevent the revival of the wanderer. The emigrant *yored* merges with the alternative (non-Zionist) Jewish myth of dispersion and Diaspora. There are *yordim* who seem to realize this and as their children grow up as Americans they become torn and troubled. Emigrants trying to return to Israel may attempt to impose an Israeli identity on their now grown-up American children. The returning father may carry a romanticized image of the Israel he left, the harshness of the country having faded like the old pictures. Becoming a 'born-again Zionist,' his reluctant teenage son will point out Israel's all too obvious shortcomings, adding a psycho-geographical gap to the generational one.

In fact, it is difficult to find a relationship between the two poles of wanderer and farmer that is adequately flexible and dialectical, each having their respective advantages and disadvantages. The wanderer searches his way to freedom, away from the Mother's restraining hand and away from the Father's strict demands. However, the wandering may be eternal since the sense of redemption resides as much in the experience of homecoming as in the experience of 'being-on-the-way,' in a simultaneous experience of inner and outer relatedness, of Eros. The natural wanderer may not be able to distinguish Eros from an engulfment into the passive Thanatos, thus feeling panic and suffocation in the overwhelming embrace of the mother, losing his independent identity.

Neumann (1970, p. 17) speaks of uroboric incest, where

> the emphasis upon pleasure and love is in no sense active, it is more a desire to be dissolved and absorbed; passively one lets oneself be taken, sinks into the pleroma, melts away in the ocean of pleasure – a Liebestod. The Great Mother takes the little child back into herself, and always over uroboric incest there stands the insignia of death, signifying final

dissolution in union with the Mother.

The reluctant immigrant protagonist in Shaham's *Rosendorf Quartet* (1988, p. 342), who eventually leaves the country, expresses it thus,

I'm afraid I'll have to find a place to stay – something I've avoided doing up to now, perhaps because of its symbolic significance. Being someone else's guest and having no home of my own means that I'm free to leave whenever the suffocation becomes unbearable, but moving out into an address of my own will mean one step toward accepting my fate.

The farmer, as an image, runs the risk of remaining fixed in a state of dependency and inhibition, a passive Thanatos which then has to give birth to the wanderer, in a search for selfhood. It is noteworthy that the young on the kibbutzim, growing up close to the earth and the cycles of nature, tend in particularly large numbers to go traveling, often for years.

Archetypal motifs are bipolar. When sinking into the ancestral earth and the embrace of Mother Earth, the farmer may feel belongingness and communion, but there is also the threat of engulfment and unconsciousness. And along with the loneliness and abandonment of the wanderer comes his search for a separate, differentiated and mature individuality, i.e., a greater consciousness. While these are internal motifs, they also reflect aspects of the collective Jewish-Israeli cycle of redemption.

Finding a way home, creating a national home, a place, a feeling of belongingness, is central to the redemption motive. Often, an emigrant's last act of disconnecting from Israel is to sell his home. Transforming it into dollars makes the way back very difficult. Indeed, many *yordim* do retain a home in Israel if only as an object onto which they can attach their hopes for a sometime return, and project a childlike wish for a peaceful future.

The concrete expression of home is a house. To build the land also means to build homes and houses. To demolish the enemy's house means to deny him that same right. Demolition of Palestinian homes became part of occupation. Political and military authorities are, of course, unaware that the denial of the *Other*'s rights reflects disconnection from one's inner sources. Where there is no soul, only concrete and tangible reality, there is loss of feeling, relatedness, value, and meaning. The enemy's home becomes insignificant. This projection is, however, re-introjected, just like everything discarded into the shadow finds its way back. Physical homelessness was until recently absent from Israeli society. While the Israeli army eventually did stop house demolitions, they were renewed as regards terrorists during the war that started after the Camp David talks failed in 2000. While demolitions of houses are dubious, the Palestinian terrorist who denies the Jew a sense of home by killing mothers, grandmothers and children in their living rooms and bedrooms, has tragically expelled Hestia from his and his family's quarters as well.

And homelessness in the history of practical Zionism can be witnessed in the cemetery around which Tel Aviv was built; there is a row of anonymous graves, possibly of destitute people who arrived alone and poor, and died penniless and nameless.

Water is the basis of life. When it dries up, there is infertility and famine. Damage to groundwater cuts off life's essence, creates alienation and illness. Making the desert bloom, bringing it back to life was one of Israel's most impressive achievements. The tedious labor this entailed eventually influenced foreign powers to recommend that the Negev desert be included in the Jewish State, incorporated into the defined boundaries of the collective ego. The scarce water resources were utilized to bring life to the dry earth. Though short of water, it is carelessly being wasted. The defunct Tsomet political party proposed continued occupation of the West Bank and its water resources as a solution to Israel's problem. This reflects the distortion of relatedness, which one-sided reliance on the sword is likely to bring about.

If water is drained of its redeeming quality, the collective soul is laid barren. Preventing the reckless depletion of water sources and the carcinogenic contamination of ground water is a subject of individual and collective ecological responsibility. Only by psycho-ecological relatedness can water retain its soul, *anima aqua*. Disregarding the essence of water as life, is to bring famine to the country, letting the myth of redemption sink back into its slumber in the unconscious, perhaps particularly so in a people who compares its holy book, the Torah, to the water of life.

The shadow of redemption entails abandonment instead of belongingness, wandering instead of dwelling, demolition of houses instead of the building of homes, uprooting and dislocating from Nature, and recklessly exhausting water resources – that is, the energy of life. The enemy makes his dubious 'contribution,' for instance by frequently setting forests on fire. For Israel, the tree is indeed the tree of life, the barren land having been redeemed by plantation, since there are no natural forests in the country. The earth, water and the tree are unmistakable insignia of Israel's myth of redemption. Their neglect holds the abandonment of the myth of redemption.

The withdrawal of the State as a narcissistically invested self-object is expressed, for example, by a sense of non-commitment and non-involvement, by decreased participation in collective processes and increased emphasis on the strictly personal and material.

The Shadow of Revolt

Revolt against the Father was necessary for the early Zionists in order to embark on their way back to their ancient homeland. The Old Way of the Father was declared dead, suppressed into the shadow. Religion and its codex were stored away in the cellar of the Zionist venture. Like most repressed phantoms, religion found its way to re-emerge, and many secular Israelis have returned to some religious observance.

The myth of revolt has another shadow side – non-revolt, or conformity. Following in their rebellious fathers' footsteps, the second generation tends to be conformist and unquestioning. The children of the new father might become dwarfed. In the shadow of the father who "married the Zionist bride" and identified with his life's work – often referring to himself as "I was one of the founders of ..." or "I established the first school in ..." – there was not enough space for the child's differentiation and separate identity. The pro-social personality that tends to come out of an emphasis on conformity has been described earlier. But the Zionist father was less of an authoritarian father than his own traditional Jewish father. In many ways he carried the youthful image, being more of an eternal youth, a puer aeternus, than a mature adult. Thus, the son's struggle against his father was often like fighting an older sibling, the way the second-born must challenge the first-born in order to gain independence.

The Shadow of Strength

The axis of fear-aggression was instrumental in the formation of Zionist-Israeli identity, with fear deflected into martial survival. However, when detached from each other, there is on the one hand an implosion of uncontrollable fear, and on the other hand aggression (Mars) without Eros.

Over the last decades, the warrior culture has changed in Israel. As reflected in Israeli films, after 1967 professionalism replaced idealism as a main theme, and after 1982 nihilism became a prominent topic (Neeman 1992). Parallel in time with the first Intifada there was an increasing concern about accidents, dangerous suicide-like games, violence, sexual harassment and suicides in the army. Aggression is not necessarily directed outward, against the enemy.

The guiding myth of the warrior is, essentially, on the retreat – which is a natural and in many ways a desirable course of history. The warrior who experiences himself as defending his home and his homeland is inspired and impelled by a sense of meaning, of fighting for survival. The myth is alive within him. But war after war, war by choice, occupation of another people, years without peace, cause the guiding myth to become rigid, to die. The myth loses its soul. And there is no possibility of artificially resurrecting a myth whose time has come to die. It needs to be replaced. It is the story of the dying king in fairy tales. A wise king will ask his three sons to bring home something new. And it is the youngest of the three, the one no one thought had anything to bring, who discovers something new and valuable just around the corner. What used to be inferior and neglected must now be given prominence (von Franz 1970). Often, however, the king is not wise, the dying myth is not relinquished, and the hero must bring change from far away, from a foreign, unknown land; that is, from what has, hitherto, been unconscious. When during the war of terror that started the year 2000 reserve soldiers were drafted, they turned up in unprecedented numbers. The feeling of physical threat, and Israel having offered to live peacefully side by side with a Palestinian state, caused very different feelings than those of the first Intifada, when many sympathized with the Palestinian fight for freedom from occupation.

In games based on Russian roulette, which disturbed the public during the years following that first Intifada, the warrior does not turn his weapon against an external enemy, but against himself and his comrade. The warrior uses the gun to endanger himself. The shadow elements of the warrior myth emerge as the myth ceases to be meaningful. In such a case, strict professionalism and discipline become merely an effort to compensate for the dying myth. In the beginning of the 1990's, the Israeli public and press expressed concern about suicides among soldiers, although, in fact, there had not been any increase in numbers. *Mythical truth took precedence over empirical reality.* In contrast to the soldier who defends his home, *the suicidal soldier* points his gun toward himself instead of at the enemy. The image of the suicidal soldier is a way in which the collective soul expresses the idea of a dying myth, the myth in which the warrior was the central image. When this does not take place consciously at the social collective level, it may be acted out by individuals who are sensitive enough to intuit where society is going, but lack adequate means of coping. Projection and aggression may be acted out as a defense against being flooded by anxiety. In extreme cases this can lead to petrification of self, since under certain circumstances it may be intolerable to simultaneously be human and to see the enemy as a human being as well. This is sometimes found in the treatment of soldiers in war, their bodies numb and their faces having lost expression, because they have been unable to do what war requires – refraining from seeing the other as human.

Death-denying strength and force seem to lay the ground for extreme vulnerability, such as happens when the former commando-fighter suffers a psychosomatic breakdown. Once able to completely trust his physical and mental capacities, he may be struck by panic, or by fear of heart failure. Once well controlled, his body betrays him. It was sometimes easier to combat the enemies from without than to come to terms with the enigmatic forces of the unconscious that upon release from the army may have to be re-introjected. The greater the need for control, the reliance on power and the conviction of one's invincibility, the more autonomous and possibly disastrous is the apocalyptic shadow.

On the political collective level, the connection between reliance on strength and its vulnerability can be seen in the case of Israel's semi-secret nuclear plant in Dimona. There, Israel has deposited its image of ultimate rage and revenge if threatened by annihilation. When confronted with this concretized capacity of rage and destruction, a technician at the plant (the aforementioned Vanunu, see page 102) gave vent to his own rage and fear by making the secret plant public – which led to his capture and imprisonment, and perhaps eradication of his psyche and soul. His exposure of the Dimona complex may have made the country more vulnerable, and Saddam Hussein fired missiles aimed at the nuclear plant during the Gulf War. Reliance on strength carries within it the seeds of vulnerability – yet, relinquishing force may sometimes be a misreading of the other.

The Intifada forced Israel to re-draw the boundaries that it had attempted to obliterate since the Six Day War. At the same time, it dictated the reconnection of fear with aggression – a reversal of the process of long to disconnect strength and aggression from fear. The Missile War in 1991 brought the collective shadow of fear closer than it had been during previous years, since Israel had been instructed to remain passive in spite of being attacked; there was no discharge of aggression.

Israeli collective reality is not only a product of an inner struggle between fear and aggression, but is itself a context for projection and identification. Terrorists have taken the place of thieves in Israeli children's nightmares. Sleeping-problems as the father goes off for his annual army service are common. Filled with headlines about dead Israelis and Palestinians, and for decades of soldiers in Lebanon and in the occupied territories, a five-year old girl's imaginary newspaper is frighteningly realistic – headlines of war and injury, pain and loss. Children's feelings know no borders; similar fears occupy the dreams of both Palestinian and Israeli children. A reality of conflict and aggression affects them similarly, making the young become carriers of the cycles of violence – but if not manipulated by incitement, they may carry the hope of reconciliation as well. The resolution of conflict by peaceful means requires wisdom and integrity, since force more easily becomes a normative way of dealing with conflict, and confrontation is often considered more legitimate than compromise (e.g., Moses 1983), certainly so where the social guiding myths are masculine.

The Shadow Side of Boundaries
The formation of boundaries is essential for the working of the ego. It is equally necessary for all the parties in a conflict. Sanity does not survive for long in a situation without boundaries. However, the quality of borders may, of course, change, as is happening throughout the world. Thus, the formation of the State of Israel within defined borders was necessary, just like the individual ego needs boundaries. In fact, there is no ego without boundaries; boundaries constitute the quintessence of ego-formation. A Palestinian State is equally necessary, for the Palestinians to build ego-constructs and institutions within the selfhood that a state provides for the collective psyche and libido, rather than these being turned toward narcissistic and archetypal aspirations.

While previously Israel's borders had been constrictive and rigid, they were expanded in an erroneous and confusing way following the 1967 Six Day War. For a long time Israel did not have the inner strength to appropriate its borders. It is less fortunate when this comes about due to external pressure and force than by internal strength.

Confusing and overly expanded boundaries cause erosion of ego-institutions. State budgets were thus transferred from infra-structure within Israel to settling occupied territories, and the judicial system was requested to legitimize political decisions, such as deportations.

Expanded boundaries, not accounting for *the other*, cause a loss of moral stature, and a narcissistic pathological need to 'fill out' the borders, thereby unduly expanding the collective self. Since *the other* is not seen, they also cause a decrease in awareness, with sudden, unexpected bursts of rage and violence.

As ego-boundaries are weakened, they become excessively permeable both from the outside in and from the inside out. External conflicts can flood the individual with anxiety or cause excessive need for denial, and internal conflicts of morality and identity may be projected outward.

The king in the fairy tale may represent the ego, the conscious identity that rules in the kingdom of man's psyche. As mentioned, there comes a time and the king is dying and his outdated modes of thinking and behavior must be replaced. When internal boundaries are weak, the "king's rule over the land" may be externalized, often aggressively against those who even momentarily are his subjects, whether the arrogant clerk or the aggressive bus driver. Individual and collective ego-weakness reduces the capacity to deal with the complexity of reality, and there is a tendency to feel inundated by anxiety, or, conversely, a need to rely on the denial of fear, or the projection of the evil within one's soul and society onto the enemy (cf. Redfearn 1990).

The Enemy as Shadow

When ego-identity takes shape, what remains outside the boundaries of consciousness comes to reside in the shadow of the unknown. It is not part of the ego and of conscious identity, yet, there can be no ego without shadow. A defensive ego, trying to deny its shadow, turns it into an even more frightening enemy, as in the following dream:

> I see a small Arab boy crawling on his knees in the street, screaming in despair, 'My hand is cut off.' It is in the grass, some meters away from where he is crawling. At the crossroad of the street are four cut-off hands, reaching up through the asphalt. The sight is too frightening for me to approach. I don't dare to extend a helping hand to bring his hand back to him, to the Arab boy. On the opposite side of the crossroad there is an overturned van. Underneath it, also on his knees, there is a Jewish man, dressed in a blue overall. His hands are tied together, and bandaged. It is Intifada.

The dream carries a personal message for the dreamer to relate to his own inner, emotional upheaval, *Intifada*. He needs to become aware of his inner, agonizing conflict. But the collective soul is, as well, reflected in the dreamer's private conflict. The despair, helplessness and entanglement are also aspects of the collective shadow. When the hand of the Arab is cut off, the ego-ideal of the down-to-earth Sabra in blue overall is inevitably wounded, as well. His hands are tied and injured, and so are the hands of the dream-ego, unable to bring the cut-off hand back to the Arab boy. Empowerment of the enemy, of the shadow, is frightening, but it is necessary for a proficiently operating ego. The enemy becomes stronger and demands to be treated as an equal. However frightening and agonizing, without empowerment of the shadow – whether collective or individual – and without relating to it, there can be no process of individuation, i.e., no vital and meaningful relationship between ego and Self. The despairing hands of the Self in the crossroads, reaching up from the earth, are oppressed by the asphalt, by the layer of collective norms and culture, i.e., collective consciousness. The dream-ego is paralyzed; the ego-ideal, the persona of the Sabra in blue overall, is wounded; and the enemy shadow is helpless. When the power of images like those of this dream is acknowledged, then the uprising of the *Other*, whether internal or external, cannot be left unattended.

The Arabs and the Palestinians have presented Israel with a vicious external enemy, just like to the Palestinian, Israel is a fierce adversary. The Palestinian terrorist is naturally a target for the projection of fear and aggression. Yet, the enemy is intrinsically necessary to institute the boundaries of ego and identity, individually as well as collectively – which does not justify abhorrent acts of violence. Israelis and Palestinians have had a mutual need for each other as enemy. The enemy, in fact, is that element of the shadow that disturbs and aggresses the ego, which evokes the Martian warrior-energy, enabling self-defense and self-assertion.

Contact between Israeli Jews and Palestinian Arabs (such as at the work place) enables them to *face* each other, which ordinarily humanizes the enemy, the other. However, these encounters – or non-encounters – are often characterized by fear, anger and mistrust, not leaving much room for friendship and mutual concern. Thus, they frequently constitute a threat rather than an opportunity, causing a crack in the sense of self-cohesion.

In order to retain a self-perception as strong and masterful, firm boundaries must be determined. The boundary between *Ego* and

Enemy is generated by aggression, and tension ensues between the two sides. This exacerbates splitting, for instance between good and bad. By tightening the boundaries, objects are externalized from *Us*, projected onto and identified as a persecutory *Them*. Aggression thus becomes a means to sustain the boundary between the *Ego* and the increasingly prevalent *Enemy*, upholding the split, even though this entails the use and justification of violence. Thus, values are differently applied as concerns *Ego* and *Enemy*. The so called "Jewish underground" had carried out acts of terror in the 1980's against Arab targets. At the time the last members of that group were released from prison, in December 1990, having served less than seven years of their life sentence, then Defense Minister Arens and others called for the death penalty for (Arab) terrorists.

An increasingly distrusting *I* (or collective *We*) will rely exclusively on itself. Rigid and constrictive ego-boundaries lead to the externalization of internal objects, projecting them onto a gradually more powerful and persecuting *Other*, which then must be dealt with by means of aggression. Force and aggression may thus be applied to reduce the power acknowledged in the very projection onto the enemy. There may obviously be a discrepancy between projection and empirical reality. Reality may then be adjusted to the projected conception, rather than projection to reality, which, as Moses (1983) says, essentially is

> an attempt to reenlist the projections of old, the notion that the enemies are all bad and we are all good, and that to trust in peace is only to be outwitted by the enemy rather than being beaten by him on the field of battle.

Disturbing as individual pathology based on projective identification may be, at the collective level the result may be disastrous. As long as the split can be maintained, everything seems to be well, and the shadow as carried by the enemy does not appear to disturb us. However, as the enemy exploits the border confusion and moves up close to attack, the *We* finds itself face to face with its own shadow. The enemy's very cruelty enables the shadow to be re-projected, split off again. It is in circumstances of boundary break-down that the frightening outside penetrates the individual, and his anxiety is projected out, and then echoed back to him by intrusive reality. These are the circumstances under which a person may "pinch or scratch himself," or inflict other kinds of harm to himself in order to realize a physical sense of his body boundaries.

The Enemy as a Threat to Israel's Identity
Actual, concrete Jewish reality in Israel is based on an *image*. The *idea* of redemption is most succinctly expressed in the short prayer "Next Year in Jerusalem," which concludes the Seder evening meal of the Passover – a festival celebrating freedom and redemption from slavery and exile, and return to the Jewish homeland. The spirit of the prayer found concrete manifestation through Zionism and modern Israel – as the previously (p. 46) referred to song goes, "I built a home and planted a tree in the Land of Israel."

Thus, the existence of the Israeli collective is highly cathected (for instance by the individual taking on the burden of years of army service), and narcissistically vulnerable, as if it cannot be fully trusted and relied upon. Healthy narcissism is necessary for an adequate sense of self-assertion and vitality. Inappropriately expanded boundaries, however, both reflect and are conducive to pathological narcissism. As Gottschalk (1988) asserts, there is an intrinsic relationship between the issue of self and non-self-boundaries, and differentiation. Failing to account for a change in close proximity such as that which followed the altered borders after 1967, can bring this narcissism toward – and fuse it with – vulnerability, paranoia and sociopathy.

There has been great difficulty in tolerating ideas, images, and symbols that were felt as impinging upon Israel's own. The Palestinian flag used to be a provocation. During the first Intifada, when Israel had yet to accept the intensification of Palestinian identity, a Palestinian could accidentally be electrocuted as he put it up, and another one may have risked his life when ordered by soldiers to take it down. Groups of Palestinian women cynically chanting slurs and abuse would easily cause excessive anger and aggression in young soldiers, because they were stripped naked of society's and their own protective layers against such provocation. In the early stages of the Intifada, foreigners commented on such situations, unable to understand why Israelis reacted so strongly to mere verbal provocations. Israelis, however, experienced them as threats to the interface between their ideational and actual existence. Only when daring to look the enemy straight in the eye, seeing his human face, can his insignia be tolerated. This was to a great degree the case as concerns many Israelis following what was felt as a break-through in relations between Israelis and Palestinians in 1993.

The enemy puts a physical boundary and causes the otherwise unlimited expansion of the collective *idea* to become confined. *The other* is, in fact, essential for the establishment of adequate ego-boundaries. Archetypal yearnings, such as the desire of rebuilding the Temple in Jerusalem, have to be brought within the confines and the boundaries of ego-based reality, rather than being acted out. Archetypal identification is dangerous and it brings madness. Were it not for its religious garment, the psychotic connotations of breeding the "red heifer" in preparation for the rebuilding of the Temple, which some persons and institutions are concerned with, would be more noticeable. And archetypal identification is dangerous, because it paves the way for individual and collective acting-out, such as political assassinations and holy war.

While the ideational realm needs to be contained within physical boundaries, it is by mourning and acceptance of loss that the spiritual dimension can be preserved. Rabbi Aha laments the destruction of the Temple (in *Lamentations Rabbah*), "As the Divine Presence was departing from the Temple, it turned back, embraced and kissed the walls of the Temple and the columns of the Temple, wept, and said: 'Farewell, My Sanctuary! Farewell, my cherished home!'" There can only be a presence if there is loss and absence, and the totality of presence (at the exclusion of *the other*, whether external enemy or internal pain) inevitably causes defeat.

The Enemy as Target for Projections and as External Persecutor
The Other, whether as internal or external object, is by definition the liable target for projections. The other may be colored by the mystique of the unknown, of secrecy, of desired but unattainable treasures. The East European pioneers and newcomers to the land were fascinated by the Oriental Jews and the Arabs, onto whom they projected the image of the Canaanite Hebrews. The attraction of the Nabatean City of Petra, as has been mentioned, also expresses this fascination.

Particularly the *enemy*, as one prominent aspect of *the other*, is the object of shadow projections, mainly of threat, anxiety and aggression. Besides the very realistic features of violence that Israel's enemies express in word and deed, the need for an external persecutor stems from Israel's dialectic struggle between fear and aggression. The more repressed the fear of annihilation is, the greater the extent to which it is projected. This leads to increased application of aggression, which amplifies the monstrousness of the enemy.

Simultaneously, there is a desire to turn the enemy into a Good Mother that can understand and contain the Israeli core fear of annihilation. The enemy is required to understand the Jewish people's special needs and its history of suffering, and protect it from annihilation. However, the enemy as terrorist acts on and augments this very core fear. Similarly, Israel tends to act on the Palestinian core fear of being expelled by deportation and having his home destroyed. The enemy is occasionally expected to provide narcissistic gratification. He is asked to appreciate and admire us, even our skills as warriors, scientists, employers, or as agricultural experts who bring progress.

The enemy may carry our weaknesses. In the state of inflated euphoria that followed the Six Day War, Israelis ridiculed the Egyptian soldiers who retreated in panic, barefoot, from the battlefields in the Sinai desert. The projected weakness was compensatory to the self-perception as strong and powerful. The shadow of frailty was forcefully thrown back at Israel in the Yom Kippur War; the attempt to reestablish mastery in the Lebanon War led to a protracted sense of impotency; and the Intifada exposed fear and vulnerability. Weakness is easily projected onto the enemy or deposited in the hands of those within society who are sensitive enough to personalize collective fears.

The predominant image projected onto the enemy is one of *evil*. The *Enemy*, whether the way he acts or as carrier of projection, takes his core energy from evil.

Death and destruction are part of nature's cycle, which encompasses birth and growth as well. Natural disasters such as earthquakes, and tragedies like premature death, occur whether man is conscious or not, but they may be conceived of as *evil* only when man consciously relates to them. And the moment man has become conscious, the choice of unconsciousness becomes evil – consider the Germans who did not know what went on in the camps nearby. As Elie Wiesel has said, what hurt the victim more than the cruelty of the oppressor was the silence of the bystander.

The closer an enemy is identified with or identifies himself with an archetypal motif, perceiving himself as absolutely righteous, as a Herrenvolk, or when his War is Holy. When enemies ensure divinity by killing the shadow as carried by the other, then they tend to perform the actual acts of evil – whether as a Nazi, as Islamic or Palestinian terrorist, as doctor-killer in Hebron or as self-appointed judge-slaughterer of the Prime Minister.

When enemies face each other, the result is usually a mutual de-demonization. To talk to the enemy implies recognizing his humanness. This requires coming to terms with the limitations of appropriate ego-boundaries, and the withdrawal of major projections. This may lead to the suffering of narcissistic injury, which has to be tolerated. In Israel's case this means to accept that places of national and religious significance are removed from the body of the collective ego, remaining in territory under foreign rule. It does oblige mutual respect of the other's holy places. Attacks on worshippers at the Western Wall and declaring this Jewish place of worship to be "exclusively Muslim" (the Mufti of Jerusalem), Arafat's and the Palestinian Authority's denial of the Jewish Temple and other holy sites, setting the ancient Shalom al Yisrael synagogue in Jericho on fire (and preventing the fire from being extinguished), the desecration of cemeteries and other atrocities, paints a painfully undeniable picture.

Intifada - Re-Establishing Boundaries
The Yom Kippur War signaled the downfall of grandiose, omnipotent illusions. The Lebanon War was an explicit though futile attempt by the nation's leaders to re-establish self-confidence and reliance on strength, and in so doing – as Menachem Begin declared at the outset of war – erase the trauma of the Yom Kippur War. Demonstrations after the 1973 War, and then large-scale protests following the onset of the Lebanon War, signified a break-up in the close proximity between individual and collective.

Confrontation with the Palestinian population in the Intifada made the denial of occupation unsustainable, and forced Israel to begin the withdrawal to geo-politically and psychologically more constricted and appropriate boundaries.

The Intifada intensified the close proximity between the individual and the collective among the Palestinians, as expressed at the time by General Matan Vilnai, due to the disturbing fact that "every Arab now has a relative that has been killed, wounded or arrested." That is, from then on there was an indivisible web of personal reasons and collective political motives that were to guide the prospective terrorist. That collective existential situation became a platform for violent acting out, based on and as if justified by the need for personal revenge. "Cultural complexes often take precedence over personal concerns and complexes," say Weisstub & Galili-Weisstub (2004). In one instance, a Palestinian woman claimed she decided to stab Jews because she suffered from headaches. It may have been her subjective truth; the Jews may have been the cause of her unbearable sense of oppressive pain. Similarly, the Jewish woman who made drawings of the prophet Muhammad as a pig, projected her intolerable shadow onto the holy of the other side. Given the explosiveness of the Middle East conflict, any disturbed person's externalization of his or her shadow may serve as the spark that ignites the fire.

The confrontation with the civilian Palestinian population in occupied territory during the (first) Intifada, including the stone-throwing children and brutal searches in families' homes, reverberated back into Israeli society. The boundaries become muddled. Banging on doors in the occupied territories was acceptable, while intolerable at home. Following the onset of the Intifada in 1987, there was an increase in violent crime, such as murder, drug traffic, sexual assault and wife abuse.

The murder of seven Palestinian workers was an extreme expression of "Intifada behavior." Though the assassin unequivocally carries his personal responsibility, the act was hastily pathologized, thereby de-politicizing it and averting essential scrutiny. The murderer claimed he killed because of a disappointed love affair, and, alternatively, he said he had been raped years earlier by an Arab. Neither serves as reason to kill, nor as grounds for projection upon an unnamed group (of Palestinians). It reflects "an ego which is still largely helpless and dominated by the unconscious" (Neumann 1990, p. 59) which does not differentiate but sees an entire group as guilty, and "blood revenge can be exacted from any given member of it" (p. 60). From a social point of view, the letting go of boundaries creates ego-weakness. The *other*, the Palestinian, is brought inside the boundaries, but there is no recognition, he remains anonymous. This is no encounter of equals, but a master-servant relationship. And so the murderer appears on the scene, merging into the picture that the collective has created, the way it has determined to deal with the existential situation since 1967. Partly dressed in army clothes, the murderer carried a gun, asking for identity papers. He acted according to the rules that the workers knew well, that is, according to the guidelines of collective consciousness, in which he acted out his psychopathic pathology.

Identification with the aggressor and the internalization of the enemy are pathological ways of dealing with fear. "By impersonating the aggressor, assuming his attributes or imitating his aggression, the child transforms himself from the person threatened into the person who makes the threat," says Anna Freud (1966, p. 113).

For a period of time after the onset of the Intifada, it was common among groups of children around the country to play so called "road-roulette," teasing drivers by suddenly and unexpectedly crossing the road in front of them. The small child challenging the big car may have been an unconscious internalization of the young Palestinians who challenged the Israeli army machine.

There were, as well, instances in which soldiers mimicked humiliation tactics of Palestinian radicals, for instance putting a fellow soldier in front of a "shock team," wearing "facial masks, just like the Hamas terrorists in Gaza."

In one instance, in an agricultural settlement near the occupied territories, stolen cows were found slaughtered in a nearby Arab village. Following this event, several handwritten notes were discovered in the cabins of a youth group temporarily staying at the kibbutz. Signed with Arabic-looking signatures, the notes read, "We will slaughter you like cows." It turned out that some of the girls in the group had written the letters. They had tried to deal with their fear of the enemy (being slaughtered like cows) by identifying with the aggressor, projecting the fear onto the group. At the same time, they were expressing repressed anger at the parental functions of the kibbutz (to whom the cows belonged) which nurtured them but also required work and discipline.

Myths in Rivalry

The upheaval of the 1992 elections, in which the Labor party with Yitzhak Rabin replaced the Likud government, was greater than the movement of voters between the political blocs indicated. In 1977, the Likud had offered a dissatisfied and insecure population an unambiguous approach to territorial issues, over which the Labor Party had been divided.

The Intifada served to re-establish the psychological boundaries of the State of Israel (a major step of de-narcisstification), and the Missile War caused a change from doing to being, restraint in the place of force, inward withdrawal rather than external attack.

Political scientists have claimed that the vote in the 1992 elections was not over the issue of territories and peace, but was pragmatic and non-ideological. In fact, this is what gave political expression to the process of de-narcisstification. People felt less need to identify with the *Collective Idea,* which had become narcissistically inflated due to the approach to the occupied territories, into which much of the country's resources had been directed at the expense of social welfare, health care, education, housing and employment. *Greater Israel* as an expression of the archetypal longing for a *Golden Age* of innocence and happiness, wholeness and fulfillment, no longer enjoyed substantial public support.

The elections provided the arena for the struggle between a hero who brings renewal and the aging king, fixated in archaic modes of thinking. Yitzhak Rabin and Yitzhak Shamir, the major contestants, came to personify these roles. The Likud attempted to disrupt this pattern by implying that Rabin was no hero, claiming that he had suffered mental exhaustion prior to the Six Day War, that he was an alcoholic, and by downplaying the image of the aging king (Shamir), emphasizing instead the party's young and upcoming so called "princes." Both claims against Rabin have since been refuted. As "proof" of his alleged alcoholism, his opponents had pointed at his characteristic "swaying" when standing upright. Not until 1997 did a medical report from a Haifa hospital disclose that as a result of being hit by a truck while patrolling on bicycle (on behalf of the pre-state *Palmach* commando unit), one of Rabin's legs had been shortened by two and a half centimeters.

The Likud also attempted to enforce the paranoid mechanism of *purity*, by demonizing their opponent, Rabin, deviously comparing him to the enemy as terrorist. Yet, Rabin managed to fuse an image of the hero, stemming from his military record and openness to renewal, with that of a father figure, moderate and balanced, renouncing extremism.

The reform of directly electing the Prime Minister, implemented for the first time in 1996 and abolished prior to the 2003 elections, was instituted because, as was claimed, "Israel needs a strong leader." This is a distortion of the hero myth. The theme of the hero is essentially a notion of renewal and courage to change. It is an idea and guiding principle rather than an actual person. The call for a strong leader, imagined as someone who will not yield to pressure, emanates from a sense of ego-weakness and insecurity. Peace and reconciliation blur the distinction between *Us* and *Them*, and therefore threaten a weak ego. Rapid social transition may be equally threatening, creating a feeling of insecurity, often leading to a demand for reverting back to previous norms and conservative leadership.

Narcissistic investment in the social collective, once carried out prominently by the pioneer, the guard, and the warrior, has been an investment of activity, deed, and doing. The process of de-narcisstification is not only a withdrawal of energy invested in the collective; it is also a change from activity and doing to a mode of being, from confrontation to greater readiness for resolution. This was the experience during the Missile War of 1991, and the elections of

1992 further promoted this change. The ideological settling of the occupied territories in order to let the idea of a *Whole, Greater Israel* take shape had been dethroned. However, the alternative myth of *Eternal Peace* (the longing for a return to the Garden of Eden) had not accounted for its shadow (to be discussed later), which then arose in murderous fervor. The myth of a *Golden Age*, whether Greater Israel, Eternal Peace, or the Messiah, is not a static condition, but an image of the road one chooses to travel.

The approach of the Israeli collective vis-à-vis the War of Terror that started in 2000 is evidence of the change that had taken place. While the majority felt betrayed and disappointed, narcissistically and physically hurt, and enraged by the terror against Israel's civilian population, the general public did not retreat from a favorable position toward political resolution, and willingness to withdraw from Palestinian territories and the establishment of a Palestinian state alongside Israel.

Chapter 8

A Crack in the Mask

The intimate relationship between individual and social processes depends upon the bond of identity that exists between them (GAP 1978, p. 503). The individual's identity embraces both his capacity to ascertain himself as a consistent entity over time and space, and his ability to identify with something beyond his individual boundaries, such as a nation, an ideology, a religion, a culture, or an era (cf. Volkan 1988, p. 51 ff.).

Different eras and societies leave their imprint on personal pathology, e.g. the hysteria of Victorian Vienna, or the prevalence of narcissistic and borderline disorders in our times. The more sensitive person will at times, often unconsciously, assume and internalize the trends and troubles of society (cf. May 1969). The cases schematically described below are not brought as clinical vignettes but as anecdotal illustrations of this close proximity between the individual and the collective. The influence of collective processes on general pathology and behavior is empirically demonstrated more validly by statistical methods. Epidemiological parameters, such as the widespread acquisition of guns following the Intifada, the increase or decrease in the number of road and work accidents, domestic violence, et cetera, can be compiled and possibly be related to political and military instability, and social turmoil.

Society is not always the cause or the trigger of personal problems. Intrapsychic conflicts and disturbances are sometimes projected onto the existential condition of the collective, and acted out in the world of shared reality. While places and events may represent personal, internal complexes (as they appear, for example, in dreams), sometimes the individual internalizes the conditions of the collective. Prevalent social features, such as alienation, aggression, absence of support systems and a lack of Eros in society may coincide with similar experiences in the individual, such as helplessness and a sense of smallness of the ego.

Basic to Zionism was its proposition to make a dramatic change in Jewish identity. While offering an idea onto which yearnings for a primal relationship to the mother or juvenile libido could be projected, Zionism has required the individual to be willing to strongly identify with society's goals – for many, too intense (Shalit 1990, pp. 122-3), and creating difficulty for the mainly Arab minority. From the times of the early pioneers struggling with the hardships of the land, to the immigrants of the 1950's living in transit camps (see Segev 1986), on to present-day Israelis drained by wars and internal strife, the individual has been asked to bear the burden of collective and often personal sacrifice.

The average Israeli has not only been exposed to these collective processes, but has actively participated in political, historical and military events. Furthermore, nation-building has not been a protracted, stable molding of society but an intensive and frenzied wavering back and forth between extremes of triumph and defeat. There have been moments of grandeur and euphoria, such as the relief following the Six Day War or the visit of Egyptian President Sadat, as well as disaster and despair, such as the Yom Kippur War, the assassination of Rabin, and the war of terror.

Close proximity between the individual and the collective was necessary for the implementation of practical Zionism. However, the excessive identification weakens ego-boundaries. In the extreme, this would be expressed by projective and introjective identification between the individual and the extended self. Alternatively, the individual may protect himself by making ego-boundaries more rigid, by aggression, by withdrawal or by separation as in emigration.

Consequently, the hardening of the external, social polarity "strength and aggression versus fear and loss" may increase the strain on the individual's own internal polarities. The native Israeli with his Sabra character, prickly on the outside, soft on the inside, would find it increasingly difficult to hold the polarity. As strength and force become more rigid collective phenomena, and the tension between them and the fear of annihilation more difficult to endure, the individual can no longer be *both* strong and weak, but tends to become *either* strong or weak. He moves with greater difficulty between these inner polarities, and when fixated on one pole, takes on a rigid character. Just as strength can be an expression of vitality, when it is rigid, it becomes numb and stale, or as Jung asserted (1969a, p. 32), "If heroism becomes chronic, it ends in a cramp, and the cramp leads to catastrophe or to neurosis or both."

The extremist interviewed by the author Amos Oz (1984, p. 87-88), referred to above (p. 82), expresses the reliance on strength with concomitant denial of fear:

> It also won't matter ... that we haven't achieved, and we won't achieve, any of our goals in Lebanon – not a friendly Lebanese regime, not the destruction of the PLO, not Major Haddad, not forty kilometers. It will still have been worth it. And if it turns out in a year that the Galilee is on the receiving end of Katyusha rockets again, even that won't make much difference to me. We'll make another war like that and kill them and destroy them until they've had it up to here.

The style and the content of the words reflect a need to rely on unrestrained strength and power, as an attempt at denial and the repression of fear. It is also apparent that the interviewee is not concerned with external reality or of attaining "any of our goals," but rather with projection. Reality assessment is absent.

The denial of annihilatory anxiety and the reliance on boundless aggression is discernible as he continues (Oz 1984, p. 88):

> ... it seems there's a good chance that this war has turned the whole self-appointed civilized world against us again. This time for good. So now maybe we've finished once and for all with that crap about the Jewish monopoly on morality, about the moral lesson of the Holocaust and the persecutions, about the Jews who were supposed to have emerged from the gas chambers pure and good. No more. We're done with all that garbage. The little destruction job we did in Tyre and Sidon, the job in Ein Hilweh (too bad we didn't wipe out that maggots' nest for good), the nice, healthy bombing of Beirut, and that mini-massacre (all of a sudden five hundred Arabs becomes a massacre!) in those camps (too bad the Christian Phalangists did it, and not us, with our own delicate little hands!), all these blessings and good deeds have finished off that bullshit about a "Chosen People" and a "Light unto the nations."

Such a person does not value feeling, but rather acts, driven by affect. He prefers force and action to introspection. He attacks, imposes his will on others, and fights his death anxiety by confrontation with danger. He rejects fear and weakness, and splits the world in black and white. Even if his armor cracks, and the persecutor who had been projected outward now threatens him from within, he does not turn to soul and psyche. His anxiety is somatized, and he may turn up at the hospital's emergency room in fear of heart failure, not realizing that it truly is his heart that has failed.

Faceless Hero
Eyal had remained on the kibbutz in the Negev desert in which he was born, until at the age of twenty-six he abruptly took his few belongings and left for New Zealand.

During the 1973 Yom Kippur war, Eyal had served in a special army unit. Later, and until shortly before his sudden departure, he had served as an officer in Lebanon, during the Litani operation in 1978 (which was a failed effort at achieving calm along Israel's northern border, and following which the so called 'security zone' in southern Lebanon was established). His masculine appearance was coupled with softness and sensitivity. He recalled how as a child he had been very fearful, often waking up at night. With a mixture of embarrassment and pride he recounted how he managed to have his father sleep with him in the children's house at the kibbutz. Parents, caretakers and other adults always forgave him for his frequent fights with other children and his generally problematic behavior. He accused his mother of not having cared sufficiently for him, claiming that "she sacrificed me for the collective." In fact, a common notion especially among children raised on kibbutzim has been, that in the efforts of reviving the collective archetypal idea of mother, as earth and homeland, and embodied within boundaries, personal mothering was often neglected. Yet, others who have grown up on the kibbutz are grateful to have experienced mothering they received from warm and competent alternatives to a sometimes dysfunctional personal mother.

From early childhood, Eyal was determined to excel. The army provided a natural outlet for his need to be "strong and heroic." Eyal's charismatic personality won him the narcissistic gratification he was looking for. He felt appreciated and was held in high esteem by others, yet there was an inner sense of inferiority and self-depreciation. In promiscuous relations with women he carefully avoided any long-term commitment for fear of responsibility, of being "seen through." For many years he saw himself as "the Israeli hero," which was also how others often related to him. He had participated in fierce battles during the Yom Kippur War and strongly believed that he, and others like him, had saved the mother country from destruction. Over the years, however, this seemed to him less to reflect his true self. Though he could not give up identifying with the hero-image, he felt it to be an increasingly stiff, unnatural, and heavy mask to wear. Rather than recognizing his repressed fears, he repeatedly turned to the foreign female volunteers on the kibbutz, trying to preserve his "Israeli hero" image, believing they would still be impressed by him. As his fears increasingly threatened to burst into the open, during his term in Lebanon, he was overcome by "an incomprehensible, strong need to leave Israel and conquer the world."

Abroad, Eyal increasingly turned to heavy drinking, attempting to keep his weakening and "aging hero-facade" intact. Impulsively, he then returned to Israel because of "a reawakened interest in the Zionist fuck," as he called it. However, this was not only an arrogant and immature desire for brief encounters with women, but a pre-oedipal search back to his personal mother and to Mother Earth. He had, as well, become increasingly concerned with his mother's health and welfare, wondering if he would see her before she died, and he felt a need to reconnect with the desert, with the fields and landscapes of his childhood, as if they soon would be gone. His death anxiety, whether expressed as his concern about his mother, or the death of his own self-image and his childhood environment, enlivened him.

Mastery Lost

In other cases, we encounter the individual who has been invaded by existential anxiety. Such a person feels weak, threatened, and unable to control his world. The ground is moving under his feet, and there may be a great sense of insecurity as regards the future. The softness of the Sabra turns into obtrusive weakness.

In the case of Miriam, an active woman of sixty-two, a personal economic crisis triggered anxiety and depression in a heretofore dependent personality. She alone had survived the extermination of her entire family in the Holocaust. She met her husband-to-be in post-war Europe. As he was determined to go to "Eretz Israel" (the Land of Israel,) she followed him there. She adopted his credo, "to be masters of our destiny and to build the future."

For many years she had helped her husband to run their hardware store, which had slowly expanded and grown into a successful enterprise. When, however, their life's work ran into financial straits, Miriam became anxious and depressed. She blamed the right-wing political leadership in power, with which she once had identified strongly. She had lost trust, and saw no possibility of a future for herself, her family, or society. She became obsessed with apocalyptic images that she in daytime tried to suppress, but which returned as soon as she went to bed. She would imagine entire cities being destroyed, and the few remaining citizens rescued onboard boats and planes with unknown destination.

She felt her efforts to build a life after the Holocaust had been in vain and had come to a dead end. Images from the war years in Europe that she thought had been buried forever would now return to haunt her. The nation's leaders, whom she felt "should care for me, my family and the future" had abused their power and did not ensure a secure, independent existence for the collective and for the individual.

Miriam needed to identify with the credo of mastery on both the personal and the collective level, as a defense against the threat of annihilation; whether the Holocaust of the past, or the threats of the future. Israel as an entirely *good mother* had failed to provide the safe haven in which a sense of mastery could be experienced unconditionally.

One of Them
According to Winnicott (1965b), the purpose of the holding environment is "the reduction to a minimum of impingements to which the infant must react with resultant annihilation of personal being." Davis and Wallbridge (1981) relate this to the area of political boundaries, claiming that "a threat to the freedom of individuals and society can come from broken boundaries because of their own insufficiency," as well as "from impingement from without." This is essentially similar to the mode of ontological insecurity that Laing (1971, p. 45) terms *implosion*, in which the individual experiences "the world as liable at any moment to crash in and obliterate all identity." It relates to the individual himself as well as his relationship to external reality and its protective quality.

Bat-Sheva was a seventeen-year-old high-school student. She was intelligent, shy and introverted. As an only child she was treated as if extremely fragile. Her parents, especially her father, tried to prevent anything they thought might cause her frustration, as if they were protecting her from evil monsters that constantly lurked behind the corner. The mother had certain anti-social tendencies that included clashes with the authorities, minor instances of shop-lifting and frequent arguments with her daughter's teachers. She accused people of not treating her with due respect. Bat-Sheva often felt embarrassed in her mother's company. She prayed that others, particularly her teachers, would be able to distinguish between the two of them, and she had "good parents" fantasies that they would "send mother to prison and bring me home with them." She avoided situations in which external boundaries and discipline were imposed upon her. She would feel it as an intrusion of her ego-boundaries, "making her choke," she said.

After a series of incidents in which soldiers were killed and civilians stabbed she said, "My parents came here from one of those places in the world where you can't walk safely in the street, where there is always unrest, and now Jerusalem and Ramat Gan have become like that." She identified with killed ones, "as if I am one of them." She asked why she and her classmates should continue to study, "we look so happy now, but in a year we're off to the army, suffocating in a uniform, and we all may be killed. If not then, then when we're just walking in the street or traveling by bus. And you know what, nobody seems to care, they're all indifferent." She felt that her mother tried to cope by constant dispute and her father by denial, repeatedly telling her that "nothing will happen, everything's all right," based on his being on the alert for whatever threat that may appear.

Bat-Sheva projected her own difficulties onto a violent and anxiety-provoking external reality. Aggression (mother) and denial (father) were identified in the outside world, as violence from the enemy and general collective apathy, "nobody seems to care, they're all indifferent." She was, as well, overburdened by carrying the shadow of mother's split-off sensitivity and vulnerability. The outside, both projected and real, flooded in on her.

Fear and Aggression
The geographical, political and existential collective condition seeps through and interacts with the individual personality. The individual also projects and sometimes displaces his personal difficulties onto the collective. Tami, a 14-year old girl, suffered from primary nocturnal enuresis. She was the only child of older, overprotective parents. When she wanted to join a youth movement, her father found the increasing independence this would entail difficult and tried to prevent her – yet he insisted that it was actually Tami herself who did not want to. The mother, as well, delivered similar double-messages. The girl's efforts at independence were obstructed. Unable to let her grow up and become independent, the parents felt that her demands for

autonomy and self-assertion stirred up intolerable conflict. Tami frequently dreamed of terrorists, and fearfully she avoided any Arab that she happened to come across. She became an ardent supporter of an extreme right wing group, trying to turn fear into aggression. Her own, individual struggle to feel secure and independent was displaced onto the external collective. She called for deportation and transfer of Arabs, which in her opinion would free the country from threat and ensure safe borders. As Tami eventually became more able to separate from her parents, and they became more able to tolerate conflict, her ego was strengthened and she could better assert herself. Gaining control over her symptoms, she dissociated herself from the extremist group.

Jerusalem and Beer-Sheba
Frequently, various places in Israel turn up in people's dreams (cf. p. 34). While *Heavenly Jerusalem* is prominent as a symbol of wholeness, the united and elevated self, *Earthly Jerusalem* is torn by conflict, divided by strife and warring groups. It is as if Jerusalem, as a living city, cannot carry the heavy load of its own archetypal symbolism. Thus, Jerusalem turns up in people's dreams both as a symbol of wholeness and as a deep wound in the core of one's existence. Other places that inhabit people's dreams are, for example, Petah Tikvah (*Gateway of Hope*, also known as "mother of the settlements," being one of the first modern Jewish villages) and Beer-Sheba (beer means *well*, sheba means *oath* as well as *seven*; legend tells us that Abraham dug seven wells here). In the same way, foreign localities, beyond the borders, turn up in some dreams. To be caught in enemy territory is sometimes experienced as frightening and as a loss of ego, but coming to a small, distant Arab village may be experienced as a beneficial encounter with aspects of one's unknown or undeveloped nature.

At a greater distance, America, and particularly the possibility of anonymity in New York, often comes to signify freedom from imposed norms, morals, hardships such as army service, too much ideology, and freedom from personal and collective parents. On the other hand, foreign places sometimes appear as the location of abandonment, loneliness and homelessness.

Father-Son
When an individual decides to leave Israel, personal reasons are often combined with collective ones. Hundreds of thousands have left the country, which touches upon deep collective feelings of abandonment

and disillusion. For instance, Yitzhak Rabin derogatively called emigrants "superfluous weaklings."

Alon was the oldest of three brothers. When drafted for the army, he asked for special status as "single soldier," claiming his father had never been at home for him. The father had been active in the Palmach, the commando unit of the Haganah pre-independence underground forces, and he had held various middle-level functions in government administration. Wherever the son turned, he felt that he encountered his father, who had not been there for *him*. There was always someone who had known his father. Alon became continuously more angry as he kept meeting his "collectivized" father instead of the absent, personal one. Frustrated, he claimed that "all these years I wanted him to play with me and he wasn't there. Then I learned to do it alone. Now, when I don't need him, it's as if he's all around, not giving me anywhere or any space to do my thing." Alon decided to leave for New York where he failed in various enterprises, accumulating debts. Whenever in trouble, he contacted his parents who helped him out financially, which only seemed to turn the situation into an escalating pattern. When from time to time his father tried to set limits, Alon would return home for an "indefinite" period of time, making his parents' life miserable, until the father again was forced to give in to his demands, and Alon would leave. He was unable to find his way in an environment dominated by the absent father, pathologically exhausting the father's resources, yet unsuccessful when trying to cope away from him.

In psychotherapy and analysis, patients reflect and introspect. They reflect on what takes place in society and towards where society is heading, since they are often conscious of what "the masses of people are able to keep unconscious for the time being" (May 1969, p. 24). Because of the proximity between individual and collective processes in Israel, patients are often acutely perceptive of society's crises and transitions. It was, for instance, the more sensitive individuals that were apprehensive of the fear and the weakness beneath the hubris after the Six Day War. Likewise, in the late 1990's it was the more perceptive individual who would detect the existential weakness behind the persona of *the strong leader*, and who would feel the anxieties that the masses tend to repress.

The Existential Condition of the Sealed Room War

The existential condition of passivity when the civilian population was threatened, which was imposed upon Israel during the Gulf War in 1991, was different from what Israelis had been used to up till then. The danger imposed by Saddam Hussein brought deep fears and anxieties to the surface. The threat of gas and chemical warfare evoked collective historical fears of annihilation. The telephone first-aid line for psychological help reported an increase in calls from thirty- and forty-year-olds, anxious about the welfare of their families (not simply their own exposure to danger), and by children of Holocaust survivors. There was a sense of betrayal by the West, including Germany, which had enabled the configuration of an apocalyptic threat from the East. It served to increase a feeling of isolation along with added elements of helplessness because of the inability to control one's fate.

A major theme in many dreams prior to the actual outbreak of war was the feeling of helplessness and inability to protect oneself, for instance due to a "lack of protective coloring with which younger women's bodies are painted," or because "Enemy planes circle over our house. As they prepare to bomb us, the walls and the roof become transparent," or because "I try to launch an umbrella-like rocket against Iraq, but it just drops to the ground." Beyond representing the dreamers' personal conflicts, these dreams seemed to tell the collective story of ego limitations. In the perspective of threats that transcend a certain point of rationality, the ego cannot be solely self-reliant.

The Israeli myth has been a masculine myth of strength, action and attack, of doing rather than *being*. Now Israel found itself in a completely different position which, significantly, gained the approval of the vast majority of the population. Were it not for external pressure, a missile-attacked Israel may have executed its right of self-defense and possibly have retaliated. Immediately after the first strike on January 17, 1991, Israeli planes took off but were called back. To some extent, Israel came to feel the strength of restraint.

Most men were not called up for army service; they did not leave home for the battle-field. Home became the front, calm and passivity the shield. Israel was attacked and injured but did not respond, in contrast to the Israeli hero-myth. Male activity and aggression were exchanged for home, family, children, care and protection. Families withdrew inward, into sealed rooms, trying to find protection in being together. The sealed room was an easily shattered protecting womb, shattered for those whose homes were hit.

It may be that this indicated the first seeds of a slow change in the Israeli collective, which has had to suffer from an unbalanced emphasis on Mars at the expense of Eros.

Pre-War Incubation

The Iraqi invasion of Kuwait was accompanied by the threat of missile attacks on Israel, including the possibility of chemical or biological warfare. Until the outbreak of war on January 16, Israel found itself in a process of preparation and withdrawal. Life became slower and more introverted. Months of tense waiting. Tourists stayed away, and Israel seemed increasingly closed off from the outside. Families went to the neighborhood school to try out gas masks, atropine syringes and decontamination powder, wondering if it was real or a cynical, apocalyptic game. Nightlife, so much part of Israeli life, slowed down, while nightmares became frequent, often referring to the collective condition. The dreams intuited a prospective state of helplessness. The former commando soldier dreams of re-uniting with his group, they raid into Jordan, but he discovers that his rifle is in the hands of the enemy who turns it against him; he is defenseless. During the war itself people appeared to be consciously centering on their anxiety, with less dreaming reported. At the end of the war nightmares again seemed to become more frequent, such as "Iraqi pilots who don't know the war has ended come here to hurl chemical bombs at us. We take cover under the blankets and escape being hit by pure luck."

The *Sealed Room War* presented the Israeli collective with two central themes – the exchange of the masculine myth for the feminine, and the apocalyptic motif of death and rebirth. The latter seemed to become particularly prominent in dreams as the war ended. Noticeably, marching Arab masses, as watched on television, appeared as a threatening force in many dreams, revealing the menacing power of the mass. In compensatory dreams such masses would appear as a large herd of animals that would suddenly stop in front of a small child, his hand raised like a policeman controlling the traffic. Images of earthquakes and storms were recurrent, as they had been before the war. Now they occasionally had a continuation; where there had been ruins, a tree with beautiful birds would suddenly appear, like the Phoenix rising from the ashes. Whereas prior to the war the dream-ego failed to deal with the threat, there was now a sense of being exposed to great destruction, but with intermittent images of rebirth.

Post-war dreaming appeared to be part of an abreactive process. The war had come to a sudden end, and at its abrupt termination the life that had come to a standstill returned in an instant, the frozen movement was suddenly unfrozen and resumed like on a movie screen. Synchronistically, the war ended the day of the Purim festival, children exchanging gas masks for costumes and masquerade. A lengthy build-up of tension is, however, not relieved instantly. Psyche and soma need more time to recover, for the experience to be integrated. Symptoms and dreams are ways the soul tells the individual not to run away too quickly.

The Intrusion
Incubation came to an end the night the war began. One room in each home had been sealed off. In the middle of the night, radio transmission was interrupted by the code word *"nahash-tsefa"* (viper), the signal to operate the air raid sirens that immediately were sounded. The sealed boxes with emergency equipment were opened, and the gas masks put on. Less than two minutes later the sound of explosions roared through the air as Scud missiles hit Tel Aviv. Then, a little late though, "Following a missile attack on Israel, air raid sirens are being sounded all over the country. You are requested to enter your sealed room, put on gas masks and await further instructions." Every evening for six weeks, the same routine of withdrawal into the sealed room.

Magical thinking was widespread. Some felt protected by drinking tea with lemon, others devising an infinite of rituals to avert the missiles.

There were those who could not bear the fear, finding safety abroad or in less exposed areas in Israel. A paradoxical response was seen among some individuals who suffered from chronic anxiety. Usually detached from their surrounding, they could now relate their fear to an external aggressor, and feel the communion of a collectively shared anxiety. Other anxious patients were not frightened by the missiles, which they experienced as much less threatening than the assaults they suffered from their internal monsters. And for some, the general sense of being alive was so vulnerable that they could not bear further imposition, whether from within or externally. To follow instructions and carry a gas mask with them wherever they go did not merely mean they had to add yet another rather useless defense to their unprotected lives, but one whose weight and visibility could not be denied, reducing even further the thin strand that connected them to life. For many Israelis going about their daily life, going to work or to shop with the gas mask as constant reminder, became a natural part of a distressing double life (cf. Lifton 1983b).

However, the Israeli population's sensitivity to what took place bears consideration. Though destruction was not negligible, it was insignificant as compared to other bombardments, e.g. during the Second World War, the bombing of Iraq, or Israel's own past history when Tel Aviv and Jerusalem endured heavy losses. The decreased willingness to sacrifice the personal ego for the collective self, and an increasing emphasis on personal welfare, independent from the demands of the collective, leads to what may be a healthy sensitivity and self-concern.

Gas

The threat was gas. No word reverberates more ominously to the Jews. Those who had survived the Holocaust, who had returned from that other planet (cf. Ka-Tzetnik 1989) made up by Auschwitz, Birkenau, Dachau, Terezinstadt and other concentration- and extermination-camps, those whose covenant with God was inscribed by numbers on their arms, were again confronted with the horrors of their past. Having escaped Europe, the home they had built in Israel, which had become their haven of safety, was threatened – and this time, again by gas. Now second and third generations of Holocaust survivors encountered the seemingly inescapable trap. They now became physically aware of what had previously been so difficult to understand; what had seemed to be the Jews' incomprehensible passivity when brought to the slaughterhouse. Now, sitting in sealed rooms wearing gas masks, passively waiting for gas that ironically had been manufactured in Germany, made the Holocaust come full circle, destroying the myth of strength and self-reliance, of action and self-assurance.

The Sealed Room

From the Israeli point of view, the sealed room became the battlefield of the Missile War. Despite several months of preparation, Israel had not anticipated the psychological circumstances of locking itself into sealed rooms, or the extent of civilian damage that was incurred. The masking tape and plastic sheets that covered the windows in the sealed rooms became the thin membrane of protection against the threat of chemical attack – a vulnerable womb which seemed like a weak protection against annihilation. Children were quoted saying, "the best thing would be to be a fetus." The sealed room was mainly a psychological *Temenos*, a secluded area of protection. In retrospect, since all the missiles turned out to be conventionally equipped, the sealed room had given no physical protection. During the war, when families debated whether to go to a conventional bomb shelter or a sealed room, many decided – it appears the children in particular – that the family should stay in the sealed room. It came to provide a sense of protective communion, and many families developed rituals of how to go about things, in which order they would sit, and so forth.

Men were accustomed to be called up for army service, going to war, leaving home, family and work and taking up the burden of battle. Now *home* had become the *front*. The instinct of Mars, of warfare, was replaced by the need to care, relate, protect and to mother. Both men and women had to face this situation, initially by command, as the country totally closed itself in for the first days of the war. Women, especially those employed in the army, in hospitals and other emergency facilities, experienced the conflict between social commands and mothering. Social responsibility and super-ego required the sacrifice of caring for their own children, just as in most of Israel's wars men had to sacrifice their personal being for the collective. Some of those who chose to fulfill their social responsibility suffered guilt feelings for not providing their children with sufficient protection; others, who followed their mothering instinct, ran into problems at work.

The Israeli masculine myth was overrun by a feminine trait. One of the many jokes that made the rounds referred to the Israeli custom of children sending letters and food packages to the soldiers at the front. Now the answer to the question, "What are the soldiers doing?" was "Writing letters to the children." Activity and aggression were exchanged for home, family, children, care and protection.

Not only was the whole country linked together by radio, but the sealed room itself became part of the global village. Boundaries broke down not only because missiles made the six hundred km route from Iraq to Israel in merely five minutes, but because the human condition carried similarities. Israel was bombed, and so was Iraq. Occasionally Israelis and Saudis would rush into the shelter at the same time – for one, it was a false alarm, the Scuds launched in the other's direction. It was characteristic of the end of the century media experience. The media not only swiftly at the place of the event, but the event taking place as images in the media; images sometimes dissociated from reality (cf. Baudrillard 1995). At night the radio would broadcast silence, coming alive only to sound the air raid siren.

The sealed room offered a special kind of togetherness. Some parents found a renewed interest in their children, engaged in playing games that had since long been put away. Others felt the suddenly imposed intimacy quiet unbearable. In some families, roles were reversed or pathological structures severed, for example when children had to care for their parents. Single men and women sometimes drifted around the country, seeking refuge with friends, often feeling uncomfortable, intruding into the family life of others. For some, it intensified their sense of being outsiders. Or, there were those like the eternally young forty-year-old bohemian who would not prepare a sealed room, but drifted from one girlfriend to the other in order to be taken care of and embraced in their protective arms.

For some, the sealed room provided an escape from their usual state of tension and anxiety. For instance, a young antisocial man found refuge as he retreated into the sealed room, knowing that he was safe from those to whom he was in debt, since they would not come to claim their money back.

There was a need to make contact with friends and family, to inform the elderly and new immigrants who might not understand all the instructions. Many found it a strange experience, nearly surrealistic, how they a few hours after an attack would hear the stories of those whose homes had been destroyed. Up to a point, they were telling everybody's story: "We heard the alarm, went into the sealed room, put on the masks, phoned friends and family, and then ..." It brought a fatalistic dimension to the sealed room experience. Within seconds your life could change – and then the relief of having survived yet one more night.

Beyond the Ego

The condition created by sudden missile attacks and exposure to collective helplessness and vulnerability strengthened the sense of close proximity that had been declining in Israel. Identification with the collective grew, and inter-group tension was temporarily put aside. The collective sharing of a common fate brought with it an increased feeling of togetherness.

The extensive physical damage precipitated a need in many to seek a spiritual dimension beyond the ego; some turned to the mystiques of the Kabbalah, others to established religion. Material possessions and physical dwellings were easily destroyed, and in lieu of annihilatory threat the smallness of the ego was discernible. There was a need to feel some deeper meaning to living in a country where physical existence is permanently threatened. There had to be something beyond material and physical reasons for existence. Sole reliance on the ego invited apocalyptic images, forcing some to reflect more profoundly and spiritually on existence.

For example, rain had not been falling for a long time and the country was dry. A week after having been forced to sit quietly at home, heavy rain began to fall. Some speculated about ecological changes caused by missiles, others found parallels in the story of the Chinese rainmaker, feeling that the nation was now perhaps in Tao, for once sitting quietly at home in contrast to the usual chaos. Others were reminded of *Honi the Circle-Maker* (Patai 1980, pp. 224-227) who told God he would not move from the circle he had drawn until He sent rain.

The Enemy

Saddam Hussein embodied the apocalyptic vision. The capacity to equip his missiles with nuclear, biological and chemical warheads could enable him to destroy the country. Palestinians in the occupied territories, including those who had held talks with Israelis, seemingly willing to dialogue and peacefully resolve the conflict, supported the Iraqi leader, to the disappointment of their Israeli counterparts. As missiles rocketed through the sky aimed at civilian targets in and around Tel Aviv and Haifa, groups of Palestinians stood on roof tops, cheering and chanting,

> Ya Saddam, Ya Saddam the beloved, hit Tel Aviv, Ya Saddam hit them with your chemical weapons, the entire West Bank will help you. SCUD, SCUD, destroy the Jews.

Enemies mutually project upon each other. A gross Palestinian projection seems to have been Israeli fearlessness, corresponding to the Israeli myth of strength. Many Palestinians appear to have found satisfaction in the bombing of Israeli cities, feeling that in this way Israelis were finally exposed to a sense of fear, the same sense of fear that Palestinians have had to experience in relation to the Israelis.

The Patient and the Therapist

With all the political and other internal conflicts that are everyday commodities in Israeli society, the collective emotional and conceptual experience is regularly shared between therapist and patient. The missile threat during the Gulf War intensified this. Patient and therapist found themselves in an existential condition of intimacy through shared anxiety. The country has frequently been subjected to collectively shared experiences, in particular hostilities, in which patient and therapist have felt concern and anxiety for the welfare of friends and relatives and for each other, as sometimes one or both have gone off to war. Now they were simultaneously exposed to the shared traumatic situation. The anxiety which a patient may find manifested in a dream image of being stripped naked, helpless under massive airplane bombardment, became external reality for the therapist and the patient at the same time and in the same place, in the temenos of the therapy room. The sealed vessel (cf. Jung 1970b, p. 15-16) of the therapy room ruptured as air raid sirens broke through and swept in, forcing many a therapist and patient to seek refuge in the therapist's sealed room. The professional persona of the therapist cracked, and often the persona of being a patient broke as well, leaving them both naked in their humanness. Hiding behind a gas mask, both patient and therapist would relinquish their personae. Therapists would find themselves unprotected, sometimes embarrassed by their human nakedness. The transitional space and its protecting frame that enveloped the clinic and the therapy hour were exchanged for exposure to the space and boundaries of the sealed room.

The invasion of the country's borders was replicated in the intrusion of the boundaries of the therapeutic encounter, similar to the more vulnerable individual's experience that his ego-boundaries are excessively exposed to penetration. And just like external circumstances penetrated the therapeutic encounter, internal problems and processes could be projected onto the external reality. One middle-aged man, for example, felt a need to hear missiles exploding nearby, as close as possible. He needed to feel that his life was endangered and then, like the Phoenix, to experience his own survival and rebirth.

One analysand was reminded of how many years earlier she had been attacked by the evil Pneuma, the harsh desert wind from the East, not in a sealed room but in the dark womb of a hijacked airplane.

This is not only her personal history, it is also the very real myth of the collective; as in so many other instances, personal history and collective myth merge in the therapeutic narrative.

Trauma
The missile attacks during the Gulf War represented a massive collective stressor. A few were killed, hit by missiles or falling debris

or while trying to find shelter. Others, while not directly hit by missiles but residing in or nearby an area struck by missiles, suffered cardiac arrest. During the first traumatic days, when confusion prevailed, some died by suffocation, handling the gas mask equipment incorrectly, or misunderstanding the all-clear signal and not removing the mask in time. In some instances anxiety and panic became fatal. (Later, German Neo-Nazis were watched on television ridiculing the tragic deaths, further emphasizing the extent to which these incidents tie into collective sentiments).

Hundreds were physically injured and thousands lost their homes. Realistic anxiety, as an appropriate response to the repeated existential threat, was widespread. For some weeks there was a great increase in reported heart failure, and the condition of asthmatic children became aggravated. After some time such symptoms decreased to their usual level. Children and adults were exposed to apocalyptic feelings and profound insecurity regarding the protective quality of "home." While some developed post-traumatic stress disorder, others discovered their coping skills, and renewed experience of child-parent relations.

The War of Terror

Since 2000, Palestinian terror has in many instances specifically targeted children and the young. They epitomize Israel as a living nation, to the resentment of those who seek its ruin. For nearly a decade – a long time in the life of a young person – prospects of peace had created a feeling that life could be 'normal' (even though 'normal' in Israel is a far cry from the West), and lessened the need to identify with the collective and of being highly ideologically motivated. While terror and threat had not been absent during the 1990's, it was believed to be carried out by extremists opposed to the peaceful solutions sought by both sides, and was therefore somehow bearable for those not directly hit.

Now terror became part of daily life, and almost any daily activity came to entail risking one's life or the life of family and friends. This obviously deepened the angst and the feelings of vulnerability among the young, and more than 40% of children has suffered post-traumatic stress.

Not only was the population not prepared for large-scale terror, but the fact that terror now openly originated with the 'partners for peace' caused frustration and bewilderment. The difficulty to comprehend the cynicism was expressed by some who rushed to the scene of slaughter, being injured as a second suicide bomber would explode when the rescue teams arrived. Similarly, there were instances when innocent, often young civilians would show the direction or help someone who slipped, only to discover the person's terrorist identity a while later.

The ever-present apocalyptic sentiments deepened, bringing about an escalating fight-or-flight response, especially among the young. While many would feel anger and a need to fight, others would desire to withdraw and possibly find tranquility elsewhere. Many would feel this as an internal split, or frequently shift between respective responses.

The extent of terror caused an unusual number of people to experience multiple trauma, injured in more than one terror attack. I meet as colleagues and in analysis those caregivers who on a daily basis deal with the victims of terror, in emergency settings as well as in the strenuous work of rehabilitation. The ubiquitous threat of burn-out and despair is always near and in need of being contained, within one's private soul and also interpersonally. Besides courage and compassion, the capacity for symbol-formation is essential. Trauma obstructs this capacity, and the traumatic reality of Israelis and Palestinians invades dreams (particularly children's; cf. Weisstub & Galili-Weisstub 2004) and fantasy life, sometimes making it dull and unsymbolic. This builds a hothouse for the growth of fundamentalism.

The Palestinians have suffered considerably from this war. Like Israel and the Israelis are obliged to scrutinize their shadow, the Palestinians will need to withdraw archetypal identifications, to mourn the loss of archetypal fantasies, to withdraw their massive projections onto the enemy as the evil to be destroyed, and to acknowledge guilt.

Chapter 9

The Death of the Mythical and the Voice of the Soul

The Death of the Mythical

Man has wrested the myths out of the hands of the gods. When approached with humbleness, myths can give meaning to the world. Mythical Prometheus does extort the fire from the gods, but understanding the mythical meaning of his deed is more important than to act it out. Prometheus means *forethinker*, the one who thinks before. Promethean fire is the capacity to plan and make use of natural transformative energy, *fire* (which like everything archetypal is bipolar, and can thus be constructive as well as destructive), for the benefit of mankind, to create consciousness and acculturation.

Prometheus's brother, Epimetheus, thinks only afterwards, after having carried out the deed, when it often is too late. He was punished for his lack of forethought, and against his brother's warning he all too easily accepted Pandora as a gift. As an artificial woman, as an artifact created by the master craftsman Hephaestus, she had no sense of Eros, of relatedness, and could unhesitatingly spread the poison of misery, disease and suffering.

Were Hephaestus alive today, he would probably be a computer freak, constructing artifacts of virtual reality. The boundary between reality and virtuality is becoming blurred. Man-made artifacts seem more real than actual events whose true nature we can no longer account for (cf. McLuhan 1996, Baudrillard 1994). Whereas in the past the media followed the event, now events take place where the camera is – even if the camera was there unintentionally, as was the case in the filmed assassination of Rabin. But it is a false and artificial *tele*-nearness (like tele-vision, vision from afar; or tele-pathy, i.e., pathos, feeling, from afar) a nearness from afar by which events lose their own reality. They become pseudo-events, as-if events. Jung (1964, p. 95) says,

> As scientific understanding has grown, so our world has become dehumanized... Natural phenomena... have slowly lost their symbolic implications. Thunder is no longer the voice of an angry god, nor is lightning his avenging missile. No river contains a spirit, no tree is the life principle of a man, no snake the embodiment of wisdom, no mountain cave the home of a great demon. No voices now speak to man from stones, plants, and animals, nor does he speak to them believing they can hear. His contact with nature is gone, and with it has gone the profound emotional energy that this symbolic connection supplied.

There is an equally false nearness to personal and internal events. Unlimited media-exposure of man's body and soul – sexual, dead, violated, raped – has little to do with closeness or freedom (Feldman 1997), but distances man from himself. There are no boundaries and no distance, no compassion nor perspective that can hold man's experience together in a unified way. Through the *Internet* everything is made public, everything is open, and it is possible to learn how to assemble bombs and suicide (homicide) belts on-line.

Or, you write a letter, send it by e-mail (instead of *snail*-mail), and it is no longer yours. Sentences are added or deleted, "forwarded" and mass-distributed – without the need for consent. Where is discretion? Privacy? Where is dialogue in contrast to *multi*logue? Where is the poet's private song, handwritten and learned by heart? Privacy is dismembered. Often people come to therapy to find *privacy*, and in privacy to find an outlet for their personal poetry.

Man's evil may be his hubris, considering himself as an equal to the gods, interfering without restraint in nature's work, and claiming godly rights. We do not know what evils may yet be unearthed by genetic engineering and computerized virtual reality, which is sometimes comprehended as more real than reality. Scientists have created electro-magnetic fields a million times stronger than what we are accustomed to, enabling fish and frogs to fly. Is that what man wants, or needs? Or, using transplants, scientists have exchanged brains, making birds behave like fish. What will the world look like

when man and computer will be cloned together?
As Rosemary Gordon (1978) says, there is

> light without visible fire; sounds and images heard and seen at a great
> distance from their source of origin; ... These and many other thousands
> of new wonders won by man through his own effort to understand, to
> control and to bend to his will and to his needs the forces of the universe
> in which he finds himself – all this has led him to dream that death also
> can be conquered.

And yet, while man may dream that death can be conquered,
whether by science or by war, we are overwhelmed by death and
deadly fears hitting back at us. As Hillman (1993, p. 111) in his
powerful, poetic language, says,

> Death lurks in things: asbestos and food-additives, acid rain and tampons,
> insecticides and pharmaceuticals, car exhausts and sweeteners,
> televisions and ions. Matter is more demonized than ever it was in the
> plague. We read labels of warning, feel invisible evils descend through
> the air, infiltrate the water, and permeate our vegetable sustenance. The
> material world is inhabited again; the repressed returns from the matter
> declared dead by Aquinas and Descartes, now as Death itself, and
> because of this resurrecting ghost in matter we are aware at last again of
> the *anima mundi*.

Awareness of the anima mundi, the world soul, may be the only
viable alternative for a world on the verge of man-made apocalypse.
But psycho-ecological awareness pertains, as yet, only to the few.

Myth-making means reaching into the creative depths of the
unconscious, bringing forth the unifying symbols of the self, but man
has wrested even the apocalyptic myth out of the hands of the gods.
The apocalyptic myth forms the other end of the paradise myth of
original, conflict-free wholeness. It is the myth of conflict between
good and evil in which the latter comes to destroy the world as we
know it, but is defeated by the forces of good, and the world is reborn.
This would mark "the end of the present era, and the initiation of a
new era of peace, harmony and general exaltation" (Ostow 1986, p.
107-108). However, the symbolic quality of the apocalyptic image
changed as man seized it from the gods and from nature. Now man
himself can cause his own actual apocalyptic destruction, and in so
doing, kill the very idea and possibility of rebirth. If we define *soul* as
the capacity to relate, imagine and reflect, then uncritical and
unimpaired, narrowly ego-centered progress causes the atrophy of
dreaming, mythologizing and symbol-formation.

Science and progress constitute our modern myth, with genetic engineering and the computer as central symbols of post-modern science. Freud (1932, p. 211) wrote to Einstein:

> It may perhaps seem to you as if our theories are a kind of mythology ... But does not every science come in the end to a kind of mythology like this? Cannot the same be said today of your own Physics?

In past myths man was threatened by the forces of nature, the wrath of the gods, and the monsters of the netherworld. What remains today is mostly the grand sin of hubris, due to man's one-sided consciousness.

In worship of the religion called science, the carcinogenic ego becomes ignorant of its shadow, intoxicating whatever lies outside the realm of restricted ego-consciousness. In the backwaters of civilization and unimpaired progress, the shadow rises against the ego and strikes back. This ego lacks feminine consciousness, the moon's reflection and contemplation, as happens when scientists are given free hand without the reflective capacities of the anima, the soul, as occasionally carried by philosophers, psychologists and others. No longer does the wisdom of Sophia (in Hebrew *hokhmah,* חכמה)

> cry aloud in the street; she does not utter her voice in the squares; she does not cry in the place of concourse, at the entrance of the gates; she is not listened to when she cries out "pride, and arrogance, and the evil way, do I hate." (From Proverbs 1:20-21, 8:13)

The unrestrained dispersal of antibiotics, for instance over-injecting milk-producing cows, has weakened our immune system, which may be one cause of activating the AIDS-virus. Jung (1965, p. 360) says,

> ... [A]t the end of the second millenium the outlines of a universal catastrophe became apparent, at first in the form of a threat to consciousness. This threat consists in giantism – in other words, a hubris of consciousness – in the assertion: "Nothing is greater than man and his deeds."

And man's consciousness is threatened by its very accomplishments, e.g. the computer, and therefore the unconscious tries to struggle with it by its ancient remedy – illness. So computers die from unknown viruses, some of them arising from the more primitive layers of our unconscious, for example "Friday the 13th virus," which however is an all too weak panacea thrown in by the shadow of superstition. The language of a computer that has gone mad is as puzzling as when God put an end to hubris in Babel.

Steven Spielberg's film *Jurassic Park* illustrates the dialectical and enantiodromic movement, whereby everything turns into its own opposite, between progression and regression. Relying on his ingenuity man acts God, and by computer-induced cloning he creates primordial images, dinosaurs, which then threaten to overtake man. What we might be creating for the future is the *dinosaur-man*, a weak link in human history, dependent on an intricate and vulnerable web of electro-magnetic fields and radio-waves.

Just imagine at what a loss man will be in the dark world of dead robots when the computers come to a standstill, causing for instance "worldwide banking chaos, air-traffic-control systems go dead, control chips open the wrong release valve in nuclear power plants, satellites get lost, deadly viruses kept under computer lock escape," as a *Newsweek* feature exclaimed in lieu of the threshold to the new millennium. Due to denial of the shadow and lack of Promethean foresight, the year 2000 (Y2K) compounded into a threatening computerized calculation of year zero-zero, from which we could have woken up to "the day the world shuts down."

In the post-modern era man is possessed by his own one-sided consciousness, having raised it to god-like proportions, not paying due respect to the compensatory efforts of the unconscious.

When we identify with the Self, as with any archetype, with wholeness, with Heavenly Jerusalem, then we create evil and hell. This is an evil of anonymity and perfection, and a hell of hubris, in which post-modern man has replaced the self, taken possession of the archetypes, and ignorant of the consequences he intervenes ruthlessly in the self-regulating psycho-ecology of the creation. This hubris of the mind may very well throw us deep into the globally overheated, yet freezing cold abyss of hell.

In *evil* man's ego has lost its stamina, its strength and vigor, and fused with the collectivity of the mass, leading to an 'abaissement de niveau mental,' may it be mass-production, mass-psychosis or mass-murder, with due respect to the difference.

In *hell*, the God-image and the Self have been projected onto the ego, whether as worship of the leader, or of man's mind.

Supreme evil arises when man uses his consciousness, which is based on differentiation and separation, for instance between good and bad, to split apart that which is not within his right to do, such as the *selection* in the death camps. Who is to live and who is to die, which race shall persist and which shall perish, are not within man's moral realm of decision making. The ultimate image of man's evil is his apocalyptic act of splitting the atom so that the enormous power hidden in that nucleus can be used for the destruction of humanity. Splitting apart is the extreme contrast of wholeness, and in nuclear destruction man's consciousness truly becomes diabolic.

We have had a hundred years of psychoanalysis, and we have had half a century of atom bombs. India and Pakistan have joined in and others, such as Iran of the ayatollahs, are following, and man's mind increasingly turns toward himself in unconscious self-destruction.

The Shadows of Peace

The Jewish people's deep fear of ultimate annihilation has crystallized through a history of persecution and destruction. As projected into the future, it now pertains, as well, to the eradication of the Jewish State, no longer a safe haven for persecuted Jews but perhaps the most dangerous place for a Jew to live in.

In the shadow of the Holocaust, death anxiety was deflected into an aggressive energy that was essential for the establishment of independence and the boundaries of statehood. Though the balance between strength/aggression and fear of annihilation altered somewhat during the first two decades of Israeli statehood, it was only because of the events that followed the 1967 Six Day War that it dramatically changed. In the weeks preceding that war, the threat of trauma repetition evoked the fear of annihilation, and the consequent release of aggressive energy threw the nation into a grandiose position of strength and fear denial. The operation of various defense mechanisms, prominently denial, splitting, repression, projection and reaction formation (cf. Falk 1992), enabled a national self-image of strength and self-sufficiency, but it prevented a healthy comprehension of reality and a modest way of dealing with it. Thus, the threat of annihilation was brought closer. When a destructive aspect of aggression is projected and then identified with, it fuses with the enemy's own reality aggression. The frightening mirror image that emerges evokes the repressed fear of annihilation. An unexpected, ego-alien sense of weakness and defenselessness may then be laid bare. In one instance, Prime Minister Rabin expressed bewilderment how it may be that one Palestinian terrorist managed to stab eight civilians in the streets of Tel Aviv. Little did he realize at the time what an easy target he himself would be, in the very heart of Tel Aviv.

Following the 1973 Yom Kippur War, an opportunity arose to

reevaluate the nation's impaired self-conceptualization, yet energy was directed mainly toward re-establishing a grandiose self-image. There was also, however, an investment of energy in the peace process with Egypt. The 1982 Lebanon War was a futile attempt at repairing the narcissistic injury inflicted by the Yom Kippur War and the return of Sinai to Egypt. It proved to be unsuccessful in re-establishing the hoped for state of strength, self-reliance, and fearlessness.

The Intifada from December 1987 till the beginning of the 1990's seemed to cause an increase in behavioral disturbances and intra-social violence, a further implosion of fear, as well as ego-Self separation between the individual and the collective.

On a collective level, increased fear is balanced by increased aggression, as evidenced by a number of parameters, such as the increase in violent crime and in the amount of guns carried by Israelis following the onset of that Intifada.

The Madrid Peace Conference was convened in October 1991. Then Prime Minister Yitzhak Shamir personally took part. Subsequently he confessed that he had meant to keep the process going for many years. His deceitful intention was to settle the occupied territories to ensure the irrevocable implementation of the Greater Israel myth, thereby preventing the prospects of peace. Rabin and Peres opened a window of hope, which a reluctant Netanyahu had to go along with by signing the Wye Plantation agreement in 1998, leading to further withdrawal from occupied territory (while this meant that Israel, in accordance with the Oslo process, still controlled more than half of the West Bank territory, which gradually would be handed over to the Palestinian Authority, more than ninety-five percent of the Palestinians now no longer lived under Israeli administration).

As noted earlier, the Sealed Room War was a marker event in so far as reliance on strength and aggression became inadequate, and vulnerability and fear were rediscovered. The psychological impact was greater than the speedy post-war suppression of the experienced fear. There is a limit to man's capacity to strain his resources. In the course of time he becomes weary, more human and less heroic. In 1981, the massive abandonment of Kiryat Shemona in lieu of Katyusha attacks from Lebanon was hushed up, enveloped in a cloud of cowardice and embarrassment. By the time of the Missile War, a massive exodus from the city rivaled the stamp of "traitor" that Tel Aviv's Mayor put on those leaving. By July 1993, during Operation Accountability in Southern Lebanon, seventy percent of Kiryat

Shemona's population left. It had now become acceptable not to expose oneself unnecessarily to rocket attacks. This attitude change does expose the very real vulnerability of the Jewish state, which faces an Arab world that in the main has not come to terms with its existence, but keeps repeating the calls for the destruction of what they call "the Zionist entity." If only a single biologically equipped warhead hits Tel Aviv, the area will be uninhabitable, thereby causing the end of the modern Jewish State.

The "make believe" peace process of Yitzhak Shamir became real when Peres and Rabin realized that one cannot appoint the other side's representatives. Israel, reluctant to deal with Palestinian representatives, had previously attempted to appoint fictitious enemy-partners. Israel had thus been playing around for decades in the battlefield of its own projections, rather than dealing with the reality of international relations. Arafat later came to prove that he was a far greater master than Shamir.

Peace and Peace-Making

Peace (shalom ,שלום) in its primitive nucleus is an image of paradisiacal harmony, a condition of unconscious wholeness and perfection, not yet disturbed and divided by the conflicts of consciousness. The naive image of peace is a reflection of our eternal yearning for paradise, the longing for a symbiotic reunion with the caring, nurturing and protective, completely *Good Mother*, rather than the *good enough* personal mother. As outlined in chapter 1, the development of consciousness and society depends upon the taboo against acting out such a desire.

Peace is an image of wholeness (shlemut, שלמות) and reconciliation (hashlama, השלמה). Yet, in living reality it can not remain an archetypal fantasy of an original, conflict-free state of harmony, without a dark side. Wholeness and reconciliation both imply a shadow side of limitation and division, aggression and hostility.

Israeli author David Grossman has spoken of the importance to imagine peace, and the difficulty this may entail for Israelis, having been exposed to constant war. However, it may be equally important to imagine the *shadows* of peace; narcissistic loss, uncertainty and mourning, which follow upon reconciliation (hashlama); and also conflict, violence, evil, and the ultimate apocalyptic splitting of wholeness (shlemut) by nuclear explosion of the atom.

Thus, peace-making entails prospects of progress, but it causes many difficulties as well:

The enemy is no longer faceless. He becomes human, with human traits and features. We face each other, and I can see him (and he, me) as good *and* bad, firm *and* forgiving. We become humanized and more of real living people to each other, less the carriers of collective projections.

Recognition of the enemy and his rights means self-limitation: Hubris is at the center of growth and accomplishment, and of victory, expansion, conquest, and inflation as well. A degree of inflatedness is inevitable as a drive into any great venture (whether we ascribe it positive or negative value), which by necessity entails narcissism and feelings of omnipotence. Hubris was indispensable during the initial stages of Zionism, as it is for any similar venture.

Having an enemy (and projecting a shadow onto him) creates external boundaries that one repeatedly confronts, antagonistically. Such boundary tension constitutes an energetic state, and the aggression that reverberates in the external wall gives shape and contours to one's existence. In peaceful relations, the sense of existence is not determined by knocking into external boundaries. One has to rely, rather, on more subtle, internal boundaries, that develop in the process of maturation.

To recognize the enemy's equal rights is to accept one's own boundaries and limitations. Mythologically, this is the workings of inescapable Nemesis (cf. Zoja 1995), daughter of Night and the goddess of Modesty. As goddess of measure and proportion she restores natural balance and order, and requires undeserved good fortune be handed back. Nemesis compensates for Hubris. She deflates narcissism – and processes of peace and reconciliation entail narcissistic loss, the loss of fantasies of archetypal completeness. For those who identify with such completeness, the loss and the shattering of the illusion become disastrous. Prospects of peace become a threat to those who see themselves as sent by God or whose wars are holy. They make up the dark shadow of suicide-bombers, doctor-killers and God's self-appointed judges. They shoot from behind. Often they do not even try to create an illusion of negotiation (and if they do, then negotiations are merely a means of deception). They blow up and dismember human bodies. In one of the computer games, cynically called *Quest*, success is measured by one's capacity to amputate the enemy's limps, one by one. It is in the beginning stages of separating from the totality of the archetype that we must imagine the mythical motif of dismemberment, at higher levels of ego-consciousness to be replaced by differentiation. Dismemberment as acted out against humans is a psychotic displacement. The insignia of the suicide bomber is neither suicide nor sacrifice, but distortion, deception and destruction.

Thus, peace causes narcissistic rage and violence among those who identify with a grandiose collective Self. In the context of a peace process, this means (for the Israeli side) to abandon grandiose fantasies, to cede historical rights and occupied territory, as well as dismantling settlements. The settlers must be understood and cared for, re-integrated into society, not left alone to carry the sacrifice of the collective myth and the re-introjected shadow.

Furthermore, the peace process is related to the change of society's guiding myths. The major transformation may be from the warrior hero-ideal to integrating the feminine. During the Missile War, Mars, the warrior, was temporarily superseded by Eros, by the need for relatedness, providing an opportunity to reclaim the soul. However, transformation in Israeli society is usually not gradual, but takes place by extreme, enantiodromic swings, and only as pathology claims headlines, changes become visible. This has been the case in the aforementioned *suicidal soldier*, followed by decreased motivation to serve in the army.

In the context of peace, the previously dominant myth ("the old king" in the fairy tales) of Greater Israel as a notion of totality becomes abstracted, *intangible*. That is, it can become incorporated in the collective memory as an idea, a dream, a yearning, but it has to be surrendered as tangible reality. In some this creates a sense of loss, and in others a feeling of having been misled over decades. The struggle for dominance wavers back and forth between the myth of Whole, Greater Israel and the myth of Peace.

Additionally, the road to peace is not only paved by formal agreements between enemies. New perceptions of the enemy are formed, simplistic, negative projections have to be withdrawn, and it entails the re-introjection of shadow projections. It is a part of the more human face that enemies take on vis-à-vis each other, but it makes for internal difficulties. At the collective level, it is the extremist, anti-peace elements in society that move forward to carry the re-introjected shadow, even acting out threatening features of the enemy. Thus, extremists among the settlers talked at some point about a *Jewish Intifada*, borrowing the enemy's uprising, and the parliamentary lobby against peace used to call itself *Force-17*, the designation of Arafat's security unit. The painful process of re-introjecting shadow projections must be consciously carried out. The Rabin assassination stands out as a tragic testimony of precisely the lack of conscious re-integration of the shadow.

It is important to accommodate for evil and apocalyptic images of destruction such as by nuclear weapons. By appropriately imagining evil we refrain from unconscious projections onto the enemy, whom we otherwise repeatedly find ourselves fighting against in order to believe that we can ever be purified from evil.

Furthermore, at the core of the myth of peace we find the idea of wholeness, a sinless paradise of innocence. However, the shadow of peace is one of conflict, war, aggression and violence that will, by necessity, be a fellow traveler on the road to peace. A major reason for this is the threat that peace (which implies recognition of the enemy) poses to those who identify with the quest for grandiose wholeness and totality, in which there is no room for *the other*. A peace process requires a constant engagement of consciousness in order to balance and control warring opposites, which thrive in the darkness of the unconscious (cf. Weisstub 1993). In its cowardliness, the Hebron massacre, February 25, 1994, was a surgeon's knife-sharp cut at the innermost point of sensitive balance of the region's polarities. The religious doctor-healer turned into evil mass murderer (cf. Lifton 1986) at Ramadan/Purim, in a place sacred to Muslim and to Jew, in the Tomb of the Patriarchs, the Cave of Abraham. This is where his two sons, Isaac and Ishmael, jointly buried him. Jews had lived here since Biblical times until the pogrom of 1929, when 69 Jewish children, women and men were murdered and the Jewish community driven away, and many Arabs will even deny that Jews ever lived here or have a right to pray at the Tomb of Abraham ("Remember that Abraham was neither a Jew nor a Christian. He was a true Muslim." Surah Ale-Imran 3:67). The pathology of the murderer (and his fellow extremists on both sides) is the personal identification with transpersonal wholeness, which carries apocalyptic destruction in its wake. The wholeness of either side (e.g., *Greater Israel* or *All of Palestine*; or either side's God) becomes the other side's Evil – while it amounts, in fact, to the evil of denial.

Then Chief-of-Staff Ehud Barak stated, that the mass murderer's irrational deed could not have been foreseen by rational means of prediction, as employed by the Intelligence Services. He was right, since rationality by definition is limited; it limits (rations) what one sees. For example, "A Palestinian who carries a gun is a terrorist; a

Jew with a gun is defending himself," as then General Shaul Mofaz, later Chief-of-Staff and Minister of Defense, has said. Under prevailing circumstances, this is paradoxically, an entirely rational yet simultaneously subjective worldview. It reflects circumstances that if unresolved become catastrophic. This worldview, simultaneously confusing and perhaps logical, becomes pathological by denial, by the failure to see how untenable it is. Peaceful solution, however, depends on *mutual* recognition of the other's rights and a willingness to compromise one's own claims.

And peace means mourning. As peace takes shape, all must mourn something and someone, and ask questions. With illusions lost, time wasted, territories given up, hopes and goals rejected, the crucial question will be "What did they die for?" Self-limitation is a state of withdrawal, sadness, and introspection. While archetypal identification was necessary for the creation of Israel, it becomes maddening and deadly when a collective ego has come into being. Yet, unaccounted for, it leads to terror, assassination, fascism and disaster.

While peace may create hope, it also blurs one's sense of identity and identification, a need strongly felt by those who are or see themselves as weak and neglected, socially or otherwise. They may desire a powerful, authoritarian leader to personify the capacities of command that they feel themselves lacking. They are willing to sacrifice personal good in exchange for identification with the collective. They request secure, firm boundaries between *us* and *them*, a definite split between *me* and *the other*. These are the ingredients that provide for fascism.

The superficial image of the strong, unyielding leader, who thrives on de-legitimization and contempt of *the other* – may it be his enemy, his political rival, a previous government, the police, the judicial system, the army, the intellectuals, or the media – constitutes a devious mask behind which lingers a lack of identity, integrity and individuality; in fact a caricature of the confident yet sensitive Sabra personality.

The peacemakers were ignorant of this shadow aspect. Just like they seemed to be in denial as regards the shadow of aggression, they failed to see the shadow of fascism that thrived on a cry for the *leader*, for hatred of the other, and for mysticism as a way of gaining a dubious sense of control in an uncertain world.

The changing quality of boundaries in peace creates hope for Eros, relatedness, but apocalyptic images are brought closer into the vicinity of consciousness as well. *A New Middle East*, which Shimon Peres envisioned during the hopeful but perhaps naïve days of Oslo, is not only an exciting venture into the future, it also brings the threat of unconventional warfare closer to awareness.

Jerusalem – City of Peace, Site of Satan

The image of *Heavenly Jerusalem* is the Jewish people's central symbol of peace and wholeness. However, the prophet Ezekiel describes the Godforsaken Jerusalem as poor and neglected, as a shameful and condemned whore. That is, *Earthly Jerusalem*, the living reality of a Jerusalem of stones and houses and people, has a shadow side of painful animosity and is split – like "the sharp cut of blood across the skyline, dripping on the crumbling houses," as in the dream mentioned previously (p. 35).

Literally, Jerusalem means *City* of *Peace*, עיר שלם, עיר שלום. The Hebrew word for peace, shalom, שלום, entails the word for wholeness, shalem, שלם. Wholeness does not mean shadow-less *perfection*, in Hebrew mushlam, מושלם, but *wholeness* holds its own shadows of fragmentation, division and partition. Evil materializes as we strive for and try to implement perfection, whereby the shadow is split off and projected onto the *other* – whether Jew, Christian or Arab, Westerner or Oriental.

The *perfection* of the machines of destruction and the chambers of petrifaction compound the cold hell of man's consciousness. Within the matter of a day I may bear witness in my clinic to, for instance, one woman whose mother for more than forty years daily drags her along the streets of destruction at *Crystal Night*, Berlin 1938, in search for refuge, within their confined symbiotic claustrophobia. And then, the now elderly man who saw his mother, having died of exhaustion, torn apart and eaten by the dogs in the camp. And then, the woman whose father was possessed by the torture he had suffered, who until his premature death tortured her, his only child, whom he had given the names of the deceased to carry as his hope for the future. But then, through the obstructive clouds of pain and anger that drives you to insanity, I also discern the nameless Gestapo officer who saved my father's life.

Evil causes people to be trapped and tormented in the hell of insanity. As a people who have suffered, should we not better understand the pledge of the other? Exposure to evil does not make anyone into a better human being. When confronted by the other's acted out evil, the cosmetics of virtue and righteousness wear off. Evil primarily seems to pertain to the paradoxically dark light of human consciousness, in which *Eros* has been raped, *Psyche* strangled, and the *Soul* slaughtered.

Jerusalem bears its name from its mythological founder, the Canaanite king, or god, Shalem, שלם, which means *whole*. But while Shalem, who became the Evening Star, spoke the words of peace and (Heavenly) Jerusalem became the archetypal site, city of Shalem, the central symbol of peace, unity and wholeness, his twin brother was Shahar, שחר, the Morning Star. Shahar (like *Shaharit*, the morning prayers), announces the arrival of light and consciousness. Shahar and Shalem were the sons from the hieros gamos, the holy marriage between the sun-god *El*, אל, and *Ashera*, אשרה, the Great Goddess of the grove. They were born out of her bottomless cavity, and, it says, "in the kiss .. and the embrace .. she bore Shahar and Shalem, the Dawn and the Evening." While every evening Shalem announces the death of the sun, Shahar pronounces the sun's rebirth in the morning. This is the consciousness-raising aspect of Shahar, who in his Christian designation is Lucifer, the Light-bringer. Satan who stands in our way as an adversary brings light and consciousness, the fire from the gods.

As Hillman says (in Shärf-Kluger, p. x),

Satan interferes, opposes and accuses. As an instrument of conflict he is fundamental to consciousness, which arises from tension.

Man's consciousness is promoted by the deeds of the devil, *diabolos*. While symbolos means casting together, diabolos means flinging apart, which is necessary for differentiation and consciousness. The devil inflicts pain and suffering, but it is in those instances in which we meet Satan, the *adversary*, when our conventional road is blocked and we feel a loss of meaning, that we have an opportunity to become conscious.

In Greek mythology Prometheus carries out the Luciferian act. As we descend from Celestial, Heavenly Jerusalem to Terrestrial, Earthly Jerusalem, when we give up the numinosity of the archetypes for ordinary human life, then Satan has blocked our way to the divine, and simultaneously he presents us with the choice of holding *some* of the divine fire, never *all* the fire, some of the water of life, since being mortal, we cannot drink all the water of life.

When in the tale of *Amor and Psyche* (Neumann 1971) Aphrodite sends Psyche to bring water from the river of life, her assumption is that she will not be able to, because for Aphrodite, as a goddess, the stream of life, the vital energy, is eternal numinous movement that defies capture. It cannot be contained, it is total. She does not understand that *Psyche*, the human soul, carries a containing and limiting vessel, defined by her ego-boundaries; i.e., she *can* take from the numinosoum, but only a small part. Sadly, perhaps, but inevitably, everything archetypal becomes partial in the human sphere.

Therefore, the archetypal *idea* of Jerusalem as wholeness can never belong to any one, contrary to the belief of fundamentalists.

One woman dreams that,

> as she enters Jerusalem, ascending ancient stone-steps, an unknown lover puts a ring on her finger. He then leads her to a huge tree in the center of the city, whose top is filled with birds in gold and red. She knows she must not come too close, as you must not come too close to the burning bush, to the divine, or you must die. She is then led to a nearby well, from which she must drink only as much as her hand can hold, and she is amazed that so little water satisfies her thirst.

It seems we need to keep a respectful distance from the divine, without running away from it, and drink from the water of life no more than we can hold.

Evil bursts forth when we try to claim it all, possess it all. In the Israeli-Palestinian conflict there are too many on both sides possessed by the zeal to possess it all, and too few have been willing to renounce the illusion of totality.

Jerusalem is the place where the sacrifice of Isaac, יצחק, took place. This is the eternal and maybe irresolvable conflict between submission to the father, whether as divine command, as social dictate or as personal authority, and the commitment to one's human offspring and future. Mothers have sent their sons to die in war for an infinite of good reasons, and Fathers have thwarted the independent lives of their daughters for reasons of protection and pride.

Abraham, אברהם, (which means 'father is sanctified') *nearly* sacrificed Isaac (or Yitzhak), יצחק, but Isaac (which means 'he laughed') was not *actually* sacrificed. In Hebrew we speak of the binding of Isaac, עקדת יצחק, indicating the dramatic cultural transition from *actual deed* to *internalized faith*, from the worship of stone-hard gods to ideational images. In Isaac's place the ram was sacrificed to God, and Isaac was to live. The sacrifice need not be complete, to make sacred is no longer engraved in stones, it need not and rather not be literal. Yet, to make sacred, to inspire the soul and ensoul the spirit, we need to sacrifice, renounce, give up the ego's hubris, the belief that the conscious ego is all and be all, which is contrary to the fundamentalist's sacrifice of himself for the purpose of killing his shadow as carried by the enemy.

When man *identifies* with the transcendent idea, in archetypal identification, he becomes possessed by evil. While Biblical Isaac, was let to live, the present day Isaac (Yitzhak) Rabin, was sacrificed on the altar of archetypal possession, reflecting the archaic forces prevalent in our society.

The Soul's Voice

Following Hillman (1983, p. 6-10), we may say that the soul is the seat of our imagination, and the soul's essence is *perspective*; to have a perspective on what we do and on the events in which we participate. Without perspective, without a way of relating to the deeds and the events in which we partake, we become soul-less and symptomatic, and tend to act out by compulsive doing or by sociopathic behavior.

The reconstruction of soul is the opus, the work of analysis. Essential to this end is the realization of woundedness and imperfection, and attending to the inner voice of the Self. There are times in a person's life, as well as in that of a society or an era, when the essential word to be heard by the voice behind the mask is a paradoxical *nothing*, as the actress Elizabeth, played by Liv Ullman, hesitantly repeats – when she finally does speak – at the end of Bergman's brilliant film, *Persona*. *Nothing* is perhaps the burning truth to be spoken in a *Clockwork Orange World* of *Pulp Fiction* in which we are fooled into believing and behaving as if nothing has any real consequence, as if there is no soul in matter, as if there is no soul that matters. To sincerely touch *nothing* and the depth of nothingness, to attend to the penetrating emptiness in the outstretched hand of the beggar in our soul, may be the call.

The soul's voice, when speaking Eros as well as Logos, relatedness and meaning, sometimes pronounces not the striving for wholeness, but rather the words of gloom and discouragement. Those are the cries of despair, expressed by the prophet Jeremiah, ירמיהו, whose name means 'God will elevate.' God-driven, he fearlessly denounced the ills of the nation, warning of the disasters that would follow.

Organized worship meant little to him, "the false pen of the scribes has made it into a lie" (Jer. 8:8). That is, he had no compassion for the treachery and falseness of collective consciousness, of the literalism that replaces soulfulness. His outspoken criticism repeatedly brought him into conflict with the authorities. Before a crowd of priests and citizens in the Valley of Hell, Jeremiah denounced their pagan practices. He smashed an earthenware jar and cried out,

> Thus says the Lord of hosts: So will I break this people and this city as one breaks a potter's vessel, so it can never be mended. (Jer 19:11)

And he proclaimed, "This whole land shall become a ruin and a waste" (Jer. 25:11). In Exodus we read, "Thou shalt not make unto thee a graven image." Hillman (1996) takes this to mean "Don't take your images literally," that is, beware of fundamentalism; let there be images, ideas, fantasy and complexity rather than "singleness of meaning that leads to dogma" (p. 113). That is, dogma, singleness of meaning, fundamentalism, fascism, worship of the Self or inflation of the ego, or annulment of the god-image, will each and every one bring malice and disorder. In the Israeli-Palestinian conflict, the light that is lit by exchange of views and ideas is exchanged for the darkness of evil and hell that come with archetypal identification with wholeness and casting the shadow onto the enemy where it hardens to stone.

> How lonely sits the city ...
> How like a widow has she become, .. (Lam. 1:1)

are the lamentations expressed by means of a *Voice*, not the persona as an external mask, but what *persona* really means, per *sona,* that is, *by means of voice.* By covering our faces as in classical Greek theatre, the voice may be heard. This may be the best the soul can do in times when the masks of virtuality lead the dance around the golden calves in post-modern deconstruction, when inflated man reproduces himself by cloning and splits the world by atoms and tears apart the human body without questioning his deeds and his values, and without having to stand trial. The anguish of the heart might be the best the soul can air when *nothing* is holy any longer and the *Voice* of the gods, of the Self, is sacrificed on the altar of triviality and deceptive virtuality, on the shrine of fundamentalism and mystification, of hubris and of evil.

The task of psychoanalysis – in society as in the clinic – may be to be the soul's guardian and attendant: to enable the individual, and perhaps also society, to gain perspective by introspection as well as *extra*spection, to listen to the whisper of the *soul* (in Hebrew, ruah, רוח) that otherwise might be carried away by the *wind* (ruah, רוח),

unheard; the soul that here in Israel, if not attended to, may be swept away by darkness at noon.

Glossary

Archetypes
Universal patterns or motifs from the collective unconscious. They are the basic content of religions, mythologies and fairytales where they appear as images. In the individual, they appear most commonly in dreams as images and themes. They are innate psychological structures, similar to instincts on the biological level. The archetype is a "purely formal, skeletal concept, which is then fleshed out with imagery, ideas, motifs and so on" (Samuels 1985, p. 25).

Boundaries
An overly *constrictive* boundary is severely limiting; it causes a diminished capacity for experience.

An overly *expansive* boundary "knows no boundaries" and does not enable recognition of a separate existence of *the other*.

An overly *rigid* boundary exerts strict control; there is no flow and no "give and take."

An overly *permeable* boundary is weak; the inside cannot be contained, and the outside threatens to flood in.

Cathexis - Object-Cathexis - Decathexis
Cathexis – Investment of energy.
Object-cathexis – Investment of energy in an external object, in contrast to its investment in the self.
Decathexis – Withdrawal of cathexis.

Close Proximity
The very special, close relationship between the individual and the collective in Israel is here called close proximity. The State of Israel came into being by the materialization of an idea, the implementation

of which necessitated the merger of single individuals into a collective. Subsequent historical, social and military developments have both strengthened and strained this relationship.

Consciousness - Unconscious
Personal consciousness – ordinary awareness.
Personal unconscious – That which is unique to the individual psyche but which has not attained consciousness, or has been withdrawn and repressed from it.
Collective consciousness – The world of shared values, ideas, culture, ideological and religious expressions; the Zeitgeist and prevailing Weltanschauung.
Collective unconscious – "The repository of man's psychic heritage and possibilities" (Samuels et al. 1986, p. 32).

Ego - self - Self
Ego – a person's conscious identity ("I").
self – a person's total psyche, including those parts that are unconscious to him.
   Often self is part of ego, as in self-image, while in analytical (Jungian) psychology, ego is part of self (often capitalized).
   Self (capital "S") denotes an image of a psychic center beyond conscious identity. It is the center of the total personality.

Ego-boundaries – Self-boundaries
Ego-boundaries are the boundaries of conscious identity. As applied to the geo-political borders of a country, ego-boundaries may be geographically equal to the self-boundaries. This is not the case in Israel. The ego-boundaries are relatively well defined – the borders within which collective ego-functions are instituted – i.e., the *State of Israel* (this excludes most of the territories occupied following the 1967 War). It includes ego-functions such as government and administration, judicial system.
   The *Land of Israel* reflects Israel's self-boundaries, which primarily covers the State of Israel, Gaza and the West Bank (Judea and Samaria).
   Sinai was, for instance, for several years considered as within Israel's self-boundaries, with efforts at giving it ego, though never formally annexed.
   (Trans-) Jordan, which is a part of historical Palestine/Land of Israel, will by some be considered within the domain of (Israel's) historical rights, and consequently within the realm of their

(expansive) self-boundaries.

It is important to note that one can perceive parts of one's collective self beyond concrete geo-political borders. Hebron is the city of the Fathers, one of the Jews' four holy cities, thus part of the collective Self, even if it remains outside the realm of ego-boundaries.

Enantiodromia
The process whereby a phenomenon is replaced by its (previously unconscious) opposite.

Energy - Libido - Numinosity
Energy and libido – used interchangeably for "psychic energy." Sometimes, but not always, libido specifically denotes "sexual energy."

Eros - Mars
Eros – the principle of relatedness. Freud identified the *life instinct* with Eros, and Jung describes five stages of Eros expression as biological, sexual, aesthetic, spiritual and a form of wisdom (as in Samuels et al. 1986, pp. 54-56).
Mars – the warrior principle. Aggression is the *life force*, necessary for the establishment of ego and ego-boundaries.

Inflation
Inflation – a regression of consciousness, whereby the ego identifies with and takes upon itself too many unconscious contents (cf. Sharp, 1991), thereby losing its capacity of discrimination, magnifying "the blind spot in the eye" (Jung 1968b, p. 24). It leads to an attitude of self-aggrandizement.

Mana
Literally, *divine power*. An impersonal supernatural force inherent in gods and sacred objects (in the native religions of Oceania). Charisma.

Myth
The term myth is often used to denote something false. However, an infinite of mythical motifs reside in the unconscious. They can be redeemed from their 'slumber' in the unconscious (by the hero) and become guiding myths, by which "human beings code and organize their perceptions, feelings, thoughts and actions" (Feinstein & Krippner 1988, p. 2). A myth may often reflect the reality of psyche and soul more truthfully than tangible reality.

Narcissism
Psychic energy invested into the self, rather than the object.
The communal collective may be considered a self-object (Kohut), an
extension of the personal self. The individual's investment of energy
into the collective is, then, narcissistic. Narcissistic energy can be
healthy – for self-preservation, self-esteem, etc.
Pathological narcissism is energy that should preferably be invested
in the object, but has become self-directed.

Object - Self-Object - Other
Object – that to which the subject relates himself; e.g. by action or
desire. Usually a person or part of a person (cf. Rycroft 1983, p. 100).
Self-Object – the mother is experienced by the infant as part of itself,
and she is therefore seen as a self-object.
Other – that other person, group or phenomenon, external or internal,
that is distinctly not experienced as part of oneself, e.g. the enemy,
who then becomes a convenient object onto whom the shadow can be
projected.

Persona
Our 'face' to the world, our 'facade.' A social role or external identity
derived from the expectations of society; it mediates between the
individual and the expectations of others. Identification with the
persona can lead, for example, to pompousness, or a loss of character.

Shadow
That which remains outside the realm of the ego, often unacceptable
to one's conscious identity and therefore rejected by the ego. The
shadow is often initially experienced in projections, e.g. onto the
enemy, whose evil or weakness must be fought, rather than recognized
as parts of oneself.

Temenos
Defines a sacred precinct, a safe place. It can be a sacred grove, or the
therapy setting.

Bibliography

Adorno, T. W., Frenkel-Brunswik, E., Levinson, D. J., & Sanford, R. N. (1950) *The Authoritarian Personality*. New York: Harper.

Ahad Ha'Am (1962) Slavery in freedom. In L. Simon (Ed.) *Selected Essays of Ahad Ha'Am*. New York: Meridian.

Almog, O. (1993) *The Army Radio Subculture: The Culture of Kibbutz Youth as Mirrored Through its Language*. Ramat Efal, Israel: Yad Tabenkin.

Alpert, C. (1971) The city that needs a psychiatrist. *Israel Magazine*, 3:11, 54-63.

Avnery, U. (1968) *Israel without Zionists*. New York: Macmillan.

Babineau, G. R. (1972) The compulsive border crosser. *Psychiatry*, 35, 281-290.

Baudrillard, J. (1995) *Simulacra and Simulation*. Ann Arbor: University of Michigan Press.

Baudrillard, J. (1995) *The Gulf War did not take Place*. Bloomington: Indiana University Press.

Bein, A. (1962) *Theodor Herzl: A Biography of the Founder of Modern Zionism*. Philadelphia: Jewish Publication Society of America.

Bleich, A., Dycian, A., Koslowsky, M., Solomon, Z., & Wiener, M. (1992) Psychiatric implications of missile attacks on a civilian population: Israeli lessons from the Persian Gulf War. *The Journal of the American Medical Association*, 268, 613-615.

Boshes, H. (1988) Aliens in the homeland. *Modern Hebrew Literature - New Series*, 1(1), 44-46.

Bowen, M. (1985) *Family Therapy in Clinical Practice*. New York: Jason Aronson.

Brown, J. A. C. (1964) *Freud and the Post-Freudians*. Harmondsworth: Penguin.

Chess, S., & Thomas, A. (1978) Temperamental traits and parent guidance. In L. E. Arnold (Ed.) *Helping Parents Help Their Children*. New York: Brunner/Mazel.

Cohen, A. (1970) *Israel and the Arab World*. London: W.H. Allen.

Davidson, S. (1987) Trauma in the life cycle of the individual and the collective consciousness in relation to war and persecution. In H. Dasberg, S. Davidson, G. L. Durlacher, B. C. Filet, & E. de Wind (Eds.) *Society and Trauma of War* (pp. 14-32). Assen, The Netherlands: Van Gorcum.

Davis, M., & Wallbridge, D. (1981) *Boundary and Space*. New York: Brunner/Mazel.

Eban, A. (1968*) My People: The Story of the Jews*. London: Weidenfeld & Nicolson.

Edinger, E. F. (1973) *Ego and Archetype*. New York: Penguin.

Elon, A. (1981) *The Israelis: Founders and Sons*. Tel Aviv: Adam.

Erikson, E. H. (1968) *Identity: Youth and Crisis*. London: W.W. Norton.

Erikson, E. H. (1977) *Childhood and Society*. 2nd ed. London: Triad/Paladin, Granada.

Erikson, E. H. (1985) Pseudospeciation in the nuclear age. *Political Psychology*, 6, 213-217.

Ettinger, S. (1979) The Jews and the Enlightenment. In E. Kedourie (Ed.) *The Jewish World*. London: Thames and Hudson.

Falk, A. (1974) Border symbolism. *Psychoanalytic Quarterly*, 43, 650-660.

Falk, A. (1975-76) Identity and name changes. *The Psychoanalytic Review*, 62, 647-657.

Falk, A. (1983) Border symbolism revisited. *International Review of Psychoanalysis*, 10, 215-220.

Falk, A. (1992) Unconscious aspects of the Arab-Israeli conflict. *The Psychoanalytic Study of Society*, 17, 213-247.

Feinstein, D., & Krippner, S. (1988) *Personal Mythology*. Los Angeles: Jeremy P. Tarcher.

Feldman, T. (1997) Personal communication.

Freud, A. (1966) *The Ego and the Mechanisms of Defense*. New York: International Universities Press.

Freud, S. (1932*) Why War?* S.E. 22. London: Hogarth Press.

Freud, S. (1946) *Totem and Taboo*. New York: Vintage Books.

Freud, S. (1949) An outline of psychoanalysis. In: *Historical and Expository Works on Psychoananlysis*. Harmondsworth: Penguin.

Fromm, E. (1965) *The Sane Society*. New York: Fawcett Premier.

Fromm, E. (1968) *The Revolution of Hope: Toward A Humanized Technology*. New York: Harper & Row.

Fromm, E. (1995) *Escape From Freedom*. New York: Henry Holt.

Fromm, E. (1976) *To Have or To Be?* London: Abacus.

Gath, G. (1983) *The Encounter Between David And Goliath: Its Significance For Our Present Situation in Israel*. Privately Circulated.

Gonen, J. Y. (1978) The Israeli illusion of omnipotence following the Six Day War. *Journal of Psychohistory*, 6, 241-271.

Gordon, R. (1978) *Death and Dying*. London: Society of Analytical Psychology.

Gottschalk, L. A. (1988) Narcissism: Its normal evolution and development and the treatment of its disorders. *American Journal of Psychotherapy*, 42(1), 4-27.

Greenberg, H. I. (1979) *Israeli Social Problems in Perspective*. Tel Aviv: Dekel Academic Press.

Greenberg, J. R., & Mitchell, S. A. (1983) *Object Relations in Psychoanalytic Theory*. Cambridge, MA: Harvard University Press.

Group for the Advancement of Psychiatry (GAP). (1978) *Self-Involvement in the Middle East Conflict*. New York: Mental Health Materials Center.

Group for the Advancement of Psychiatry (GAP). (1983) *Community Psychiatry: A Reappraisal*. New York: Mental Health Materials Center.

Guntrip, H. (1977) *Psychoanalytic Theory, Therapy and the Self*. London: Maresfield Reprints.

Guvrin, N. (1982/3) The great fear and the striving for redemption. *Modern Hebrew Literature*, 8(1-2), 28-32.

Hazelton, L. (1977) *Israeli Women: The Reality behind the Myth*. New York: Simon and Schuster.

Hertzberg, A. (1969) *The Zionist Idea*. New York: Atheneum.

Herzl, T. (1946) *The Jewish State*. London: Rita Searl.

Herzl, T. (1961) *Altneuland*. Haifa: Haifa Publishing.

Hesse, H. (1975) *Wandering*. London: Picador.

Hillman, J. (1983) *Archetypal Psychology: A Brief Account*. Dallas: Spring.

Hillman, J. (1993) *The Thought of the Heart and the Soul of the World*. Dallas: Spring.

Hillman, J. (1996) Psychology - Monotheistic or Polytheistic: Twenty-five years later. *Spring* 60: pp. 111-125.

Jansen, M. (1987) *Dissonance in Zion*. London and New Jersey: Zed Books.

Joseph, B. (Ed.) (1982) Addiction to near-death. *International Journal of Psycho-Analysis*, 63(4).

Jung, C. G. (Ed.) (1964) *Man and His Symbols*. New York: Doubleday.

Jung, C. G. (1965) *Memories, Dreams, Reflections*. New York: Vintage.

Jung, C. G. (1966) *Symbols of Transformation. Collected Works, 5.* (2nd edition) London: Routledge & Kegan Paul.

Jung, C. G. (1966b) *The Practice of Psychotherapy. Collected Works 16.* (2nd edition) London: Routledge & Kegan Paul.

Jung, C. G. (1968) *The Archetypes and the Collective Unconscious. Collected Works 9i.* London: Routledge & Kegan Paul.

Jung, C. G. (1968b). *Aion. Collected Works 9ii.* London: Routledge & Kegan Paul.

Jung, C. G. (1969a) *Two Essays on Analytical Psychology. Collected Works, 7.* London: Routledge & Kegan Paul.

Jung, C. G. (1969b) *The Structure and Dynamics of the Psyche.* Collected Works, 8. (2nd edition) London: Routledge & Kegan Paul.

Jung, C. G. (1970a) *Civilization in Transition.* Collected Works, 10. (2nd edition) London: Routledge & Kegan Paul.

Jung, C. G. (1970b) *Mysterium Coniunctionis.* Collected Works, 14. (2nd edition). London: Routledge & Kegan Paul.

Jung, C. G. (1971) *Psychological Types.* Collected Works, 6. London: Routledge & Kegan Paul.

Ka-Tzetnik (1989) *Shivitti.* San Francisco: Harper and Row.

Kernberg, O. F. (1975) *Borderline Conditions and Pathological Narcissism.* New York: Jason Aronson.

Kluger, Y. H. (1976) *Israel: The Archetypal Background of its Current Reality.* San Francisco: Jung Institute.

Kluger, Y. H. (1999) *A Psychological Interpretation of Ruth.* Einsiedeln: Daimon Verlag.

Koestler, A. (1949) *Promise and Fulfillment: Palestine 1917-1949.* New York: MacMillan.

Kohut, H. (1971) *The Analysis of the Self.* New York: International Universities Press.

Laing, R. D. (1971) *The Divided Self.* Harmondsworth: Penguin.

Laplanche, J. & Pontalis, J. B. (1988). *The Language of Psychoanalysis.* London: Karnac.

Lichtenberg, J. (1978) The testing of reality from the standpoint of the body self. *Journal of American Psychoanalytic Association*, 26, 357-385.

Lifton, R. J. (1983a) *The Broken Connection*. New York: Basic Books.

Lifton, R. J. (1983b) *The Life of the Self*. New York: Basic Books.

Lifton, R. J. (1986) *The Nazi Doctors: Medical Killing and the Psychology of Genocide*. New York: Basic Books.

Luz, Z. (1988) Sovev veHolech. Interview. *Kibbutz*. [In Hebrew.]

Mahler, M. S., Pine, F., & Bergman, A. (1975) *The Psychological Birth of the Human Infant*. London: Hutchinson.

Maidenbaum, A. & Martin, S. (1991) *Lingering Shadows: Jungians, Freudians, and Anti-Semitism*. Boston: Shambhala.

Masterson, J. F. (1981) *The Narcissistic and Borderline Disorders*. New York: Brunner/Mazel.

May, R. (1969) *Love and Will*. New York: Norton.

McLuhan. M. (1996) *The Medium is the Massage*. San Francisco: HardWired.

Moses, R. (1983) Psychological aspects of stress in Israel. In S. Breznitz (Ed.) *Stress in Israel*. Princeton: Van Nostrand.

Moses, R. (1984) Projection, identification and projective identification – their relation to political process. Jerusalem: Sigmund Freud Center Conference.

Ne'eman, J. (1992) *The Male and the Army as Reflected in Israeli Cinema*. (Lecture) Tel Aviv.

Neumann, E. (1963) *The Great Mother*. London: Routledge & Kegan Paul.

Neumann, E. (1970) *The Origins and History of Consciousness*. Princeton, NJ: Princeton University Press.

Neumann, E. (1971) *Amor and Psyche*. Princeton: Bollingen Series.

Neumann, E. (1973) *The Child*. London: Maresfield Library.

Neumann, E. (1990) *Depth Psychology and a New Ethic*. Boston: Shambhala.

Odajnyk, V. W. (1976) *Jung and Politics: The Political and Social Ideas of C.G. Jung*. New York: New York University Press.

Ofrat, G. (1979) Eretz Israel skepticist drama. *Modern Hebrew Literature*, 5(1-2), 42-60.

Orlov, L. A. (1912) Alla Karim. *HaShiloah* [In Hebrew.]

Ostow, M. (1986) Archetypes of apocalypse in dreams, fantasies, and in religious scripture. *Israel Journal of Psychiatry and Related Sciences*, 23, 107-122.

Oz, A. (1984) *In the Land of Israel*. NY: Vintage.

Patai, R. (1980) *Gates to the Old City*. New York: Avon.

Perls, F., Hefferline, R. F., & Goodman, P. (1973) *Gestalt Therapy*. Harmondsworth: Penguin.

Rabin, I. (1989) Radio program "24 hours." *Israel Army Radio*. [In Hebrew.]

Redfearn, J. W. T. (1990) Dreams of nuclear warfare: Does avoiding the intrapsychic clash of opposites contribute to the concrete danger of world destruction? In N. Schwartz-Salant & M. Stein (Eds.) *Dreams in Analysis* (pp. 181-198) Wilmette, IL: Chiron.

Reich, W. (1970) *The Mass Psychology of Fascism*. New York: Farrar, Straus & Giroux.

Reich, W. (1972) *Listen, Little Man!* London: Souvenir.

Roazen, P. (1979) *Freud and His Followers*. Harmondsworth: Penguin.

Rycroft, C. (1983) *A Critical Dictionary of Psychoanalysis*. Harmondsworth: Penguin.

Sachar, H. M. (1958) *The Course of Modern Jewish History*. New York: Delta.

Samuels, A. (1985) *Jung and the Post-Jungians*. London: Routledge & Kegan Paul.

Samuels, A. (1993) *The Political Psyche*. London and New York: Routledge.

Samuels, A., Shorter, B., & Plaut, F. (1986) *A Critical Dictionary of Jungian Analysis*. London: Routledge & Kegan Paul.

Satinover, J. (1986) Jung's lost contribution to the dilemma of narcissism. *Journal of the American Psychoanalytic Association*, 34, 401-438.

Savir U. (1998) The Process: 1,100 Days That Changed the Middle East. New York: Random House.

Scholem, G. (1974) *Major Trends in Jewish Mysticism*. New York: Schocken.

Schulman, M. (1963) *Moses Hess: Prophet of Zionism*. London: Thomas Yoseloff.

Segal, H. (1974) *Introduction to the Work of Melanie Klein*. New York: Basic Books.

Segev, T. (1986) 1949: *The First Israelis*. New York: The Free Press.

Selzer, W. J. (1984) Treating anorexia nervosa in the somatic hospital: A multisystemic approach. *Family Systems Medicine*, 2, 195-207.

Shachar, Y. (1999) Personal Communication.

Shaham, N. (1988) *The Rosendorf Quartet.* New York: Grove Press.

Shaked, G. (1988) Waves and currents in Hebrew fiction in the past forty years. *Modern Hebrew Literature/New Series,* 1(1), 4-12.

Shalit, E. (1987) Within borders and without: The interaction between geopolitical and personal boundaries in Israel. *Political Psychology,* 8, 365-378.

Shalit, E. (1990) Experiential supervision as an adjunct to regular supervision of psychotherapy. *The Clinical Supervisor,* 8(1), 109-130.

Shalit, E. (1994) The relationship between aggression and fear of annihilation in Israel. *Political Psychology,* 15(3), 415-434.

Shalit, E. (1996) An interview from Israel. *Spring,* 60, 93-109.

Shalit, E. (2002) *The Complex: Path of Transformation from Archetype to Ego.* Toronto: Inner City Books.

Shalit, E., & Davidson, S. (1986) Intensive family intervention in a community consultation framework. *Journal of Family Therapy,* 8, 61-78.

Shavit, A. (2003) The Definition Fence. *Haaretz,* Aug. 7.

Sharp, D. (1991) *Jung Lexicon: A Primer of Terms and Concepts.* Toronto: Inner City Books.

Shärf-Kluger, R. (1967) *Satan in the Old Testament.* Evanston, IL: Nortwestern University Press.

Spiro, M. E. (1969) *Children of the Kibbutz.* New York: Schocken Books.

Stein, M. (1989) Hephaestus: A pattern of introversion. In J. Hillman (Ed.) *Facing the Gods* (pp. 67-86) Dallas: Spring.

Talmon, J. L. (1970) *Israel Among the Nations.* London: Weidenfeld and Nicholson.

Tripp, E. (1974) *The Meridian Handbook of Classical Mythology.* New York: Meridian.

Volkan, V. D. (1972) The birds of Cyprus: A psychopolitical observation. *American Journal of Psychotherapy,* 26, 378-383.

Volkan, V. D. (1985) The need to have enemies and allies: A developmental approach. *Political Psychology,* 6, 219-247.

Volkan, V. D. (1988) *The Need to Have Enemies and Allies.* Nortvale, NJ: Jason Aronson.

von der Tann, M. (1989) A Jungian perspective on the Berlin institute for psychotherapy: A basis for mourning. *San Francisco Jung Institute Library Journal,* 8(4), 43-73.

von Franz, M. L. (1970) *Interpretation of Fairytales.* Dallas: Spring.

Watzlawick, P., Weakland, J., & Fish, R. (1974) *Change: Principles of Problem Formation and Problem Resolution*. New York: W.W. Norton.

Weisstub, E. (1993) Questions to Jung on 'Answer to Job'. *Journal of Analytical Psychology*, 38, 397-418.

Weisstub, E. & Galili-Weisstub, E. (2004) Collective Trauma and Cultural Complexes. In T. Singer & S. Kimbles (Eds.) *Cultural Complexes*. London: Routledge.

Wiesel, E. (1970) *A Beggar in Jerusalem*. New York: Random House.

Winnicott, D. W. (1958) Aggression in relation to emotional development. *Collected Papers: Through Pediatrics to Psycho-Analysis*. London: Tavistock.

Winnicott, D. W. (1965a) *The Family and Individual Development*. London: Tavistock Publications.

Winnicott, D. W. (1965b) *The Maturational Processes and the Facilitating Environment*. London: Hogarth.

Winnicott, D. W. (1980) *Playing and Reality*. Harmondsworth: Penguin.

Wistrich, R. S. (2002) Muslim Anti-Semitism: A Clear and Present Danger. http://www.ajc.org/InTheMedia/Publications.asp?did=503.

Ya'ari, Y. (1934) What he didn't tell her until now. *Gilionot*. [In Hebrew.]

Zoja, L. (1995) *Growth and Guilt*. London: Routledge.

Index

Abraham, iii, 2, 30, 92, 138, 161, 165
Abu Ala, 91
Abu Mazen, 24
Adorno, T, 101
aggression, 5, 36-41, 52, 60, 64, 72, 76, 83-85, 133, 137, 140, 144, 158-159, 161-162; and enemy, 116-117, 120-121, 123-125, 156; and fear, 65-69, 74-75, 79, 115, 118, 132, 137-138, 156-157
aggressor, identification with, 126
Agranat Commission, 81
Ahad Ha'Am, 52
a'liyah (immigration), 35, 51
alienation, 1, 6, 8, 35, 36-41, 42, 48, 56, 60, 85, 105-106, 109, 114, 132
Aliens in the Homeland, 60
Alla Karim, 36
Almog, Oz, 41
Alterman, Natan, 62
Altneuland, x

Amalek, xii
ambivalence, 31, 78-79, 81-82
Amir, Yigal, 19
Amor and Psyche, 164
anima aqua, 114
anima mundi, 153
annihilation, xi, xii, 46-50, 56-58, 61, 65, 90, 95-96, 102, 105, 109, 112, 124
anorexia, 1, 70
anxiety, xi, 1, 11, 15-17, 19-20, 64, 65-69, 71, 76, 78, 86, 97, 103, 105, 117, 119, 121, 123, 133-135, 137, 141-148, 156; death, 68, 76, 133, 135, 156; ontological, 19, 68, 136
Aphrodite, 164-165
Arafat, Yassir, 17, 24-25, 28-29, 38, 40, 91-92, 125, 158, 161
archetype, archetypal, xii, 4, 41, 43, 48, 52, 58, 71, 90-93, 96-97, 104, 106, 111, 113, 127, 134, 138, 155,

159, 164-165, 169;
identification with, 4, 29,
36, 39, 93, 123, 149, 162,
166-167; fantasy, 25-26, 85,
149, 158-159; possession,
34, 155, 166
Ashera, 164
atonement, 89
Avnery, Uri, 62
Babel, 154
Babineau, G R, 71-72
Barak, Ehud, 21, 24, 87, 96,
161
Bar-Ilan University, 19
Bar-Lev Line, 77
bar mitzvah, 5
Beaufort, 14
Beer Sheva, 138
beggar, ix-x, 167
Begin, Menachem, 14, 81-82,
84-85, 125
Beitania, 56
Bellow, Saul, 30
Ben-Gurion, David, 53, 74, 80
Berdichevski, Micah Joseph,
62
Bergman, Ingmar, 166
Bible, xii, 46, 53, 59-60, 166
Bilu, 49-50
birth, 8, 49, 57-58, 113, 124;
and boundaries, 69, 73-74;
of nation, ix, 51
Boaz, 60
Book, the, 46, 114
border, xi, 13-17, 42, 45-46,
67-68, 69-74, 76-79, 82, 85-
87, 118-119, 121-122, 131,
134, 138, 147, 170-171
borderline personality, 1, 70,
131
bread, 47

boundary, 6-7, 17, 39-40, 45-
46, 49-50, 64-74, 76-79, 82-
83, 86, 96-97, 99-100, 108,
114, 117-123, 125-127, 131-
132, 134, 136-137, 144,
147, 151-152, 156, 159,
162, 165, 169-171
bystander, 3, 31, 38, 124
Caduri, Rabbi, 106-107
Camp David, xi, 21, 24, 77,
91, 114
Canaan, Canaanite, 60, 123,
164
carpet, 47
cathexis, 67, 75, 98, 111, 169
Cave of Abraham, 2, 161
childhood, 5, 34, 72, 100, 104,
134-135
Childhood and Society, 8
Clinton, Bill, 17, 24
close proximity, x-xi, 15, 45-
46, 49, 61, 71-72, 83, 88,
95-105, 109, 122, 125, 131-
132, 145, 169
complex, 20, 37-38, 55, 81,
85, 117, 119, 125
consciousness, collective, xiii-
xiv, 1, 9, 42, 48, 59, 64, 72,
78, 81, 83, 97, 100, 105,
109, 120, 167, 170
consensus, 8, 43, 83, 104, 106
corruption, 21, 98, 102
Crystal night, 163
Davidson, Shamai, 1, 74
death, xi, 5, 11, 15, 16, 20, 23,
28-29, 34-37, 39, 55, 64-68,
75-77, 80, 85, 92-93, 96,
112, 117, 124, 141, 148,
153, 163
death camps, 40, 155
deception, 21-30, 159, 160

Deir Yassin, 69
Demjanjuk, John, 96
Depth Psychology and a New Ethic, 9
deportation, xiii, 119, 124, 138
diabolos, 164
diaspora, 46, 75, 103, 112
Dimona (nuclear plant), 104, 117
dinosaur-man, 155
dismemberment, 97, 160
displacement, 36, 160
dual union, 57-58
earth, ix, 5, 22-23, 35, 46-50, 52, 56, 59-62, 74, 82, 111, 113-114, 120; Mother 5, 6, 34-35, 49, 52-53, 55-57, 59, 61, 113, 134-135
Eban, Abba, 63
Edinger, E, 57, 58
ego, boundary, 64, 69-71, 76, 119, 121, 123, 125, 132, 137, 147, 165, 170-171; ideal 36, 97, 120; consciousness, 4, 77, 81, 118, 154, 160; loss of, 4, 71, 74, 101, 138; weak, 4, 100-102, 119, 126, 128
Eichman, Adolf, 96
Einstein, Albert, 154
El (sun-god), 164
Elazar, David, 81
Elimelech, 59
enemy, as shadow and projection, xii, xiii, 3, 10, 14, 16, 29, 32, 37, 46, 64, 66, 72, 78, 81, 86, 95, 98, 101, 119-125, 146, 149, 159, 161, 166
Enlightenment, 48

Epimetheus, 151
Erikson, Erik, 7-9, 58, 63, 69, 70-71, 79, 100-101
Eros, 5, 36-40, 60, 84, 97, 112, 115, 132, 141, 151, 160, 162, 164, 166, 171
Ezekiel, 53, 75, 163
exile, 51-52, 60, 63, 72, 122
evil, iii, xi, 3, 7, 9, 10, 17-19, 21, 23, 29-30, 68, 88-89, 106, 119, 124, 136, 147, 149, 152-155, 158, 161, 163-167, 172
Falk, Avner, 49, 52, 71, 73, 82, 156
Fallaci, Oriana, 21
farmer and wanderer, 112-113
Father(s), 3, 21, 30, 50, 52, 55, 61-63, 72, 74, 97, 101, 112, 115, 128, 165, 171; and son; 61, 101, 138-139; way of 5, 52-53, 61-62, 72, 109
Fedayeen, 75
fight-or-flight, 149
fire, 5, 6, 21, 56, 89, 114, 125, 151, 153, 164
fear, denial of, 80-81, 85, 119, 133
Freud, S, 2-8, 36, 154, 171
Freud, A, 126
Fromm, Erich, 7- 8
Gaia, 47
Galili-Weisstub, E, 125, 149
Garden of Eden, 57, 129
Gath, G, 37, 52
Gaza, 21, 24, 42, 76, 78, 79, 127, 170
Gestapo, 163
Golan Heights, 76, 81
Golden Age, 20, 58, 127, 129
Goldstein, Baruch, 2

Gordon, A D, 34
Gordon, Rosemary, 153
Gorodish, (Shmuel Gonen), 20
Greater (Whole) Israel, 18, 29,
    39, 41, 108, 127, 129, 157,
    160, 161
Green Line, 13, 78, 79, 87
Grossman, David, 158
Group for the Advancement of
    Psychiatry (GAP), 1, 45, 78,
    131
guiding myth, xiv, 18, 39-40,
    51, 60, 83, 96, 116, 118,
    128, 160, 171
Guntrip, H, 66-67
Gush Emunim ("Bloc of
    Faith"), 81-82
ha'apala, 99
Habib, Philip, 86
Haganah, 139
Hamas, xiii, 27, 127
Hanegbi, Zachi, 18
Hebron, 2, 124, 161, 171
Hebrew University, 73
hell, 25, 155, 163, 167
Hephaestus, 151
Hermes, xii
hero, heroism, ix-x, xiv, 6, 18-
    19, 25-26, 49, 52, 64-65, 76-
    77, 96, 108, 116, 128, 133,
    134-135, 140, 157, 171;
    ideal, xiv, 19, 134-135, 160
Hertzberg, Arthur, 34, 52, 53,
    55, 62
Herzl, Theodor, ix, x, 33-34,
    49, 51, 53
Hess, Moses, 49
Hesse, Herman, 52
Hestia, 111, 114
Hillman, James, 153, 164,
    166, 167

holding environment, 67-68,
    136
Holocaust, 9, 17, 27, 31, 45,
    68, 74-76, 93, 96, 99, 103,
    133, 135-136, 140, 143, 156
Holy Land, 22, 25
home, 13, 16, 17, 35-37, 47,
    52, 58, 60, 63, 72, 88, 103-
    105, 111-114, 116, 123-124,
    126, 137, 139-148, 159
homeland, 35-36, 58, 60-61,
    115-116, 122, 134
homelessness, ix, 34, 52, 60,
    113-114, 138
Honi the Circle-Maker, 146
Hovevei Zion, 49
hubris, x, 9, 31, 49, 59, 77, 80-
    81, 84, 106, 108, 139, 152,
    154-155, 159, 166-167
Hudaibiya, Treaty of, 25
Hula swamps, draining of, 75
Hussein, Saddam, 17, 87-90,
    117, 140, 146
hysteria, 1, 131
immigration, xi, 35, 45, 51, 99
incest, xi, 60, 72, 112,; taboo 5
integrity, 22-23, 38, 79, 104,
    118, 162
internalization, 67, 126-127
Ishmael, 91-92, 161
Isaac, 30, 91-92, 161; binding
    of, 92, 165-166
Ivan the Terrible, 96
Jenin, 27-28. 93
Jeremiah, 16, 20, 166-167
Jericho, 42, 125
Jerusalem, 9, 21-22, 28-29,
    32, 34-35, 37, 45-49, 61, 64,
    71-73, 106-107, 112, 122-
    123, 125, 137-8, 143, 155,
    163-166

Jewish underground, 121
Judea and Samaria, 80, 170
Jung, C G, 2, 4-7, 9, 35, 37,
    56, 61, 65, 100, 133, 147,
    152, 154, 171
Jurassic Park, 155
Kabbalah, 52, 145
Kafr Kassem, 69
kibbutz, 39, 55-56, 59, 61, 73,
    97, 113, 127, 134-135
Kibieh, 69
Kiryat Shemona, 13, 84, 86,
    157-158
Kluger, Yehezkel, 34, 52, 60
Koestler, A, 64
Labor party, 41, 81-82, 127
Laing, Ronald, 67, 69, 131
Lavi (plane), 108 109
leader, leadership, 6, 8, 21, 28,
    40, 80, 82-84, 86, 88, 91,
    98-101, 105, 125, 128, 136,
    139, 155, 162
libido, 1, 5, 6, 37, 56, 66, 70,
    111, 118, 132, 171
Lifton, R J, 2-4, 68, 70, 74,
    76, 143, 161
Likud party, 62, 99
Logos, 5, 47, 166
Lot, daughters of, 60
Lucifer, 164
Mahler, M 57, 67, 69
Mahlon and Chilion, 60
Maidenbaum, A, 2, 4
Mandelbaum Gate, 73
Mars, 36-41, 69, 84, 115, 141,
    144, 160, 171
Masada, xiv, 39, 64-65, 74, 82
May, Rollo, 20, 131, 139
Mecca, 21, 92
Menorah, 47
Meridor, Yaakov, 109

Messiah, 33-35, 47, 49, 58,
    129
Mezuzah, 47
Michael, Sami, 10
Milgram, Stanley, 104
Moab 60
Mofaz, Shaul, 162
Muhammad, 29, 92, 126
Mordechai, Yitzhak, 20
"more of the same," 81, 83
Mossad, 104
Mother, 3, 5-6, 19, 26, 37, 48,
    52, 56-59, 66, 70, 72-74, 97,
    104, 109, 112-114, 123,
    132, 134-138, 144, 158,
    163, 165, 172; Great
    Mother, 5, 52, 61, 65, 71-
    72, 74, 112
Motherland, 52, 55, 60, 107,
    111
Mount Scopus 73
Naomi, 59-60
narcissism, narcissistic 31, 34,
    42, 70, 81-82, 102-103, 106,
    108-109, 118-119, 122, 127,
    131, 159, 172; defense, 106,
    108; gratification, 50, 103,
    124, 134; injury, 86, 125,
    129, 157; investment, 19,
    42, 49-50, 58-60, 80, 97-98,
    105, 128; loss, 82, 158-159;
    rage, 32, 160; withdrawal
    of, 41-43, 97, 104, 106, 109,
    115
Nathan, Abie, 38
national unity, 43, 106
Nazi, Nazism, xi, 2, 4, 18, 31,
    68, 69, 96, 99, 108, 124, 148
Neeman, Judd 115
Nemesis, 159

Netanyahu, Benjamin, 18-20,
41, 105, 107, 157
Neumann, Erich, xiii, 2, 3, 4,
6, 7, 9, 10, 50, 55, 57-59,
62, 65, 101, 104, 112, 126,
164
New York, xi, 138-139
night journey, of Muhammad,
29, 92
nihilism, 115
Oedipus, 3, 40, 59
ontogeny, 4, 40, 62, 65
Orlov, L A 36
Orpah, 60
Oslo, 2, 24-25, 40, 42, 91,
157, 163
Ostrowsky, Victor, 104
Oz, Amos, 84, 133
Pandora, 151
paradise, 19, 25, 57, 100, 104,
106-107, 153, 158, 161
participation mystique, 7
Passover, 17, 29, 122
peace, 17, 18, 24-32, 35, 41,
74, 77, 80-82, 85, 99-101,
116, 121, 127-128, 148;
image of, 35, 41, 58, 113,
129, 153, 158, 163-166
process, xiii-xiv, 18, 20-21,
24-25, 90-93, 108, 148, 158-
163; shadow of, 41, 129,
156-158
Peres, Shimon, 17, 19, 86,
107, 157, 158, 163
persecution, persecutor, 2, 11,
63, 66, 68, 75, 85, 95, 98,
121, 123-125, 133-134, 156
persona, ix, 9, 81, 97, 102,
120, 139, 147, 167, 172;
film 166
Petah Tikvah, 138

Petra, 74, 123
Phoenix, 141, 147
phylogeny, 4, 65
pioneer, ix, x, xiv, 34-36, 49,
52-53, 55, 59, 61, 96, 111,
123, 128, 132
PLO (Palestine Liberation
Organization), 24-26, 29,
40, 86, 90, 92, 108, 133
possession, 34, 81, 155, 166
power, 16, 37, 41, 64, 68, 75,
77, 80, 83-85, 101-102, 104,
117, 121, 133
primal relationship, 57-58,
106, 132
pro-social personality, 100,
115
Prometheus, 6, 151, 155, 164
Psyche, 50, 164-165
psycho-ecology, 114, 153, 155
puer aeternus (eternal youth),
58, 115
Purim, 17, 99, 142, 161
Rabin, Yitzhak, x, xiii, 17-19,
24-25, 40-41, 82, 86, 92,
100, 108, 127-128, 132,
139, 152, 156-158, 161, 167
ram, 165
Ramadan, 167
Ramallah, 21, 2
Ramat Gan, 137
ram's horn, 60
rebirth, 10, 35-36, 141-142,
147, 153, 164
redemption, ix, x, xiv, 33-36,
51-52, 55-57, 60-61, 75, 80,
83, 111-115, 122
Red Heifer, 9, 123
Redfearn, J, 106, 119
Reich, Wilhelm, 39, 101
return to religion, 43, 63, 109

revolt, 51, 52-53, 61-63, 115
Ross, Dennis, 29
Russian roulette, 116, 126
Ruth, 60
Sabbatai Sevi, 49
Sabra, 69, 75, 120, 132, 135,
    162
Sadat, Anwar, 17, 80, 85, 100,
    132
Samson, xiv
Samuels, Andrew, 2, 6, 57
Saramago, J, 27
Savir, Uri, 90-91
Satan, 22, 26, 93, 163-164
Satinover, J, 4
scapegoat, 10, 22, 88-90
Scholem, Gershom, 34, 52
sealed room, xi, 17, 40, 88,
    140-148, 157
selection, 25, 155
self-object, 42, 70, 106, 115,
    172
Sha'at, Nabil, 40
Shachar, Yoram, 53
Shach, Rabbi, 61
Shaham, Nathan, 60, 113
Shahar, 164
Shaharit, 164
Shalem, 164
Shamir, Yitzhak, 107, 128,
    157, 158
Sharon, Ariel, 14, 24, 43, 82
Shekhinah, 52, 61
Shomrim (guards) 46
Sicarii, 38, 65, 108
Sinai, 76, 81-82, 124, 157,
    170
Smolenskin, Peretz, 53
sociocide, 29, 32
Sphinx, 81
Spielberg, Steven, 155

Stalin, 27
strength, ix-x, xiv, 16, 51, 52-
    53,60, 63-65, 68-69, 75-78,
    80-86, 101, 105, 115-118,
    125, 132-133, 140, 143,
    146, 155-157
suicidal soldier, xiv, 39, 116,
    160
suicide bomber, 19, 25-29, 32,
    93, 149, 152, 159-160
symbiosis, 69, 72
symbolos, 164
Talmud, 61, 92
Tashmad, 11
Tel Aviv, 19, 20, 50, 53, 93,
    114, 142, 143, 146, 156,
    157, 158
temenos, 2, 144, 147, 172
Temple, Temple Mount, 9-10,
    24, 29, 34, 92-93, 123, 125
terror, terrorism, xi, xiv, 2, 23-
    32, 39, 41, 75, 77, 78, 84,
    87, 101, 112, 121, 162 ; war
    of, 21, 23-32, 90-93, 129,
    132, 148-149
terrorist, xii, 19, 26-29, 31-32,
    38, 65, 79, 91, 93, 101, 114,
    118, 120-121, 124-125, 127-
    128, 138, 149, 156, 161
Thanatos, 5, 37, 112-113
theater of doubt, 35
The Nazi Doctors, 2
The Rosendorf Quartet, 60,
    113
thirty-six, legend of, 34-35
totem, totemism, 3, 4
tree, 15, 25, 46, 59, 114, 122,
    141, 152, 165
Tu b'Shevat, 15
Ullman, Liv, 166

Us and *Them*, 6, 10, 38, 72,
    78, 121, 128, 162
Valley of Hell, 167
Vanunu, Mordechai, 104, 117
victim, 4, 27-28, 36, 53, 63,
    74, 80, 89, 124, 149
Vilnai, Matan, 125
violence, mystique of, 63
Voice, 6, 20, 22, 31, 32, 38,
    39, 92, 104, 151-152, 154,
    166-168
von Franz, M-L, 116
Volkan, Vamik, 10, 71, 72,
    87, 131
warrior, ix, x, 37, 96, 115-116,
    120, 124, 128, 160, 171
water, 28, 35, 46, 50, 56, 59,
    75, 88, 114, 153, 164, 165
weltanschauung, 2, 23, 100,
    170
Weisstub, Eli, 125, 149, 161
West Bank, 17, 39, 51, 76, 78-
    82, 87, 107, 114, 146, 157,
    170
Western Wall, 37, 76, 125
Wiesel, Elie, x, 124
wine, 47
Winnicott, D W, 19, 66-67,
    69, 100, 136
World Parents, 62
World Trade Center, 31
Ya'ari, Yehuda 36
Yamit, 82
yerida (emigration), 41
yeshiva, 61
yishuv, 50-51, 63
yored (plural *yordim*), 72,
    104, 112, 113
Zealots, 64, 65
zeitgeist (spirit of the time), 1,
    100, 170

Zoja, Luigi, 159

About the Author

Erel Shalit, author and Jungian psychoanalyst, is a graduate of Uppsala University, Sweden, 1978. He is training and supervising analyst with the Israel Society of Analytical Psychology (ISAP) and member, International Association of Analytical Psychology (IAAP). He is a member of the Council for Peace and Security.

He has been Director of the Community Mental Health Clinic, Shalvata Psychiatric Center, and served as officer in the Medical Corpse of the Israel Defense Forces.

Dr. Shalit lectures and teaches at the Israel Society of Analytical Psychology; at the Dept. of Psychotherapy, Tel Aviv Medical School; the Institute of Dream Psychology, Stockholm, and other institutes and centers in Israel, Europe, and the United States.

In addition to *The Hero and His Shadow: Psychopolitical Aspects of Myth and Reality in Israel*, Dr. Shalit is the author several books, including: *The Cycle of Life: Themes and Tales of the Journey, Enemy, Cripple, Beggar: Shadows in the Hero's Path, The Complex: Path of Transformation from Archetype to Ego*, and *Requiem: A Tale of Exile and Return*.

Further information can be found at www.eshalit.com

The Hero and His Shadow introduces a psychological perspective on the history, development and myths of modern Israel.

The realization of Zionism relied on the pioneer, who revolted against the Way of the Father and sought spiritual redemption through the revival of Mother Earth in the ancient land. Myth and history, psyche and matter are constantly intertwined in the birth and development of Israel, for example when in the Declaration of Independence we are told that pioneers make *deserts* bloom, the text actually says they make *spirits* blossom.

Pioneer, guardsman and then warrior were admired hero-ideals. However, in the shadow of the hero and the guiding myths of revolt, redemption, strength and identity-change, there were feelings of despair, doubt, weakness and fear. Where there has been renewal, lurks the threat of annihilation.

The suppressed aspects of past and present myths, which linger in the shadow, are exposed. The psychological consequences of Israel's wars, from independence to the present war of terror, are explored both on a personal note and from a psychoanalytic perspective, with social examples and clinical vignettes.

Shadow aspects of the conflicting guiding myths *Peace* and *Greater Israel* are examined, as well as mythical connections, such as between Jerusalem and the respective archetypal images of *Wholeness* and *Satan*.

Made in the USA
San Bernardino, CA
30 March 2016